Dewi Candraningrum

The Challenge of Teaching English in Indonesian's Muhammadiyah Universities (1958 – 2005)

Mainstreaming Gender through postcolonial Muslim Women Writers

UNI PRESS
Hochschulschriften Bd. 157

Gedruckt mit Unterstützung des Deutschen Akademischen Austauschdienstes

D 6

Bibliographic information published by the Deutsche Nationalbibliothek
The Deutsche Nationalbibliothek lists this publication in the Deutsche Nationalbibliografie; detailed bibliographic data are available in the Internet at http://dnb.d-nb.de.

ISBN 978-3-8258-1742-8
Zugl.: Münster (Westf.), Univ., Diss., 2008

A catalogue record for this book is available from the British Library

Verlagskontakt:
Fresnostr. 2 D-48159 Münster
Tel. +49 (0) 2 51/620 32 - 22 Fax +49 (0) 2 51/922 60 99
e-Mail: lit@lit-verlag.de http://www.lit-verlag.de

Auslieferung:
Deutschland/Schweiz: LIT Verlag Fresnostr. 2, D-48159 Münster
Tel. +49 (0) 2 51/620 32 - 22, Fax +49 (0) 2 51/922 60 99, e-Mail: vertrieb@lit-verlag.de

Österreich: Medienlogistik Pichler-ÖBZ GmbH & Co KG
IZ-NÖ, Süd, Straße 1, Objekt 34, A-2355 Wiener Neudorf
Tel. +43 (0) 2236/63 535-290, +43 (0) 2236/63 535 - 243, mlo@medien-logistik.at

Distributed in the UK by: Global Book Marketing, 99B Wallis Rd, London, E9 5LN
Phone: +44 (0) 20 8533 5800 – Fax: +44 (0) 1600 775 663
http://www.centralbooks.co.uk/html

Distributed in North America by:

Transaction Publishers
New Brunswick (U.S.A.) and London (U.K.)

Transaction Publishers
Rutgers University
35 Berrue Circle
Piscataway, NJ 08854

Phone: +1 (732) 445 - 2280
Fax: + 1 (732) 445 - 3138
for orders (U. S. only):
toll free (888) 999 - 6778
e-mail:
orders@transactionspub.com

Zusammenfassung

Diese Dissertation untersucht die Herausforderungen, denen sich die Lehre der Anglistik an indonesischen Universitäten in dem Zeitraum zwischen 1958—das Gründungsjahr der Universitas Muhammadiyah Hamka (UHAMKA)—und 2005, als die letzte Muhammadiyah Universität, Universitas Muhammadiyah Sukabumi (UMMI) eröffnet wurde, stellen musste. Die islamische Muhammadiyah Organisation unterhält momentan 38 Universitäten in ganz Indonesien, 22 davon sind anglistische Fakultäten angegliedert. Muhammadiyah, die zur Zeit mehr als 12000 moderne Schulen, 168 Universitäten, 345 Krankenhäuser und über 600 Polikliniken und Gesundheitsdienste besitzt, befürwortet die Aufnahme weltlicher und religiöser Fächer in ihre Curricula, eine Einstellung, die sich auf die Ära Ahmad Dahlans (1912–1923) zurückführen lässt.

Indem sie Bildungseinrichtungen errichtet, unterstützte Muham-madiyah erfolgreich eine rationale Herangehensweise an die Identi-tätsdiskurse des Islams. Allerdings hat der momentane globalpolitische Kontext dazu geführt, dass die muslimische Gemeinschaft in Indonesien nicht bereit ist, die Unvermeidlichkeit multikultureller Werte im globalen Zeitalter anzuerkennen. Als Reaktion darauf haben die anglistischen Fakultäten der Muhammadiyah Universitäten einen monokulturellen westlichen Literaturkanon in ihre Curricula aufgenommen, der außerstande ist, den Geist der Multikulturalität wiederzugeben. Studierende der Anglistik in Muhammadiyah Universitäten sehen sich häufig mit Schwierigkeiten konfrontiert, wenn es darum geht, westliche Werte durch die Rezeption westlicher Literaturkanons wahrzunehmen und wertzuschätzen.

Aus diesem Grund ist es dringend erforderlich, diesen "clash of cultures" beizulegen. Es ist notwendig, einen speziellen Kanon für muslimische Studierende in Indonesien zu entwickeln, der den kulturellen Graben schließt, mit dem sie sich bei der Analyse englischer Texte konfrontiert sehen. Muslimische Studenten benötigen den Kontakt mit einem multikulturellen Literaturkanon, in welchem westliche und islamische Werte zusammentreffen und in zeitgenössischen Dialogen analysiert werden. Studierende sollten ebenfalls die Möglichkeit erhalten, Werke muslimischer Autorinnen zu lesen, die sowohl islamische als auch westliche Werte kritisch hinterfragen, wie zum Beispiel Leila Ahmed aus Ägypten, Fatema Mernissi aus Marokko oder Kartini aus Indonesien, genauso wie andere Autorinnen, die kulturelle und religiöse Grenzen überschritten haben.

Muhammadiyahs Auffassungen zur Stellung der Frau sind hauptsächlich von den Schriften des Korans und der Hadith beeinflusst. Diese Schriften werden als heilige Texte angesehen und häufig mit einem wortgetreuen oder textlichem Ansatz interpretiert, wodurch der historische Kontext verleugnet wird. Das wortgetreue Lesen dieser Texte beeinflusst sodann die innere islamische Kosmologie, die die Wahrnehmung der Geschlechterrollen und verhältnisse beherrscht. Wenn der Seminarraum der Muhammadiyah Universitäten ein Mikrokosmos der muslimischen Gesellschaft ist, so ist Geschlecht ein einflussreicher Faktor in den Anglistikseminaren und die Auseinandersetzung mit Geschlechterfragen muss sich sowohl an die Studierenden als auch an die gesamte muslimische Gesellschaft richten. Diese Dissertation versucht, diejenigen Entschei-dungen der Muhammadiyah Universitäten in einen theoretischen Zusammenhang zu stellen, die zur inhaltlichen Ausrichtung der anglistischen Fakultäten geführt haben.

Im Speziellen versucht sie, die folgenden Fragen anzusprechen: welcher Text, von wem unterrichtet, mit welchen Methoden, zu welchem Zweck, welche Hausarbeiten nach sich ziehend, von wem wie ausgewertet, und mit welcher Zielsetzung? Diese Studie wäre nicht in der Lage herauszuarbeiten, welche positiven Resultate das Behandeln von Gender Studien in Universitäten haben kann, ohne vorher bis zu einem gewissen Grad festgelegt zu haben, wie die pädagogischen Grundwerte des Islams lauten und welche Position er gegenüber Gender Studien in Lehre und Studium einnimmt. Die Einstellung muslimischer Studierenden zu Geschlechterfragen und dem Studium der Anglistik insgesamt werden von ihren individuellen Erfahrungen als Teil der internationalen muslimischen Gemeinschaft geprägt. Die postkolonialen muslimischen Autorinnen, die ich meinem vorläufigen neuen Kanon für den Prosalehrplan aufgenommen habe, behandeln mit großer Mehrheit für das Überschreiten von Grenzen; weiterhin spielen ihre Interpretationen von Geschlechterbeziehungen eine bedeutsame Rolle in der Umgestaltung der muslimischen Gemeinschaft im Allgemeinen und lassen aufgrund dessen Studien und Rückschlüsse auf die möglichen Veränderungen der kritischen Einstellung der Studierenden zu.

Diese Dissertation möchte Studierende dazu animieren, Literatur aus einer geschlechterkritischen Perspektive heraus zu rezipieren um damit in der Lage zu sein, einseitige und voreingenommene Meinungen kritisch zu hinterfragen und den künstlerischen Wert eines Werkes sowohl im Detail als auch im großen Ganzen zu erkennen. Sie soll den Studierenden eine differenziertere Haltung gegenüber ihren eigenen Werten im Vergleich mit Werten außerhalb ihrer Gemeinschaft vermitteln. Der gegenwärtige Lehrplan erfordert eine gründliche Analyse unter gender-theoretischen Gesichtspunkten, damit das Potential der Studierenden andere, selbst islamkritische, Meinungen, deutlich wahrzunehmen, voll entwickelt werden kann. Der Kontakt mit den Texten postkolonialer muslimischer Autorinnen, hergestellt durch die vorgeschlagene Reform des Kanons, könnte das kritische Verständnis der Studierenden erhöhen und ihnen helfen, ihre eigene Welt zu verstehen, mitzugestalten und zu teilen; weiterhin könnte es dazu führen, dass sie auch Welten, die der ihren gänzlich unähnlich sind, wertschätzen lernen. Diese Dissertation sieht sich als Versuch, einen solchen Prozess zu initiieren.

Table of Contents

Preface and Acknowledgments

This study is the publication of my PhD thesis (Doktorarbeit) at the Englisches Seminar, Philosophische Fakultät, Westfälische Wilhelms-Universität Münster. I would like to express my gratitude for the constant support from DAAD (Deutscher Akademische Austausch Dienst). My sincere gratitude for the comments and unending care as well as support from my Doktorvater, Prof Dr Klaus Stierstorfer, Englisches Seminar, Universität Münster, where I conducted most of the research. I also benefited a lot from the Gutachten of Prof Dr Laurenz Volkmann, Universität Jena. It is an honor that Prof Dr Stephanie Hellekamps (Universität Münster) could be the examiner of this work. My special gratitude is extended to Assoc Prof Harry Aveling, La Trobe University as well as Assoc Prof Brenton Doecke, Monash University who gave thoughtful input to the project proposal. My special gratitude is extended to Dr Soe Tjen Marching (SOAS, London) as well as Dr Wendy Mee (La Trobe University) who helped me a lot in polishing my English. Berthold Damshäuser, Universität Bonn, and PD Fritz Schulze, Uni Frankfurt during my stay in Germany, have provided insightful input as well to this research.

I could not conduct my field research in Indonesia without the support of the following prominent Professors in Muhammadiyah: Prof Dr Ahmad Syafii Maarif, Persyarikatan Muhammadiyah; Prof Dr Amin Abdullah, Rector of Universitas Islam Negeri Yogyakarta; Prof Dr Bambang Setiaji, Rector of Universitas Muhammadiyah Surakarta; Prof Dr Edi Suandi Hamid, Rector of Universitas Islam Indonesia; as well as Prof Dr Med Rasjid Soeparwata, Uniklinikum Munster, Head of Muhammadiyah Special Branch of Germany. I got an important robust input from the discussion with Muhammad Thoyibi, MA., Universitas Muhammadiyah Surakarta (UMS); Maryadi MA., UMS; Musiyam, MPT, UMS; as well as Muhammad Sayuti from DIKTI Muhammadiyah.

I would like to express my gratitude to the constant help from R. Husna Mulya (Komnas Perempuan) who supports the data of Perda Sharia and Mariana Amiruddin & Eko Bambang Subiyantoro (Jurnal Perempuan Indonesia) who provide news on Indonesian women's movements against the discrimination contained in Perda Sharia. I owe a lot to the help from Lukman Hakim, Universitas Paramadina, who supported me with the collection of Muhammadiyah Curriculum. I also benefited from discussions with Soe Tjen Marching (SOAS London), Gadis Arivia (Universitas Indonesia and Yayasan Jurnal Perempuan), Arif Harsana (SOAI, Essen), Lena Simanjuntak (DIG

Koeln), and Sri Tunruang (1 Welt Forum Aachen). My special gratitude is extended to the generous SOAI team: Kristina Grossmann, Nicole Weydmann, Rolf Jordan, Patrick Ziegenhain, Mela Badruddin, Ratna Noviani and Sara Asu Schroer. They deserve my deep gratitude.

Finally I have to thank to my husband, my dearest friend, Ahmad-Norma Permata, who supported me constantly. My sincere gratitude to my parents, Ibu Dewi Ngaenah and Bapak Soekirno who have been taking care of our Ivan-Ufuq Isfahan, my eight-year-old son. They all deserve my deepest gratitude.

List of Abbreviations

AMS	Algemeene Middelbare School (Senior High School, Dutch era)
BAN	Badan Akreditasi Nasional (National Accreditation Board)
DOM	Daerah Operasi Militar (Military Operation District)
EFL	English as Foreign Language
ELT	English Language Teaching
ELTTP	English Language Teacher Training Project
EMDP	English Materials Development Project
ESL	English as Second Language
ETUP	English Teachers Upgrading Project
FLP	Forum Lingkar Pena (Pen Circle Forum)
HEC	Higher Education Curriculum
HIS	Hollandsch-Inlandische School (Dutch colonial elementary school)
HTI	Hizbut Tahrir Indonesia
IELTS	International English Language Testing System
IKIP	Institut Keguruan dan Ilmu Kependidikan (Education and Training Institute)
KOMNAS	Komisi Nasional (National Comission)
KOPASSUS	Komando Pasukan Khusus (The Special Forces Command)
KOPERTIS	Koordinasi Perguruan Tinggi Swasta (Private Higher Education Coordination)
KOPWIL	KOPERTIS Wilayah, Koordinasi Perguruan Tinggi Swasta Wilayah (Private Higher Education Coordination, regional sector)
MDGs	Millennium Development Goals
MKK	Mata Kuliah Ketrampilan dan Keahlian (one of university subjects which develop students' skills)
MPB	Mata Kuliah Perilaku Berkarya (one of university subjects which develop students' creativity)
MPK	Mata Kuliah Pengembangan Kepribadian (one of university subjects which develop students' personality at university level)
MULO	*Meer Uitgebreid Lager Onderwijs* (Advanced Elementary Education/Junior High School)
NTB	Nusa Tenggara Barat (West Nusa Tenggara)
NU	Nadlatul Ulama (Awakening of Religious Scholar)

Perda	Peraturan Daerah (District Ordinances)
PKI	Partai Komunis Indonesia (Indonesian Communist Party)
PKS	Partai Keadilan dan Sejahtera (Justice and Prosperous Party)
PTM	Perguruan Tinggi Muhammadiyah (Muhammadiyah Higher Education)
PTPG	Perguruan Tinggi Pendidikan Guru (Higher Education for Teacher Training)
RUU APP	Rancangan Undang-Undang Anti Pornografi dan Pornoaksi (Bill Draft on Anti Pornography and Porno Action)
SCTV	Surya Citra Televisi (one of Indonesia TV channel)
SLTP/SMP	Sekolah Menengah Pertama (Junior High School)
SMU	Sekolah Menengah Umum (Senior High School)
STC	Standard Training Course
TBC	Tahayul, Bid'ah, Churafat (belief in mystical spirits, heresy, and unlawful rituals from Islamic practices in Indonesia)
TEFL	Teaching English as Foreign Language
TOEFL	Test of English as Foreign Language
TOEIC	Test of English for International Communication
TPA	Taman Pendidikan Al Quran (Al Quran education for the children and the youth)
UAD	Universitas Ahmad Dahlan
UHAMKA	Universitas Hamka
UI	Universitas Indonesia
UKIT	Universitas Kristen Indonesia Tomohon
UKK	Universitas Kristen Klabat
UKP	Universitas Kristen Petra
UKSW	Universitas Kristen Satya Wacana
UMMAT	Universitas Muhammadiyah Mataram
UMJ	Universitas Muhammadiyah Jakarta
UMM	Universitas Muhammadiyah Malang
UMMI	Universitas Muhammadiyah Sukabumi
UMS	Universitas Muhammadiyah Surakarta
UNAS	Universitas Nasional
UNDIP	Universitas Diponegoro Semarang
UNM	Universitas Negeri Malang
UNESCO	United Nations Educational, Scientific and Cultural Organization

UNKLAB	Universitas Kristen Klabat Sulawesi Utara
UNSRI	Universitas Negeri Sriwijaya
UNSU	Universitas Negeri Sumatera Utara
UNSYIAH	Universitas Negeri Syiah Kuala
UUD 1945	Undang-Undang Dasar 1945 (1945 Indonesian Foundation Constitution)
UNY	Universitas Negeri Yogyakarta
VOC	Vereenigde Oostindische Compagnie (Dutch East Indies Company)

PART I
THE CHALLENGE OF TEACHING ENGLISH IN INDONESIAN'S MUHAMMADIYAH UNIVERSITIES (1958-2005)

Chapter I
Introduction

1. Who Reads the Canon?

At present Muhammadiyah has 22 English Departments in about 38 Muhammadiyah Universities throughout Indonesia. The 22 English Departments and the years of establishment at Muhammadiyah Universities are as follows: Universitas Muhammadiyah Ahmad Dahlan Yogyakarta (1984), Uni Muh Bengkulu (1991), Uni Muh Buton (2001), Uni Muh Gresik (2001), Uni Muh Jakarta (1989), Uni Muh Jember (1989), Uni Muh Makasar (1993), Uni Muh Malang (1987), Uni Muh Mataram (1992), Uni Muh Palembang (1994), Uni Muh Palu (1987), Uni Muh Pare-Pare (1999), Uni Muh Ponorogo (1993), Uni Muh Pontianak (1993), Uni Muh Prof Dr Hamka (1958), Uni Muh Purwokerto (1995), Uni Muh Semarang (1999), Uni Muh Sukabumi (2003), Uni Muh Sumatera Utara (1976), Uni Muh Surabaya (1984), Uni Muh Surakarta (1984), and Uni Muh Tapanuli Selatan (1983). The positive attitude taken by Persyarikatan Muhammadiyah (which now owns more than 12,000 modern schools, 168 universities, 345 hospitals and more than 600 polyclinics and health services in the educational sector) in introducing secular and religious subjects into its curriculum construction dates back to the era of Ahmad Dahlan (1912-1923), during which Dutch and three other European languages—English, French and Latin—were introduced and taught in Muhammadiyah schools. During the period of Sukarno's presidency (1945-1966), Muhammadiyah saw English as an inseparable part of modernization by establishing its first English Department at Universitas Muhammadiyah Dr Hamka Jakarta in 1958. The positive attitude of Sukarno's successor (Suharto) towards English was manifested by the widespread establishment of the English departments in Muhammadiyah University: almost 20 English Departments were established in Muhammadiyah universities during his presidency. From 1996, however, the literary canon taught in the English Departments has not been reformed to meet the present context, in which discourses on Islamic identity versus the coming of globalisation are heavily contested. Detailed inquiries will be undertaken into the following English Department Curricula: Kopwil I, Uni Muh Sumatera Utara; Kopwil II, Uni Muh Palembang; Kopwil III, Uni Muh Prof Dr Hamka Jakarta; Kopwil IV, Uni Muh Sukabumi, Jawa Barat; Kopwil V, Uni Muh Ahmad Dahlan Yogyakarta; Kopwil VI, Uni Muh Surakarta, Jawa Tengah; Kopwil VII, Uni Muh Malang, Jawa Timur; Kopwil VIII, Uni Muh Mataram, NTB; Kopwil IX, Uni Muh Makasar, Sulawesi Selatan. KOPWIL stands for *Kopertis Wilayah*, KOPERTIS stands for *Koordinasi Perguruan Tinggi Swasta*, meaning Regional Coordinator of Private Universities.

During Ahmad Dahlan's era, the discourse on Islamic identity was mainly designed to purify Islam from the non-Islamic elements such as *tahayul*, *bid'ah*, *churafat* (irrational beliefs), popularly known as TBC. Ahmad Dahlan was educated under the western education system, i.e. the Dutch colonial formal school, and Islamic traditional schools. His hybrid educational backgrounds were quite unique at his time, and this had inspired to establish the most successful modern Islamic educational institution in present day Indonesia. By establishing an educational institution, he had successfully promoted a rational approach to addressing discourses of identity in Islam by eradicating the superstitious debris of the TBC. The present global-political context has found the Indonesian Muslim community as being unable to accept the inevitability of multicultural values in the global era. In response to this situation, the English departments in Muhammadiyah universities have adopted a mono-cultural western literary canon in the formation of their curricula, which is unable to reflect the spirit of multiculturalism.

These conclusions are based upon my close observations of the classrooms in which Muhammadiyah students often find it very difficult to perceive and appreciate Western values in reading Western literary canons. For this reason, it is very urgent to resolve these "cultural clashes". A single work by Shakespeare, for instance *Henry VI*, would be read and interpreted differently by Muslim students. There are always pedagogical considerations in forming a literary canon. And the question of "Who reads the canon?" is rarely addressed compared with the question of "how to read the canon?", which has long been established in literary theory. It is necessary to develop a specific canon for Islamic students in Indonesia to bridge the cultural gulf that they face when reading texts in English. These students require exposure to a more multicultural literary canon, in which Western and Islamic values meet and negotiate in contemporary dialogues which are manifested in the formation of multicultural literary canons. Novels written by V.S. Naipaul or Salman Rushdie could be read, interpreted, and appreciated rationally and critically instead of being condemned irrationally and even violently. The students at Muhammadiyah Universities will be aided by strategies that enable them to read critically. Students will also have a chance to read novels written by Muslim women writers who have integrated Islamic values as well as Western values, for example Leila Ahmed, from Egypt or Attia Hosen, women writers from India; or even Kartini, an Indonesian Muslim women writer.

The present context calls for an urgent need to offer multicultural literary canons which can enhance Islamic students' critical awareness in perceiving the rapid changes of globalization. Globalization should be made more open to dialogues between the West and the East, between Islam and the West. Instead of perceiving globalization as an agent leading to the homogenization of particular values, in this case Western values, it may be possible to perceive it as a chance to create a space for the discussion of diversity in values. In other words, Islamic values as well as texts can be incorporated into the formation of literary canons in English Departments. Many contemporary writers, be they from the UK (for example, the contemporary novels of Hanif Kureishi), from the US, Australia, Canada, India or many other postcolonial Muslim regions such as Pakistan, Bangladesh, Malaysia, Tunisia, Morocco, Aljazair, Algeria, or even Indonesia deserve to be placed in the canon to enhance dialogue between the West and the East, and specifically to enhance Muhammadiyah students' skills in negotiating between their own Islamic values and the Western values they encounter in English texts.

2. How to read the canon?

Postcolonial scholarship in the context of Teaching English as Foreign Language (TEFL) has been growing in the last few decades, and this has significantly contributed to the availability of diverse impressions and more varied information about practices of TEFL apart from those found exclusively in countries in which English operates as a first language. English in Indonesia is still a foreign language; at the same time, however, it is also regarded as the most indispensable second language to be learned from kindergarten to university. There have recently been important developments in the use of English as global language. Haneline argues that English is no longer a 'White' language (Haneline, 2001: 669-672). It is used throughout the world by people of every race and culture. Haneline's argument has undone the binary opposition of the ownership of English in the postcolonial discourse.

Discussions of the Center versus the Other in Postcolonial discourse have, sometimes, led to fixed binary oppositions. It tends to "essentialize" and thus separate diverse phenomena into two categories. Stierstorfer argues that the basic situation of two contrasting spheres is often caught in the paradox of being forced to enter a communication which will always be characterised by "violent appropriation", such as Foucault's opposition between madness and sanity, the relationship of colonizer to colonized in post-colonial theory... (Stierstorfer, 1999:164). All these discourses, in their insistence on positing an absolute opposition between some notions of *essential* [Other] and the West, between *us* and *them*, obscure more fundamental questions of vast differential social formations—the complex cultural heterogeneity, and the distribution of economic and political power within a certain society. This also undermines the possibilities for ideological/political contention and change (Joshi, 1994:3). Binary oppositions depend on what Bhabha calls "the separation from origin and essences" that characterize the postcolonial as it moves away from binary anti-colonialism to a more nuanced examination of the ways in which the position of both colonizer and colonized are inwardly conflicted (Bhabha, 1994:4). It calls into question assumptions of homogenous national cultures in host/home/ center versus guest/away/periphery.

Since the early 1980s, historians have progressively shifted their focus away from the political and constitutional framework of the British Empire, to the impacts of imperial ideologies and practices of British culture and society (Ward, 2001:1). The position of the British at the Center of the discourse of Postcolonialism can be problematized in certain way. Ward further argues that as far as the post-1945 era is concerned, rigid conceptual barriers between metropolis and periphery are still very much intact. There remains a firmly entrenched assumption that the broad cultural impact of decolonization was confined to the colonial periphery, with little relevance to post-war British culture and society (Ward, 2001:2). Yadav has argued that, throughout the early modern period, English-language writers have been part of a traditionally marginal literary culture in the European world, far behind the Italians, the Spanish, and the French in international recognition and renowned (Yadav, 2004:1). He has noted that such views tended to misconstrue imperial ambitions in the eighteenth-century British literary culture as an assurance of metropolitan centrality, rather than recognizing these ambitions as marks of an effort to overcome provincial secondariness in the world of European cultures (Yadav, 2004: 2).

Burton adds that the binary existence is not fixed between *home* and *away*. She recommends that the "history of the United Kingdom be revised in order to account for the impact of empire, ex-colonial migration and non-white communities and constituencies in contemporary British life" (Burton, 2001:xi). She exposed a variety of colonial "Others" circulated at the very heart of the British Empire before the twentieth century (Burton, 1998:6):

> They were, as Gretchen Gerzina has noted, a "continued and very English presence" from the Elizabethan settlement onward. Empire was, in short, not just a phenomenon "out there", but a fundamental and constitutive part of English culture and national identity at home, where [as Benita Parry has noted] "the fact of empire was registered not only in political debate…but entered the social fabric, the intellectual discourse and the life of the imagination".

Thus, to organise the post-colonial discourse around simple, binary oppositions results in gross oversimplifications. "The 'Orient' and the West are not merely opposites, but work dialectically in culture and through cultural imagination" (Burton, 1994:229). Europe and the West are not homogenous, the Other and the third world are not self-evident and self-contained entities. These simple binaries could repeat the imperialist and colonialist mythologies that are supposed to be deconstructed. This deconstruction aims at "unravelling the oppositions which ordinarily sustain and legitimate the hierarchies of race (white/black, civilized/savage, human/subhuman)" (Plasa, 2000:4). This research aims to produce a more complex picture and a non-monolithic definition of binary oppositions which certify the "undoing of the opposition between East and West" (Moore-Gilbert et al, 1991:5). Such rigid binary taxonomy could be "both the trap of essentialism and the vice of agency-versus-determination (Burton,

1998:20). Burton furthermore argues that identity has historically always been "compromised" (Burton, 1998:20). Stoler also highlights that "an effective colonial history of the present does not rest on some generic distinctions between the rigid taxonomies of the colonial state and postcolonial disruptions to them, but on the attention to the scrambled categories in which people lived" (Stoler in Pieterse & Parekh (eds.), 1995: 145 and Burton, 1998:23). In this light, Indonesia becomes the site of interaction among values coming from home, the West or the East. In this case, the hybrid status of Indonesia is unavoidable. This thesis reveals the plurality rather than the duality of Indonesia. Considering the former review, with particular emphasis on English teaching in Indonesia, the present study is developed to explore the contemporary Muhammadiyah universities, which could become sites of invention and construction in educational praxis—for the simple reason that the local is, at present, also a site for the global.

Since the focus of the present research is to construct an alternative curriculum, the history and theory of curricula will need to be taken into account. Richards suggests that before a curriculum is constructed, a goal must be established. Several sources will have to be taken into account, such as Burlbaw & Field (2005), *Explorations in Curriculum History*; Edwards & Usher (2003), *Space, Curriculum, and Learning*; Seel & Dijkstra (2004), *Curriculum, Plans, and Processes in Instructional Design: International Perspectives*.

After setting up several aims, a curriculum should have its own basic philosophy. The plan will have to focus on how the teaching will be delivered, and in relation to this, the methodology of teaching. The final step will be the plan to provide material and teaching apparatus (in the form of a syllabus). The syllabus is generally conceived as a list or inventory of items or units with which students are to be familiarized. As one aspect of the apparatus of the curriculum, the syllabus specifies "the content of a course of instruction and lists what will be taught and tested" (Richards, 2001:2). A syllabus designer at the very least should provide a rationale for the design of the syllabus. And this will emerge from an approach that "selects language units for progressive assimilation by [students]" (Crombie, 1985:1). I will employ this theory to construct an alternative multicultural literary canon in the curriculum of an Indonesian English Department.

3. What to Read?

Recent research on critical pedagogy adopts values that resistance is the political site where teacher and students can raise "pertinent questions of canon, culture, identity and representation in literary texts" (Hardin, 1999 and Johnston, 1996). Ashcroft et al. (1989) furthermore explain that "[O]ne of the main features of imperial oppression is the control over language and this becomes the medium through which a hierarchical structure of power is perpetuated (Ashcroft et al., 1989:7). This power supports the very basic concern of the emergence of "*canonical texts*" (a set of definitions of the canon has been further explored by Guillory, 1995). The canonical literary texts produce a set of fixed discourses maintained by a particular group to define the center and marginal texts. The discourse of post-colonialism has therefore been grounded in a struggle for power—that power focused in the control of the metropolitan language (Foucault in H. L. Dreyfus and P. Rabinow (ed.), 167). The metropolitan literary texts reflect the centralization of the will of power. "Canonization is the most extreme form of what Nietzsche called interpretation or the exercise of the will-to-power over texts" (Bloom, 1975:100). "A canon is not a body of texts 'per se', but a set of reading practices [...] and these reading practices, in turn, are residents in institutional structures, such as education curriculum and publishing networks" (Ashcroft et al, 1989:189). The Western literary canon experiences total exposure because of the frequent representation through the discourse of English language teaching. Questions over value, meaning, social function, and canonicity have become subjects of controversy in the recent history of literary theory (Gerald Graff in Myers, 1994: 9). And one of the struggles within the English Department, as Tiffin highlights, is "the relationship between canonized and deeply institutionalized 'mainstream' British literature and other literatures in English" (Tiffin in J.M.Q. Davies (ed.), 1994:41). As the discourse of Western-oriented literature has been investigated critically by Said, he does not mean to annihilate the canon but rather to "search for a more flexible, more provisional canon answering to a broader range of immanent cultural needs" (Gorak, 1991:209). This proposal of an open canon reveals a place for the peripheral and marginal texts to have their representation.

Volkmann further argues for a new privileged status for literature—especially minority/post-colonial literature—because of its exemplary staging of the current human condition and the insights it offers into the evolving new value-systems of the ethical turn of postmodernism as a means of dialogic competence in the EFL-classroom (Volkmann in Heinz Antor and Kevin L. Cope (eds.)., 1999:132). He adds that such competence entails in great part an understanding of the recent theoretical debates on post-colonialism and *Fremdverstehen*, the intricacies of cross-cultural understanding (Volkmann, 1991:33-37). Stein further warns that by concentrating disproportionally on a small number of recognizable voices, post-colonial polyphony is in danger of being transposed into homophony, with many writers being confined to the margin. Paradoxically, this is a marginalization that occurs under the sign of celebrating diversity (Stein, 2004:183). This helps "to defeat the monolithic, one-way Western narratives of cultural domination" (Walder, 1998:114). The canonical works are expected to provide knowledge of the world represented, to exemplify powers for making representations that express possible attitudes or produce artistic models, and to articulate shared values in a past culture that influence the present or to clarify means of reading other works we have reason to care about (Altieri, 1990:41).

As suggested by Tiffin, the starting point in teaching post-colonial theory remains the literary texts, since in spite of the recent turn to theory "the literary texts remain the focus of most English department curricula" (Tiffin, 1994:42). The particular reason why the literary texts become the center of the curriculum is that "for most post-colonial literary critics, a return to post-colonial literary texts comprises an absolutely crucial gesture within the politics of critical writing and the *sine qua non* of a literary critical engagement with the structures of neo-colonialist power" (Tiffin, 1994:42). Further, Tiffin suggests that teaching post-colonial literary theory involves more than teaching the relevant literary texts and relevant theorists. It involves "an approach which necessarily impacts on literary study generally and the current structures and ideologies of English departments as they are still generally organized" (Tiffin, 1994:46). It opens a more critical and interrogative awareness of the teaching process, an influence that operates "*against the grain*" (Tiffin, 1994:49). It teaches the students the current canon not in the traditional way but rather teaches them to read against it—by understanding the values and meanings of the texts in students' contexts.

Teaching against the grain suggests inquiring into relations of power. Power is not only repressive but also productive. The location of productivity within the text should be inquired into, not in a traditional way in which the fetishization of a Western canon becomes absolute. This inquiry is structured to address questions of gender, colonialism, and representations between the Centre and its Other. Instead of questioning the character and characterization, style, point of view, plot and theme within the structuralist framework, teaching against the grain questions the positions of the characters, how these positions might be exchanged, or how the texts could possibly be rewritten from different points of view. And the textual analysis should be combined with an analysis of practices that produce power. This will deal with how the author positions him/herself, how characters are positioned, how the readers are positioned by the author, how the reader positions her/himself in reading the texts. The curriculum construction will envisage the way Volkman scrutinizes recent prominent observers such as Beck, Habermas, or Morley and Robins, finding that "very few curricula have yet tackled explicitly" any intercultural contact which required critical awareness in the multicultural society within the era of globalization (Volkmann in Antor & Stierstorfer (eds.), 2000:406-407). This curriculum aims to what Volkmann envisaged from Habermas' proposal on "die gleichberechtigte Koexistenz der Lebensformen"—"the co-existence of differing ways of life" in an interdependent world society.

Ashcroft, Griffiths, and Tiffin in *The Empire Writes Back* (1989) demonstrate the counter-canonical textual strategies in post-colonial writing and post-colonialism as a reading strategy. In counter-canon writing, English, which is used by colonial discourse as a means of speaking from the centre and of drawing diversity into the metropolis, is adopted by post-colonial writers as a cultural means of writing back. In order not to repeat the master's command and in order to liberate their writing from the standard of the canon, the English language has to undergo transformative processes: abrogation and appropriation. Ashcroft, Griffiths, and Tiffin give the definition of the terms as follows: abrogation is a refusal of the categories of the imperial culture, its aesthetics, its illusory standard of normative or 'correct' usage, and its assumption of a traditional and fixed meaning 'inscribed' in the word. It is a vital moment in the decolonizing of the language and the writing of 'english'. Appropriation is the process by which the language is taken and made to 'bear the burden' of one's own cultural experience, or, as Raja Rao puts it, 'to convey in a language that is not one's own the spirit that is one's own' (Rao cited by Ashcroft et al, 1989:38-39).

The denial of standard English which leads to the use of a variety of 'Englishes' and the usurpation of the language to articulate social and cultural identities of post-colonial societies aims to diversify the centralized notion of correctness and redefine the concept of 'difference'. For post-colonial writers, it is the difference in the diverse cultural experiences of the post-colonial society that needs to be acknowledged. One interesting aspect of post-colonial writing back is the 'rewriting' of mainstream English texts, such as the rewriting of Shakespeare's *The Tempest*, of Daniel Defoe's *Robinson Crusoe*, of Charlotte Bronte's *Jane Eyre* in Jean Rhys' *Wide Sargasso Sea*, and of Joseph Conrad's *Heart of Darkness* in Chinua Achebe's *Things Fall Apart*, for example. In writing back of this kind, canonical texts no longer contain, to quote Ashcroft, "their centrality or 'greatness' which dominates, no longer their revelation of the 'universal human condition', but the newly revealed cultural horizons of their hybrid and transformative 'counters'" (Ashcroft, 2001:34). Here, English is used to write from the specific culture of post-colonial experiences and with the standpoint of the margin. Therefore, the post-colonial texts become, according to Ashcroft, Griffiths, and Tiffin, a site of struggle for linguistic control (Ashcroft, 2001:115).

In post-colonial counter-canonical discourse, writing strategies are accompanied by a reading strategy. In the post-colonial reading of the canon, English texts are read from points of view that are different from those of the centre. Aiming to uncover the silent voice of the repressed in specific canonical texts, in the 're-reading' of such a literary text such as *The Tempest*, Caliban is regarded not as a sub-human creature, but as an important individual and human-being. In the subversion of canonical texts via re-reading, the value judgments of the master are no longer the fixed standards that control the interpretation of meanings. The transferral of power from the centre via post-colonial reading strategies conveys the political dimensions of discarding the Orientalist discourse—the stereotyping representation of the Other. Instead, what is valued and emphasized is cultural plurality, differences and diversity rather than binary oppositions.

4. The English Language as a Melting Pot

Before English became an international language, English had experienced constant changes and influences. To scrutinize this will help the readers of postcolonial literature to understand the position of English before European colonization in the 18th century. This exploration shows that English has long been a melting pot of all European languages. This melting pot position was further influenced by European exploration of other continents such as Asia, America, Australia, and Africa. Loan words and cohabitation have continued up until the present.

This short sketch of the history of the English language will inquire into the origin of the word "anglo-saxon". The frequent phrase "anglo-saxon" is used by postcolonial critics to illustrate the relation of the English language and its metropolitan position. Before English achieved its metropolitan standing in the early nineteenth century, the English language possessed relatively minor status in the face of Latin and other European languages such as French. It is a strenuous effort of the historical imagination to picture an early modern world in which English occupied only a relatively minor place (Yadav, 2004:27). Yadav asserts the traditionally marginal status of English literary cultures in the European world (Yadav, 2004:175). By providing this brief sketch from the fifth century onward, "anglo-saxon" experienced constant hybridization through its history along with the development of its language, *Englisc*, up until the present. This supports the thesis of Pratt's "contact zone" in which metropolitan and periphery interact and influence one another. The stream of influences is not only determined by the center in relation to the marginal but also the other way around.

After the withdrawal of the Roman legions from Britain by the early fifth century, in the mid fifth century AD (A.D. 449) three Germanic invaded Britain: the Teutonic Invaders (Morris, 1883:27) from European mainland; the Angles (from the south of the Danish peninsula); the Saxons (from the coastal areas to the west of the Danish peninsula); and the Jutes (from Jutland, in the north of the Danish peninsula). These tribes, referred to as Anglo-Saxons, settled permanently in the south and east coast of the British Isles (Knowles, 1997; Baugh, 1993; Graddol et al, 1996; Penhallurick, 2003). They called the land they had won ´ngla-land (the land of the Angles) (Knowles, 1997; Baugh, 1993; Graddol et al, 1996; Penhallurick, 2003). The British Isles spoke a variety of Celtic languages such as Manx, Cornish, Welsh, Scots, Scots Gaelic, Norn, and Irish. These settlers used their diverse dialects which stem from one of the Proto-Indo-European languages, the West Germanic language. Morris explained that the name *German* was probably given to the Teutons by some continental Celtic tribes. Some philologists argue that the word German is said to have meant howlers, shriekers (from Celtic *gairm-a*, to cry out), on account of their warlike shouts. Other theorists connect the name with the Celtic stem *germo* 'hot' (cognate with the English adjective *warm*), referring to hot springs near Aachen (Brook, 1958:37). Another theory regards it as derived from Latin *germanus* 'genuine' (Brook, 1958:37). The Germans still call their language *Deut-sch* (or *Deutch*). The origin of the term is found in Old High German *diot*, people, *duit-isc*, national. In the oldest English *theod* and *theodicy* refers to people (cf. Umbrian Latin *tuticus*, from *tuta*, a city). The Teutons were *the people*, in contradistinction to the Romans and others, whom they called *Welsh*, or foreign (Morris, 1883:3). The Danes, the Dutch, the Germans, and the English, are all considered as nations of Teutonic origin. They occupied a large portion of central Europe at the same time that the Celts spead over the western parts of Europe which scattered along the western shores of France and Spain, several centuries before the Christian era (Chambers Educational Course, 1888:1-2). The indigenous people spoke the Celtic language and the newcomers practiced their dialects, which by the ninth century had been labeled as '*Englisc*' (Penhallurick, 2003). Some scholars, however, argue that the formation of the English used by the Anglo-Saxons did not occur on the European mainland, but rather in the islands of Britain (Graddol, Leith & Swann, 1996). DeCamp further argues that "the origin of English dialects lie not in pre-migrational tribal affiliations but in a certain social, economic, and cultural development which occurred after the migration was completed" (De Camp, 1958:232). Wood adds that the term West Germanic through which English is connected to its earlier ancestors is purely theoretical. He explains that there is no written, documentary evidence of it. However, he highlights that from a comparative study of certain tongues (notably Anglo-Saxon, Dutch and German), philologists believe that these must have been derived from a third branch of Primitive Germanic, differing in certain respects from both Gothic and Scandinavian, and they have agreed on the term *West Germanic* as a designation for English (Wood, 1950:21). According to Penhallurick and Wood, the term "Indo-European" is chosen instead of "Aryan" or "Indo-Germanic" to give rise to the Indo-Iranian languages such as Sanskrit and Persian and to give prominence to their relationships with the Romance and Slavonic groups) (Wood, 1950:21).

DeCamp's thesis was supported by the fact that the original Old English (450-1100 AD) had been influenced by two other Proto-Indo-European languages. The first influence was from the indigenous inhabitants of the British Isles, the Celts. It was argued that in many cases the Saxon invaders married

British women, who spoke their own language, taught their children to speak their mother tongue, and whose words took firm roots in the kitchen of the new English household (Meiklejohn, 1897:283). The second influence was the Scandinavian branch of the Germanic family from the Danes, who colonized part of Britain in the 8th and 9th centuries (797). And the third influence was the Normans in the 11th century (1066) who spoke a variety of French called Anglo-Norman. From both languages, English received some loan words. English was not actually mixed with the two languages, rather they experienced cohabitation. The cohabitation with the Scandinavian language resulted in a significant grammatical simplification, including loss of grammatical gender and lexical enrichment. The cohabitation with the Norman language led to an influence on the spelling. Before these three languages influenced English, English had formerly been influenced also by Latin-Roman. English also received some loan words from Latin.

During the Norman reign in the British Isles for three hundreds years, English was spoken by the lower classes (Knowles, 1997:17; Sheridan by Yadav, 2004:46), while the upper classes spoke French. French was the language of the Royal courts and the ruling and business classes. During French domination it was called Middle English (1100-1500). English became a minor language in the world of literature since most of the literary works were written in Old French or Latin. Later, English cohabitated with influences from the Anglo-Norman culture. A large number of Norman words were assimilated into Old English. English received the continuous tense of –ing. Some of French spelling also influenced it.

During the 15th century, Middle English was transformed by the Great Vowel Shift. This transformation dated back to the emergence of so-called Modern English (1500-1800) in the late 15th century. After the middle of the 14th century, English started to gain its victory, the victory which was progressing until the Renaissance and Reformation in the 16th century (Knowles, 17; Sheridan by Yadav, 46). This century also led the British to expand into other regions, and is otherwise known as the era of imperialism. During this period there were two main influences which reshaped English: firstly, the Industrial Revolution which needed new words; and secondly, the British Empire, which at its height covered one quarter of the globe. This last principal factor led English to adopt foreign words from many territories.

Despite the previous periodization of English by some scholars and historians, others also regard this periodization as being based on the influence of Latin upon the English language. Latin was the language of the Romans and has influenced almost all languages in Europe. Apart from language-internal contact between variants of English, the four aforementioned languages which played a major role in the shaping of English are Latin, Celtic, Scandinavian and French. Of these four, Latin had the most extended influence, temporally speaking, especially in relation to vocabulary (Kastovsky & Mettinger, 2001:10). There are more Latin words than English in the English language, although the grammar is distinctly English and not Latin at all (Meiklejohn, 1897:281). The influence of Latin upon English is described by Wood as follows (Morris, 1883:27-32). The Latin First period consists of words that have had no influence upon the language itself, but are only to be found in names of places, as *castra*, in Doncaster, Chester, etc. The first contribution of Latin was made by the Roman not directly to the English but to the Britons. From 43 AD until 410 AD, Roman held the British Isles. The Romans left the Celts with words from Latin that mostly became the names of places. The Latin of the Second Period is when the English were converted to Christianity around A.D. 596 by Augustine and his forty missionary monks from Rome. They were granted land to settle in Canterbury by the King of Kent. During the four following centuries many Latin words were introduced *directly* by Roman ecclesiastics, and by English writers who translated Latin works into their own language. At this period, literature was not neglected by the Anglo-Saxons. Their first known writer was *Gildas*, a historian, who flourished about the year 560. Another was called *Bede*, a priest, who lived in the eight century and was celebrated all over Europe for his knowledge and literary productivity. But the majority of the writers of that age thought it necessary to compose their works in Latin, as it was only by that means they could make themselves intelligible to the scholars of other countries, who were almost their only readers (Chambers Educational Course). Latin of the Third Period refers to the Norman-French *indirect* influence during its invasion of Britain (the Norman-French having originated from the Latin language brought into Gaul, or Celtic, by the Romans). Latin of the Fourth Period is from the Revival of Learning in the beginning of the sixteenth century up to the present time by the introduction of a large number of words from Latin. Meiklejohn states that this period was rather a process than an event, the dates of which are vague, but which may be said to have taken place in the sixteenth and seventeenth centuries (Meiklejohn, 1897:285).

From the previous two broadly sketched outlines of the periodizations of the English language, it is clear that its history has been determined variously by social changes. The English language from its initial development has been subjected to constant foreign influences. From the very beginning, English was also positioned as one of the minor languages among many other proto-Indo-European languages. History indicated that the superior European language among others was Latin. This fact shows that the position of English as the solid center in the postcolonial perspective is problematic and unstable. The history of English shows that from the very beginning of its development, English had already became a melting pot, since English has borrowed many words and undergone grammatical changes during its development. English has always been in close contact with other European languages. This constant exposure was followed by its meetings with other languages outside Europe in the course of British Imperialism. Yadav has called this the transformation of the status of the English language in relation to the larger European world of letters and in relation to the global stage (Yadav, 2004:45).

5. The Teaching of English as Second and Foreign Language

During British imperialism, English was experiencing constant dynamic changes. Its encounters with Spanish during the discovery of the New World in 1492 led to some Spanish words being integrated into English. And its commercial dealings with the Dutch also enriched its vocabularies. In the late 15th century, the European Age of Discovery led to global maritime explorations. British overseas explorations outside of Europe and the British Isles led to the establishment of the British Empire. This was pioneered by the reign of King Henry VII (1485-1509) and developed and expanded gradually by King Henry VIII. During his reign, he established the Royal Navy as the backbone of further British overseas explorations. This basic navy system was developed further during the reign of the Tudor Queen Elizabeth I (1553) who was succeeded by Elizabeth in 1558. In 1562 Hawkins began the slave trade (Meiklejohn, 1897:449). During her reign the concept of British Empire had been coined by John Dee (a Welshman who derived this concept from Dante's book *Monarchia*). Following this era, America was founded and emigrational settlement was promoted to other lands such as Canada, Australia, New Zealand and South Africa. This has been labeled as the "first British Empire". In this case, English was being spread by its native speakers. In Howatt's terminology these were called the *Colonies of Settlement* in which English was the mother tongue from the beginning, and which led to "new English" being born from long term contact between settlers and indigenous people (Howatt & Widdowson, 2004:128). Such English is popularly called English as the First Language (EFL) in the discourse of English Language Teaching.

At the end of the "first British Empire" with the loss of America in the 17th and 18th centuries, the British moved to the "second British Empire" which expanded into Asia and Africa. In this era, the British exercised Mercantilism; the economic doctrine of competition between nations for a finite amount of wealth under the spirit of Adam Smith's economic liberalism. The loss of America led Britain to grant self-governing colony status to Canada, Australia, and New Zealand. During this period, the British government also banned slavery in 1834.

The second British Empire has been divided by Howatt into second and third categories. His second category comprises territories where the British presence had political and economic purposes, but which explicitly excluded permanent settlement, examples being India and other parts of Asia such as Hong Kong, Singapore, Ceylon, and Malaya. And the third category is a colony of settlement with imported slave and workforces who inevitably experienced the most extreme dislocation particularly during the independence process, as in Kenya and Zimbabwe. Within this second Empire, English has been labeled as English as Second Language (ESL).

The decision to make English the second language was partly due to the inauguration of English as the official language in the former colonies of the British Empire. The numbers of English speakers of the several sovereign states and territories where English was an official language was a total of 2,135 million people who occupied 15,583,152 square miles. India represented over half of this population.

The categorization of English as the first language, second language, and foreign language (in the case of nations other than those previously mentioned, such as Indonesia) proved it to be a living and diverse entity. As a living language English has been undergoing changes and modifications (Morris, 1883:48). With the interruption of the history of the British imperialism, English has also been in close contact with other non-European languages. And these contacts have created a dynamic "giving, taking and borrowing" relationship among languages.

The earliest major example of English in this role was provided by India, where the language was adopted in the nineteenth century as a medium of general education, largely because at the time no other language seemed available for the purpose (Perren, 1968:1). The medium of teaching in English was then widely spread in neighboring countries in Asia and Africa. At the same time, some countries where there has been no former colonial dependence on Britain have extended the teaching of English as an essential second language—Indonesia and Thailand for example (Perren, 1968:1). The spread of English in the educational sphere in Africa and Asia inaugurated its position as "pre-eminent even among the languages of the West", to borrow the following prophecy made by Macaulays's in 1835:

> The claims of our language it is hardly necessary to recapitulate. It stands pre-eminent even among the languages of the West...Whoever knows that language has ready access to all the vast intellectual wealth which the wisest nations of the earth have created and hoarded in the course of ninety generations...it is likely to become the language of commerce throughout the seas of the East (Macaulay quoted by Perren, 1968:1-2).

The status of English as a metropolital language was acquired mainly not by the "erasure" of other languages in the periphery, but rather by the recognition of linguistic and cultural diversities within the Empire. Yadav has argued that the central elevation of English as a metropolitan language is mainly due to the negotiation of the metropolitan and provincial standing within the imperial culture as a project of hegemony and at the same time as a project of cultural assimilation (Yadav, 2004:45). It was the most important modality of the British Empire.

Such a modality was also supported by the attitude of spreading the language to the Empire by the teaching English language.

However, the spread of English after 1600 had not been accompanied by much in the way of English teaching (Morris, 1883:48). In the late eighteenth century and nineteenth century England, education meant learning Latin and Greek (Blake, 1996:274). To use correct English, the educated had to learn the Classics. And literacy meant knowing the language and culture of the Classics. William Cobbet took his role to be providing the less educated with the means of fighting against these exclusions. He strove to achieve a powerful weapon in which the lower classes could improve their position and status through education, particularly grammar. He published his English Grammar book in 1818 in New York (Blake, 1996:275-277). Cobbet opposed the idea that language was an attribute of class. His Grammar book was intended for the illiterate and lower classes in general. Besides providing an easy and simple course in English grammar, he also continued attacking the use of Latin in Education as a means of excluding the layman. His book provided easy access to the unfortunate masses who could not afford education. Further he brought common sense rather than prejudice, leading to a situation in which the poorly educated classes could improve their position and their status through education. His efforts offered no sudden revolution, but rather a new climate in which the class struggles of the early nineteenth century took place. He believed that education was a powerful weapon for the lower classes.

Cobbet's English Grammar Book marked the birth of the independence of the English language from the privileged Latin teaching at schools and universities in Britain. Such a phenomenon was influenced by four major factors before 1789 when the use of a "polite" language of the eighteenth century was under strain. This also supported the use of the "real", concrete and popular language instead of an abstract and classical one. The first was the freeing up of restrictions on newsprints and copyrights; the second was the American Revolution; the third was the French Revolution, which led to democratic movements; and the fourth was the discovery by Sir William Jones that Sanskrit [the language of India—part of British Empire] was related to Latin and Greek (Blake, 1996:272-273). The superiority of Latin was thus challenged by the acknowledgement of the language of a British colony (in this case, India). This factor placed the old system under pressure. The discovery of the development of the Proto-Indo-European languages encouraged the view that all languages were equal. This equality was also supported by the way in which German influences exerted themselves in England. Johann Michaelis from Goettingen University recognized that the use of language was democratic, that is, its use was decided by the majority of the speakers of a language, whereas the learned formed an infinitesimal part of those speakers (Blake, 1996:282-283). This concept questioned the view that a proper language is the preserve of educated elites.

The Independence of America brought a new spirit of rejecting dictated norms and standards from England. Noah Webster published *The American Spelling Book* (1783) and *An American Dictionary of the English Language* (1828) which marked the birth of another genre, American English which then became another source of Standard English after World War II. Cobbet and Webster had to undergo constant opposition from those who wanted to set up a Britain-centered Standard English.

Following the outbreak of the First World War 1914, America was becoming a superpower vis-à-vis Soviet Union. During the early twentieth century, despite the growing tension of the First World War (WW I) and the Second World War (WW II), there were also some other growing advancements in science and technology. This led to a revolution in travel and communication. After WW II, some former colonized countries were made independent. Malaysia and India were freed from the British government and Indonesia was freed from the Dutch, just to mention a few examples among many other new nations which tried to free themselves from their former European colonizers.

After the communication revolution, which was marked by the arrival of computers and recently the internet, the world has shrunk and been labeled as a "global village". During this revolution, English has played a significant role. English has been labeled as an international language, as many people communicate in this language. Quirk et al have argued that English has become the "primary medium" for twentieth-century science and technology (Quirk et al, 1972:2). Kachru argued that competence in English and the use of this language signify a "transmutation": an added potential for material and social gain and advantage in which English is considered as a symbol for modernization, a key to expanded functional roles, and an extra tool for success and mobility in culturally and linguistically complex pluralistic societies (Kachru, 1982:1). Its position was first supported by the emergence of America as the Superpower and the many areas in which English became the Second Official language (in the former British Empire) and Foreign language (in the non-British Empire in which English is seen as indispensable, people must learn this language to enable them to survive in the global world, and even to have more political, social, and economic power).

Despite the existence of the American language which was followed by Australian and Canadian English, a new attitude of 'linguistic tolerance' which grew out of the post-WW II had created another arrival of English variants; Hall has described this situation with the expression "hands off pidgin" (Kachru, 198317). By supporting the existence of Pidgins and Creoles within the English variants, certain linguists have rejected "the time-honored slogan 'There are no mixed languages' not because [they] necessarily consider it disaproven but because they do not find in it a useful guideline for the study of linguistic variation in general and contact vernaculars in particular" (DeCamp et al, 1974:70). Another factor which drove this change was the publication of *Cours de linguistique general* (which contained the lectures of Ferdinand de Saussure) in 1916. Saussure's structuralist approach led to a shift from the historical study of language to the study of language as a meaningful entity in its own right during a particular period of time. This also paved the way for upgrading the study of the varieties of English within the former Empire (Blake, 1996:309). In addition, this challenged the supremacy of Standard English. Kachru's life has been devoted to Indian English, to name an example. Other variants have also occurred such as Nigerian English. Kachru proposes that the arrival of these new variants is caused by the acculturation of the English language in the linguistically and culturally pluralist context of the former British Empire (Kachru, 1986:1). He further suggests that the new varieties have their own linguistic and cultural ecologies or socio-cultural contexts in which the adaptations to these new ecologies have given non-native Englishes new identities (Kachru, 1986:12).

In line with the variants of English, Kachru argues that it is difficult to raise a question of the model in discussing English as International and intra-national language (Kachru, 1983:238). He further asserts that the teaching of English is based on a dynamic model which embraces polymodels with reference to the local, intranational and international uses (Kachru, 1983:238). In his perspective, interference should be regarded as *deviation* rather than *mistake*. The term "deviation" describes the cultural and linguistical nativization of a variety of English. Blake, in his conclusion, states that "a corollary of this development has been greater status for these different varieties, both in England and abroad, and those who try to re-establish norms in Britain will find it difficult to control the development of English within Britain, let alone in the rest of the world" (Blake, 1996:332).

The variety of English has elevated English into a position of an International language. This variety is supported by the existence of other languages which came into contact with the English language during British colonization and the recent "global village". English becomes the "other tongue" or as a second or foreign language. The "other tongue" is not an innocent tongue, but rather a multi-faceted concept with a long history and different manifestations in various regions of the world (Kachru, 1982:1). He classifies the non-native varieties of English worldwide (30-40 percent of English speakers) into the institutionalized and the performance varieties and suggests a need for an attitudinal change toward the institutionalized non-native Englishes (Kachru, 1982:325-344). The non-native Englishes practice English as a Second or Foreign Language on the institutional level.

In 1978, some specialists were fully conscious of the visible shift in emphasis within the field of the study and Teaching English as Foreign/Second language (annotated as TEFL or TESOL) (Strevens, 1980:91). The term TESOL (Teaching English to Speakers of Other Languages) is widely used to include both TEFL (Teaching of English as Foreign Language) and TESL (Teaching of English as Second Language). *TESOL Inc.* was founded in 1966 and has its corporate headquarters in Alexandria Virginia. It was designed under the United Nations Department of Public Information as an NGO. It had more than 13,000 members in more than 120 different countries and had nearly one hundred affiliates within other language education groups, representing approximately 47,000 members (about half of the affiliates were outside of the USA). TESOL is commonly and widely known in American English. In British English the equivalent term is ELT (English Language Teaching). (Some of the previous data is taken from the various TESOL and TEFL website).

English as a foreign language is spoken in the non-English-speaking regions such as Indonesia, Japan, China, and other countries which were not previously colonized by the British Empire. In these countries, teaching English as a second language has been required in the national curriculum from school until university level. Typically, EFL is learned either to pass exams as a necessary part of one's education, or for career progression while working for an organization with an international focus, and TEFL presupposes literacy in the mother tongue. EFL may be part of the state school curriculum in countries where English has no special status (as in the case of most European Union nations). People of these countries may also be supplemented by private lessons, whether for school children or business people.

Besides professional associations, learners of English are often keen to get accreditation via a number of international exams such as: IELTS (International English Language Testing System), accepted by most tertiary academic institution in the UK, Australia, New Zealand and Canada. TOEFL (Test of English AS Foreign Language), and Education Testing Service test of English language proficiency for academic purposes, are accepted primarily in the USA. TOEIC (Test of English for International Communication), is an Educational Testing Service test of English language proficiency for business purposes.

Those who work in the area of English teaching as a Second or Foreign language are founding professional associations to support their programs. TESOL Inc. refers to Teachers of English to Speakers of Other Languages, a professional organization based in the United States. IATEFL is the international Association of Teachers of English as a Foreign Language, a professional organization based in Britain. Several other professional organizations for teachers of English exist at national levels such as SPELT in Pakistan, BELTA in Bangladesh, SLELTA in Sri Lanka, NELTA in Nepal, MELTA in Malaysia, TEFLIN in Indonesia, ASIATEFL in the region of Asia.

The previous brief sketch of the history of the English language clearly shows constant influences coming from the outside of the English language. Being brought to the British Isles by the Anglo-Saxon-Germanic-Tribes from mainland Europe, English was shaped mainly by other proto-Indo-European languages, especially the Latin. In the course of history, English deconstructed the center position of Latin among the educated-elite in England and absorbed a large numbers of Latin words. This inauthenticity of English formed a process of living-hybridity, which has seen it become the most used living language in the contemporary world. Constant exposures were also experienced because of British colonization, whether in the first or second phase, in which English was spread as the First language or the Second language. English has also emerged through histories of cultural transactions with multiple others. These others remain constitutive elements in the process of consolidating English as an International language. English is itself fundamentally hybrid.

Open exposures to other influences whether from inside or outside Europe paved the way for the deconstruction of elite English education both in the center and periphery of the British Empire. Within the heart of the British Empire, English Grammar Book signaled the rise of the illiterates to study English and to gain social status within the struggle of the classes. Outside the British Empire, the most populated former colony, America, departed from standard (British) English. America inaugurated its own American English which was later followed by Canadian English, Australian English, etc. The regions outside the British settlement also proclaimed their own Englishness in the form of pidgins and creoles, such as Nigerian English. The rise of English from the language of "the illiterates and the vulgars" to the International language brought with it other consequences.

Some nations of the former British Empire retained English as their official language. This decision had its effects, one of them was the teaching of English as a Second and a Foreign language. As English was growing as an International language, some professionals English teaching organisations were founded to cater for the demand. Along with this, several associations were also established to handle the tests for those who learn English as a Second or a Foreign language, such as the famous TOEFL and IELTS tests.

At the national levels, similar professional memberships and associations were also founded in connection with the organizations at the international level which are based in Britain and America. Indonesia, as a country in which English operates as a Foreign language, could not escape from the powerful influences of English as an International language in the interplay of economical, cultural, and political effects of globalization. The previous brief historical sketch envisions the further development of an English language curriculum in Indonesian Higher Education.

6. Situating the Indonesian Curriculum

A free market economic system was activated by the Indonesian government in 2003, and this has been affecting the educational sector in Indonesia. Competitiveness is the spirit behind this economic system. Indonesian universities are predicted by many experts to be unable to compete with foreign qualified universities. The current Indonesian curriculum has the following weaknesses: (1) a monolithical educational material design which is provided for all universities; and (2): a closed-system development in which students' creativity has had limited room to grow, and which has failed to cater local wisdom. Although local values are not denied, due to the vast diversities in Indonesia, they are not fully appreciated as well by the Indonesian educational system.

The department of National Education has introduced a new curriculum for the higher education, called the 2000 Higher Education Curriculum (Kurikulum Pendidikan Tinggi Tahun 2000). This new curriculum changed the basic paradigm and philosophy of the previous 1994 Higher Education Curriculum (hereafter HEC). The paradigm of 1994 HEC applied a content-based approach. The 2000 HEC also applied content-based approach in which students' competences play a basic role in the educational policy. This new version of curriculum was developed in reaction to the UNESCO educational philosophy, that is learning to know, learning to do, learning to be, and learning to live together. This philosophical change in the paradigm of education, however, was found to be difficult to apply at a practical level.

The problems faced by many higher education institutions in applying this paradigm are as follows: the external factors, (1) globalization which, in being characterised by flows of people, information, technology, capital, images and ideas, has been inclined to homogenize multidimentional cultural values. (2) The politicization of higher education in relation to the economic and political factors outside of the educational sector. (3) The wide gap in technological advancement between the first and third worlds. The internal factors are as follows: (1) the demands of educational distribution throughout Indonesia have been difficult to tackle; (2) the large gap between advanced / qualified and non-advanced institutions; (3) a lack of educational experts and resources in advancing the quality of education in Indonesia.

With the previous problems the policy being adopted by the Educational Department is to manifest three educational pillars in the Indonesian Higher Education system: the Board of the Chancellor that provides visions, paradigms and philosophy; the Board of the Executor, which works at the practical level; and the Board of the Evaluator, which evaluates the educational output. Besides forming the basic pillars of the higher education system, the Department of Education also cooperates with the stake holders in the economic, social and political sectors, as well as transposing the educational paradigm into strategies of accountability, autonomy, self-evalution, accreditation, working competency, and morality in practice.

In the development of curriculum materials, many Indonesian academic institutions have misunderstood the meaning behind the 2000 HEC. They thought that the main factor behind curricula should be that of students' acquring specific competence, regardless of the academic content which was outlined in the 1994 HEC. But the 2000 HEC was intended as a follow up to the 1994 HEC, which meant that in order to have a particular competence, students would have to be able to master the academic content as prescribed in the previous (1994) curriculum. Students should master the basic knowledge prescribed in the curriculum as well as being ready to have particular competence in order to be able to work at the professional level.

The formulation of competences in the 2000 HEC contained three basic aspects: (1) students' competencies in their own daily lives as an individuals; (2) professional competence in the workplace; and (3) competence as part of the community as a whole. This affected the formulation of each subject in the university curriculum. Subjects were formulated into the following divisions: (1) 4%-6% to develop individual characters, *Mata Kuliah Pengembangan Kepribadian* (MPK); (2) 50%-60% to develop creativity, *Mata Kuliah Keterampilan dan Keahlian* (MKK); (3) 30%-40% to develop competence in a real practice, *Mata Kuliah Keahlian Berkarya* (MKB); (4) 10%-15% to support students' innovation, *Mata Kuliah Perilaku Berkarya* (MPB); (5) 6%-8% to support students character as part of the community, *Mata Kuliah Berkehidupan Bermasyarakat* (MBB). These divisions are cited from the Government Regulation No. 60/1999 Article 13.

The shift from a content-based to a competence-based approach in the educational sector was conspicuously a consequence of the economic crisis faced by Indonesia since 1998 as well as the AFTA (Asian Free Trade Action) in 2003, when qualified foreign experts flocked to Indonesia, and the issuing of International Certification in the professional workplace affected the local and unqualified human resources. The 2000 HEC is a curriculum designed to secure the future, specifically in the competitive arena of globalization. This is meant to accelerate Indonesian university outputs in the following areas: (1) The developmental sector in which social justice, chances in the workplace, as well as the supremacy of law emphasise competencies which had previously been ignored in the 1994 HEC. (2) The 21st Millennium Development Goals (MDGs) in which students are encouraged to master foreign languages, information and technology skills as well as entrepreneurship. (3) *Kuliah Kerja Nyata* (KKN), practical field works for students in which particular stakeholders train and use them in the work place. (4) The understanding of the local, national and international cultural values formulated in *Ilmu Budaya Dasar*, Basic Cultural Education, through which students are expected to have empathy, solidarity and respect for other cultural values in the frame of global ethics. Cultural understanding is intended to increase the appreciation of diverse cultural values to minimize ethnic, religious, national conflicts. (5) Excellence in specialized fields of study and professionalism in the workplace. This encourages universities to select particular deparments as areas of excellence.

7. Situating the Muhammadiyah Curriculum

Universities with excellence in special areas thus become specific trademarks, leading to empowerment as well as market orientation. In the context of Islamic/ Muhammadiyah Universities, the area of excellence is mostly determined by the values of Islamic morality. Muhammadiyah universities are established on the ground of the Quran and the Hadits, as the two pillars of the Islamic way of life. Despite being grounded on the Quran and the Hadits, there are two other important sources of morality: Ijma and Qiyas. Ijma refers to the words of ulama and clerics, while Qiyas is a form of rational deduction. The previous four sources play significant roles in moulding the concept as well as identity of Muhammadiyah universities. The source of authority in exercising the previous four sources is often disputed. There is always a debate between ultra-conservative ulemas and liberal-progressive ulemas in defining the philosophy of Islamic education. The Internal dynamics within Muhammadiyah educational bodies manifest the struggle for authority, played out by important ulemas, whether conservative or progressive. Besides being characterized by ulemas, the philosophy of Islamic education is mostly defined by Professors in Muhammadiyah universities who graduated in the West. This tradition dates back to policies introduced by the Dutch Government in 1930. The development of Muhammadiyah Higher Education was started in 1958 when it established its first university, Universitas Muhammadiyah Hamka (UHAMKA). The establishment of such a university was actually planned shortly before Indonesian Independence in 1945. World War II, however, affected the development of the educational sector in Indonesia, which had been established by the Dutch in 1900.

There was a great struggle within Muhammadiyah in 1950, regarding the question of establishig a Jawiyah or a University as a form of Higher Education. These debates were exhausted when the proponents of Jawiyah (North African Model) had to accept that the University, as a European model, was the best form of Higher Education. This was as a significant era in which the first blueprint of the form of Muhammadiyah education began to follow Western models. The adoption of Western educational models had, however, actually had been intitiated by the founder of Muhammadiyah, Ahmad Dahlan, in 1912, when he established modern schools based upon the Dutch model of schooling. When universities were about to be established, the courses offered by Muhammadiyah were similar to those of state-owned universities. There was no difference in the curriculum except for additional Islamic studies subjects from semester 1 until 3.

8. Research Questions and Methodology

a. Research Questions

This research investigates the challenge of teaching English in Indonesian Muhammadiyah universities from 1958—when Universitas Muhammadiyah Hamka (UHAMKA) was first established—until 2005, when the last of the Muhammadiyah universities, Universitas Muhammadiyah Sukabumi (UMMI) was established. An analysis of the history of English language teaching in Indonesia as well as an inquiry into Muhammadiyah English Departments' curricula aims to answer the following questions:

1. How did the English language enter Indonesia? What role did English play during the Dutch and Japanese colonial eras? How did indigenous Indonesians perceive English at that time? What was the language policy being implemented from the early period of Indonesian independence (1945) onward, through the [Soekarno (1945-1965), Soeharto (1966-1998), and Post-Soeharto periods (1998-2005)? How did each government perceive foreign languages? How important was English at these times? What measures were implemented in order to disseminate English?
2. What are the main internal and external factors that have influenced the construction of curricula development within English departments in Islamic Muhammadiyah Universities? In what ways have these factors influenced the curricula in articulating its students' critical engagement with literary texts? How does the curriculum present itself within the wider context of teaching English literature at the tertiary level in Indonesia?
3. How did Muhammadiyah policy makers, rectors, lecturers, as well as students perceive the existence of English language? Were there problems in viewing Western cultural values as manifested in the literary canon in the English curriculum? Are there problems faced by Muslim students in perceiving Western values? Are there any clashes? How did lecturers and students usually overcome these problems?
4. What kinds of curricula will best promote the students' critical engagement with English literary works? How can gender issues contribute to the making of the curriculum? How can post-colonial literary works by Muslem women contribute to the development of students' critical thinking as well as empathy, solidarity and tolerance?

b. Theoretical frameworks

This proposed research is interested in investigating the dynamics of English teaching in Indonesia, especially in Islamic Muhammadiyah universities. The first methodological issue will be to decide which disciplines and approaches should be covered or employed in the research. Since the study is dealing with the power of both Islamic education philosophy and the teaching of English, which also represents an educational-political phenomenon as experienced by Indonesian students, it accordingly requires inter-disciplinary approaches.

In order to understand the historical background of how English entered Indonesia, the present study needs to examine the genealogy of the history of English and English language teaching, which serve as the backgrounds for how English became the imperial language. The history of English and English language teaching which have been stated as the basis of the imperial language in this context will be analysed to find how it relates to the present globalization and how it relates to the power of Islamic education philosophy stated in the Muhammadiyah curriculum. In other words, this study is interested in analysing the ways English plays a role in the present situation as the international language as well as how Islamic education philosophy adopts it at the practical level. The history of Imperialism and English will be examined using the perspectives of those who have had a long active engagement in the history of European imperialism, such as Howatt (2004), Penhallurick (2003), Groeneboer (1998), Knowles (1997), Graddol et.al (1996), Baugh (1993), who provide a basic knowledge of how English became an international language through European imperialism.

Since the focus of the present study is to construct an alternative literary canon in Muhammadyah English department curriculum, the history and theory of curricula will need to be taken into account. Richards suggests that before a curriculum is constructed, the goals of the curriculum need to be established. After setting up several aims, the curriculum should have its own basic philosophy. These decisions will then affect the kind of teaching methodology to be deployed. The final step will be providing material and a teaching apparatus (in the form of a syllabus). The syllabus is generally conceived as a list or inventory of items or units with which students are to study. As one aspect of the apparatus of the curriculum, the syllabus specifies the content of a course of instruction and lists what will be taught and tested. A syllabus designer at the very least should provide a rationale for the design of the syllabus. I will employ this theory to construct the alternative literary canon in the English department curriculum which is aiming to introduce gender issues to Muhammadiyah students.

c. Research Methodology

In order to analyse the genealogy of English and English language teaching this study is interested in examining two main aspects of discourse, namely the history of the English language itself and the history and development of the profession of the teaching of English, namely the "industry of English" as a second language. The methodology of this thesis is developed from my aim to transform English classroom activities into political praxis, which deconstructs the absolute traditional Islamic morality which influences students' perceptions of the literary canon. My thesis will be conducted by using two methodological analyses. The first will be literary discourse analysis in the post-colonial context; the second, which is equally important, is constituted by the construction of an alternative literary canon for use in the curriculum.

d. Research Scope

Muhammadiyah was chosen from among many other Islamic universities due to its positive attitude in implementing English language teaching since the very beginning in 1958. Other Islamic universities have only recently established English departments. With the 38 existing Muhammadiyah universities, there are around 22 English departments. Muhammadiyah is one of the leading national 'modernist' Islamic social organizations, which has branches throughout the country and has approximately 30 million followers. Founded in 1912, Muhammadiyah runs mosques, prayer houses, clinics, orphanages, poorhouses, schools, public libraries, and universities.

Students of Universitas Muhammadiyah Surakarta (UMS) are chosen to be interviewed due to my previous position as a lecturer at UMS. This prior experience has made it easier for me to access policy makers as well as classroom activities. UMS is the second biggest Muhammadiyah University which was founded on 18 September 1984. It has 7 faculties. It is located in Surakarta, central Java which has 554,630 inhabitants (Surakarta Central Statistic Bureau, 2002). Although an Islamic university, UMS also accepts non-Muslim students. In 2005, the number of Muslim students at the University was approximately 23,000. The dynamics of English language teaching can be seen through the lens of UMS, where the English department recruits about 600 students annually.

e. Significance of the Research

The proposed research has potential significance in a number of areas. As an academic staff member of the English Department at the Education Faculty of Universitas Muhammadiyah Surakarta (UMS), I cannot detach myself from the English teaching context (Candraningrum, 2004:59-70). Hence the present research must also be seen within that context. In addition, it is not very difficult to find texts with discussions of post-colonial theory in relation to English teaching in areas such as Canada, Australia, India, South Africa, and Malaysia, all of which were the colonies of Britain. Careful research on English teaching in Indonesia, particularly due to its status as a territory isolated from British colonialism, will become a valuable resource in the discourse of post-colonialism. Such research certainly contributes to providing a more comprehensive picture regarding TEFL. However, what has been done so far is still far from being sufficient, especially in relation to Indonesia, the most populous Muslim country in the world, where English plays a dominant role. It is ironic to find such a situation; very little is written about the impact of the English language in Indonesia, especially in Islamic universities. Most research on TEFL in Indonesia, regard English as (to borrow Penny Cook's term, 1992:5) "natural, neutral, and beneficial". Many researchers on TEFL in Indonesia have conducted their research under the assumption that English is not embedded by social, cultural and political interests: see Abdulhamied, 1982; Alip, 1993; Anita, 1994; Kasbolah 1988; Latief 1990; Martani; 1996; Zainil, 1987. Therefore this study is designed to supply an academic study on English language teaching in Islamic education, literary study as well as gender study, in Indonesia.

In Education, the study is expected to bring more insights on teachers as agents of change in their own classrooms at universities. Resistance cannot be separated from the realm of political process of the societies. I am trying to contribute a curriculum of an English department for specific Indonesian contexts in a given period, and within a limited locality.

9. Chapters charted

This research will be written in two parts: firstly, historical inquiries into the history of English language teaching as well as research on the Muhammadiyah curriculum; and secondly discussions of gender issues through an analysis of postcolonial Muslim women writers. **Part One** will focus on historical challenges in teaching English in the Indonesian Muhammadiyah universities from 1958 (UHAMKA establishment) until 2005 (UMMI establishment), and will consist of three chapters.

Chapter One introduces the educational backgrounds of English departments in Muhammadiyah universities. In this Chapter, an analysis of who reads the canon will create a framework for later chapters. After examining Muslim students' perceptions of English language teaching at Muhammadiyah universities, the necessity of equipping students with better tools in reading the English literary canon will be discussed. The questions of who reads the canon, and how to read the canon, are then followed by the question of what should be read. This research argues that Muslim students, specifically, need a different literary canon, in which Islamic and non-Islamic (Western) values meet together in the forum of literature.

After explaining the background to this research, Chapter one continues with discussions on situating education in Indonesia as well as situating the current curriculum in Muhammadiyah universities. This is then followed by more practical and technical questions on conducting the research; i.e. the formulation of research questions, methodology, theoretical framework, research scope as well as significance of the research.

Chapter Two charts the socio-political factors involved in the emergence of teaching English in postcolonial Indonesia. It introduces *Bahasa Indonesia* as the contesting melting pot by discussing the interplay of *Sanskrit* with Hinduism and *Arabic* with Islam. It then discusses European languages (1602-1942) as well as investigating the Dutch disengagement with education for indigenous Indonesians. After charting the previous development of foreign language teaching prior to Indonesian independence, the chapter discusses the dawn of English Language Teaching (ELT) and the role of America in the "new" Indonesia (1942-1965). This is followed by a discussion of the Suharto period (1965-1998), during which English Language Teaching (ELT) gained its stronghold. The chapter is concluded by a brief sketch of the development of a National English Syllabus.

Chapter Three explains the existence of English as a means of *Dakwah* (religious propagation): a survey on the history of English Departments in the Indonesian Muhammadiyah Universities (1958-2005). It discusses *Madrasas* in relation to their encounters with both traditionalists and the forces of modernity. This is followed by a discussion of how Muhammadijah established modern Islamic schools and universities (1912-2005). This chapter extends to the history of English Departments in Muhammadiyah Universities (1958-2005). It investigates 7 English Departments, Universitas Muhammadiyah Prof Dr Hamka (1958), Universitas Muhammadiyah Surakarta (1984), Universitas Muhammadiyah Ahmad Dahlan (1984), Universitas Muhammadiyah Malang (1987), Universitas Muhammadiyah Mataram (1992), Universitas Muhammadiyah Makasar (1993), as well as Universitas Muhammadiyah Sukabumi (2003). This chapter concludes that English can become a means of *Dakwah*, while also placing limits upon Islamic education.

Part Two focuses on mainstreaming gender through postcolonial Muslim women writers. This part will be divided into five chapters (Chapters Four to Eight). **Chapter Four** investigates the quests of Muhammadiyah students for Islamic identity by observing the literary works of Helvy Tiana Rosa (an Islamist literary women writer), whose works accentuate the calling for universal brotherhood (*Ummah*) and the return to the totalism of Islam (*Kaffah*). It starts with contextualizing new-Islamism in Indonesia: propagating Islam *kaffah* and *ummah*; followed by situating literary resistance: the emergence of new-Islamist literature. The works by Helvy Tiana to be discussed are *Jaring-Jaring Merah* (The Red Net), *Maut di Kamp Loka* (the Death at Camp Loka), and *Hingga Batu Bicara* (Until the Stones Speak). This chapter concludes that Muslim students are looking for the Ideal Norm, *Darul Ummah*.

Chapter Five concentrates on gender biases in contemporary Indonesian Sharia-Ordinances (*Perda Sharia*) in the 63 districts in Indonesia which directly affect the obligation of Muhammadiyah female students to wear headscarfs or veils. It argues that Sharia law is implementing democracy, but not yet considering women's rights. It highlights women's resistance and the suppression of women's voices as well as the under-representation of women during the enactment of Sharia Law. It then proposes "Sharia education" and "gender-mainstreaming", as well as legal assistance, with a concluding discussion of diverse gender constructions among Indonesian women.

Chapter Six reports the findings of my fieldwork conducted from mid July until mid of September 2007. It describes the situation of Muhammadiyah at a crossroads between sacred texts and pragmatism. Following this, it introduces the interviews conducted, followed by a report on Muhammadiyah positions that mediate between ideology and pragmatism in the establishment of English Departments. The second part of this chapter reports on how Islam and Muhammadiyah transform the cognitive into the affective. It also investigates how the current Western literary canon is still considered to be sacred. Finally, it examines how there is clash of values in classroom activities, concluding with a discussion of tensions in Islamic curriculum reformations within the framework of Muhammadiyah universities.

Chapter Seven illustrates the mainstreaming of gender through postcolonial Muslim women writers. Firstly, it discusses the Islamic cosmology of Muhammadiyah students, examining the religious setting in connection with the choice of literary texts. This is followed by questions of theory relating to multicultural education, post-structuralist critical pedagogy, the untangling of gender inequalities, and classroom practices. The chapter then examines the merits of teaching postcolonial Muslim women writers by introducing the works of five women: Cornelia Sorabji, Nawal el-Saadawi, Leila Ahmed, Fatema Mernissi, and Kartini. It concludes with a discussion of using works by postcolonial Muslim women writers' in the prose syllabus, accompanied by discussions of themes related to gender.

Finally, this research is concluded in **Chapter Eight**, which summarizes the problems faced by Muslim students at Muhammadiyah universities in terms of their reception of English language texts. It sets out proposals for future educational policies that could build a specific canon for Muslim students, in order to bridge the cultural gulf that appears during the reading process. It concludes that the formulation of a prose syllabus containing Muslim women writers from postcolonial countries could help in tackling these problems. In the classroom in Muhammadiyah universities, detailed discussions on Muslim society and gender are powerful factors in teaching English, and the study of gender issues must be delivered to both the students and the Muslim society.

Diagram 1

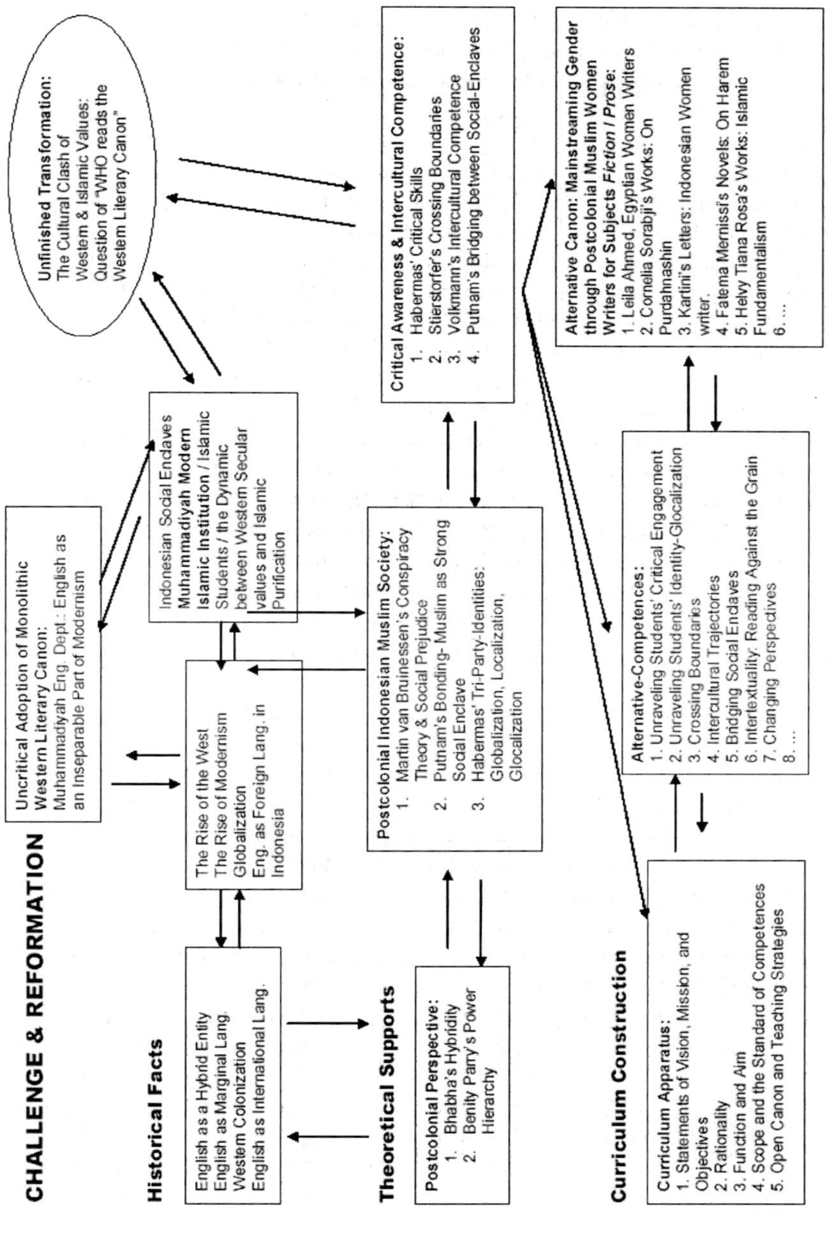
CHALLENGE & REFORMATION
Historical Facts
Theoretical Supports
Curriculum Construction
Uncritical Adoption of Monolithic Western Literary Canon: Muhammadiyah Eng. Dept.: English as an Inseparable Part of Modernism
Unfinished Transformation: The Cultural Clash of Western & Islamic Values: Question of "WHO reads the Western Literary Canon"
Indonesian Social Enclaves Muhammadiyah Modern Islamic Institution / Islamic Students / the Dynamic between Western Secular values and Islamic Purification
The Rise of the West
The Rise of Modernism
Globalization
Eng. as Foreign Lang. in Indonesia
English as a Hybrid Entity
English as Marginal Lang.
Western Colonization
English as International Lang.
Critical Awareness & Intercultural Competence:
1. Habermas' Critical Skills
2. Stierstorfer's Crossing Boundaries
3. Volkmann's Intercultural Competence
4. Putnam's Bridging between Social-Enclaves
Postcolonial Indonesian Muslim Society:
1. Martin van Bruinessen's Conspiracy Theory & Social Prejudice
2. Putnam's Bonding- Muslim as Strong Social Enclave
3. Habermas' Tri-Party-Identities: Globalization, Localization, Glocalization
Postcolonial Perspective:
1. Bhabha's Hybridity
2. Benity Parry's Power Hierarchy
Alternative Canon: Mainstreaming Gender through Postcolonial Muslim Women Writers for Subjects Fiction / Prose:
1. Leila Ahmed, Egyptian Women Writers
2. Cornelia Sorabji's Works: On Purdahnashin
3. Kartini's Letters: Indonesian Women writer.
4. Fatema Mernissi's Novels: On Harem
5. Helvy Tiana Rosa's Works: Islamic Fundamentalism
6. …
Alternative-Competences:
1. Unraveling Students' Critical Engagement
2. Unraveling Students' Identity-Glocalization
3. Crossing Boundaries
4. Intercultural Trajectories
5. Bridging Social Enclaves
6. Intertextuality: Reading Against the Grain
7. Changing Perspectives
8. …
Curriculum Apparatus:
1. Statements of Vision, Mission, and Objectives
2. Rationality
3. Function and Aim
4. Scope and the Standard of Competences
5. Open Canon and Teaching Strategies

Chapter II
The Socio-Political Factors of the Emergence of Teaching English in Postcolonial Indonesia

1. Introduction

This chapter addresses the question of how English entered Indonesia in relation to European Colonialism in the early sixteenth century. In order to identify more closely the place occupied by English in postcolonial Indonesia, the rest of the chapter will be devoted to sketching the position of the "surrounding" colonial languages (Portuguese and Dutch) in the interplay with the position of Bahasa Indonesia, the Indonesian national language in the mid-twentieth century. This sketch will be framed from the perspective of foreign languages which entered Indonesia during the pre- and post-colonial periods. Bahasa Indonesia as one of the Austronesian or Malayo-Polynesian languages had been used as the lingua franca in the Indonesian archipelago before the seventh century. It is a modern dialect of Malay language which borrowed heavily from many foreign languages, the notable ones are Sanskrit, Arabic, Portuguese, Dutch, Japanese and English. This chapter will untangle the sedimentation of foreign languages into the history of foreign language teaching in Indonesia, beginning with the arrival of Sanskrit along with Hinduism and Buddhism, followed by the arrival of Arabic accompanied with Islam, the arrival of Portugese, Spanish, English and Dutch with Christians and Catholics missions, and finally the appearance of Japanese language during the Second World War.

In exploring further the impact of English on Indonesian, I will provide a brief history of Dutch colonization. In discussing this, I will supply some information of the language policy of the colonizer to provide a better picture of the existence of English. I will analyze how the significance of English was different from and/or similar to other European languages in the course of Dutch colonization. I will use a critical perspective in outlining the history of the arrival of the English language during the Dutch era as well as uncovering the socio-political factors that imbued the establishment of English departments in Indonesian universities through the policies developed by the Indonesian government. I argue that the existence of the English language in Indonesia, besides being normal, neutral and beneficial, was also embedded by other significant social, political, economic, and religious factors. These factors played significant roles in the emergence of English language teaching in pre and post colonial Indonesia.

2. *Bahasa Indonesia* as the Contesting Melting Pot: The Interplay of *Sanskrit* with Hinduism and *Arabic* with Islam

Indonesia came into existence as a nation after World War II. *Indonesia* originated from Greek: *Indus* = India and *nesos* = islands. *Republik Indonesia* came into existence on Independence Day (17 August 1945) following Dutch and Japan colonization, during a period in which other regions in Africa and Asia also gained their independence from European colonization. The physical boundaries of Indonesia were established by the Netherlands when they took over the many islands and made them into a single colony: the Netherlands East Indies (Vickers, 2005:2). At present Indonesia is a home to more than 200 million people and is the biggest Muslim-country in the world and the fourth most populous country in the world. The present Indonesia was formerly named by the Dutch as the "East Indies". Why East Indies? Since the largest British colony was India, Indonesia was named after India. The "East Indies" refers to thirteen thousand islands located to the East of India. Indonesia is located in the South Eastern area of the Asian Archipelagos. Sumatra, Java, Kalimantan, Sulawesi, and Papua are the five largest islands. Within those islands there are more than 300 ethnic groups and 200 local languages. The total number of languages and ethnic groups are more than 742. The East Indies was a complex entity before the arrival of foreign influences. The term Indonesia or East Indies which means "the islands of India" was given by a German ethnologist, and has been used since 1884 (Vlekke, 1943:6).

The first primary foreign influence on Indonesia was exerted by the cultures of the Indian subcontinent. Compared to the Indian population, 78% of which adopts the Hindu way of life, the majority of present-day Indonesians (around 82%) are Muslim. Hinduism which apparently originated from India, however, was deeply rooted in the formation of many of the former dynasties in Indonesia before the arrival of European colonialism as early as the sixteenth century. For nearly seven centuries, the Hindu and Buddhist empires challenged each other for supremacy in the archipelago east of India. These influences combined with local "pagan" traditions to form the basic identity for present-day Indonesia. The Hindu Mataram was located in Java, and the Buddhist Srivijaya was centred in Sumatra. The famous Hindu empire of Majapahit was located in Java in the thirteenth century. These three previous kingdoms had moulded the sediment of the basis of social and cultural legacies for most people in the Indonesian archipelago. The so-called "Pagan-Indonesia" with its Malay language, incorporated its first foreign language, *Sanskrit*, in the 7th century. Sanskrit was introduced on the islands of Sumatra and Java from the 7th to the 14th century under the influence of Hinduism and Buddhism, and their local kingdoms. All coastal areas of India contributed to the eastward expansion of its culture and southern India had much more influences than others (Vlekke, 1943:25). It is estimated that there are some loan words in modern Bahasa Indonesia from Sanskrit whether directly (around 750 words) or indirectly, and far greater amounts of loan words exist in the old Javanese languages (the dialects spoken by the people of Java). Almost half of the old Javanese language was based on loans words from Sanskrit. Sanskrit was taught among the high-rank of the nobility. The middle class spoke a low form of the Malay language. The spread of Sanskrit was used to advance Hinduism as well as Buddhism, which were circulated in their ritual exercises. The schools were named *Padepokan*, a three-in-one system of teaching-learning-working (Sadtono, 1997:2). A small number of students studied under the supervision of a religious teacher. The school dealt with the study of Shivaism, Buddhism, literature, language, science, astronomy, arts, and architecture (Mestoko, 1979:25-29). This was supported by evidence found in many Hindu-Buddha temples in different parts of Java and South Sumatera. Hinduism and Buddhism were then challenged by the arrival of Islam in Indonesia through Gujarati and South Indian traders as early as the thirteenth century. The Majapahit of Java slowly lost its ground and moved to East Java, and finally resided in the island of Bali where most of its present population adhere to Hinduism. Islam began to spread widely to the East Indies in the fifteenth century with the rise of Sultanate of Malacca in the straits between Sumatra and the continent. The oldest Islamic Kingdom was established in Perlak, Aceh in 1292. Merchants from Gujarat who came to Indonesia formerly did not come there with the intention of propagating Islam; rather they wanted to trade spices. This spice trade undermines the assumptions of former historians, who thought that foreign visitors from India arrived in order to establish Hindu, Buddhist, and later Islamic missions. Their first footholds in the East Indies were established through commercial relations, especially the spice trade. Before the arrival of the Portuguese, Indian merchants were the main connection between the Asian spice trade and the European continent, with other competitors including Persian and Chinese merchants.

Along with the commercial business, Islamic dynasties then transformed most of the Hindu-Buddhist kingdoms, with Bali being an exception. The most notable Hindu-dynasty which was transformed into Islam was Mataram, located in Yogyakarta. The second new foreign language, Arabic, was then introduced to the natives. This teaching, however, was only disseminated among the noble-ranks and those who converted to and studied Islam. At the level of everyday usage, Arabic was assimilated by and transformed the Malay language. 21,000 Arabic, Persian and Hebrew words were loaned into Bahasa Indonesia and a greater amount into the Malay language (with its variants: Malaysian language). The teaching of Arabic transformed the previous *Padepokan* system. Some traditions of Islamic teaching introduced during this period can still be found today. The *Pesantren* system separated between the school for the boys and for the girls. The stark contrast between two systems was: the previous schools were only for the nobility, whereas the *Pesantren* was not only for the nobility but particularly for natives who had converted to Islam. Despite this intention, however, in the first phase of its application only the nobles attended the schools. Only after the arrival of the European merchants were the middle class able to access the traditional Pesantren schools. The teaching of Sanskrit and Arabic among the natives was not an alien system, as it used the Malay as the language of instruction in both traditional systems. The interstices between Malay language and its foreign influences such as Sanskrit and Arabic moulded the assimilation among those three languages. The choice of the transliteration of Bahasa Indonesia, however, was not as in the present Latin form (the influence of Latin teaching by Portuguese), but in the Arabic transliteration called Jawi, meaning Arabic transliteration read by the Malayan.

Previous sketches of the history of foreign languages in Indonesia prior to European colonialism offer a perspective of hybridity in the formulation of an East Indies identity. The first economical influx of Indian spice traders led to the introduction of Hinduism, Buddhism and Islam, and produced a syncretic and hybrid identity that influenced both language and religion. Despite the three religions, the most notable and primary influence was the formation of the Malay language before the arrival of European colonialist. Some of the historians of Indonesia have argued that the pre-European colonization was a peaceful one, the arrival of Indian traders had not been accompanied by military interventions. The establishment of kingdoms under Hindu, Buddhist, and Islamic influences suggests, however, a colonial reality in which religious missions spread to the so-called "pagan" East Indies Archipelago. In this way, Indonesia had become a contesting ground of values where many foreign influences gained footholds. Despite its peaceful approach, the spice trade had, in a broad cultural sense, colonized Indonesia. The different and varied approaches used by those foreign influences have been written in the history of Indonesia. Most of the historical approaches see European forces as the sole colonizers of Indonesia. By contrast, I argue that the former foreign influences of Hinduism, Buddhism, and Islam pursued similar economical, religious and cultural aims to those pursued by European colonisers.

Such influences were moulded into the formation of the Low-Malay language, now popularly known as Bahasa Indonesia. The High-Malay language was spoken among the high-ranking elite at the Courts and was used in matters pertaining to the Mohammedan religion; and Low Malay or Pasar, the Market Malay was spoken as the everyday language in the community (Valentijn 1724, II-1: 244 cited by Groeneboer, 1998:25). Before the arrival of the Portuguese, the Low-Malay language had become the *lingua franca* that united people in South East Asia during the spice trade. The next discussion will analyse how the struggle amongst three foreign influences was further contested by the arrival of the European colonialists, which was represented by the economical aims of the Portuguese and the Dutch. During the period of colonialism, the British interfered for only five years from 1811-1816.

3. The European Foreign Languages (1602-1942): The Dutch's Disengagement with the Education for the Indigenous in Indonesia

The sixteenth century marked the arrival of the Portuguese, the first Europeans who came to Indonesia, and their intention was to search for the source of spice commodities which were previously distributed and traded by the Indians, Persians and Chinese to mainland Europe. The Portuguese was the third foreign language which influenced Bahasa Indonesia significantly. Besides Low-Malay language, Low Portuguese language was the second lingua franca in South-East Asia in the sixteen century. High Portuguese language was considered as the language of Christianity and European literature. Just like how the Europeans viewed Latin to be the means of understanding European cultures, High-Portuguese was posited in a similar position in the archipelago. High Portuguese was taught in seminaries which were built by the first Indonesian colonizer. Great difficulties for this language teaching were found in areas which were densely populated by Muslims. In the areas which were not Islamic, the Christian missionarists could assert their influence, and this remains so today. The Muslim areas were usually around the coastal area of Sumatra, Java, Borneo and Celebes islands. The arrival of the Portuguese with their missionary activities remained in certain regions which were later governed by the Dutch colonizers such as the Highland of Batak in Sumatra, Highland of Toraja and Manado in Celebes, Papua and the areas of Flores and Timor islands. The multiethnic East Indies were exploited by the new colonizer's imperial policy, *divide et empera* (divide and conquer) in such a way that the Dutch could gain more and more power.

The seventeenth century marked the arrival of the Dutch in the East Indies. The ambition of the Dutch was to win over the spice trade in the East Indies which was formerly under the Portuguese's control. Dutch was introduced as the official language of the colonial government and Portuguese as well as Malay languages remained the lingua franca. In 1602, the VOC (The Dutch East Indies Company) had taken over the control of the spice trade from the Portuguese except for the east islands of the archipelago but they finally fell into the VOC's hand later on. The VOC was a chartered private enterprise but had quasi-governmental powers. Complete with its own fleet and army, the VOC gradually expanded more influence and grip on political matters. The VOC was formerly established by seven chambers which represented each state in the Netherlands. Like the British East Indies Company in India, the VOC relied and depended mainly on "indirect rule" through "feudalism", characteristics of the former Indonesian kingdoms which spread throughout the East Indies. The VOC used traditional native elites—the Kings and their personnels—as their media while imposing their wills and extracting major income under the supervision of the Dutch colonial officials. In 1799, the VOC was dissolved and awarded to the United Kingdom of the Netherlands.

The political effect of the Napoleonic war in Europe had great impacts on the people in the East Indies. The Dutch officials in the East Indies were supposed to have practical and sufficient knowledge of the French language. A small private school for the French language was also opened in 1811.

A few months later, the East Indies archipelago was brought completely under the English rule with the assignment of T.S. Raffles as the first English colonial Lieutenant-Governor. English was introduced as the official language of the government. In order to promote Malay to the English officials and English to the indigenous officials, the first English grammar as well as dictionary (Malay-English and English-Malay) was compiled and written in 1812 with the effort of W. Marsden. During the short British interregnum 1811-1816, education was left entirely to private initiatives. In 1813 a missionarist opened a small school with English and Latin as part of the curriculum, and there may well have been more private schools of this sort during these years (F. de Haan, 1922-1923, *Oud Batavia; Gedenkboek uitgegeven het Bataviaasch Genootschap van Kunsten en Wetenschappen naar aanleiding van het driehonderdjarig betaann der stad in 1919*, Batavia: Kolff. 3 vols., II p. 262 in Groeneboer, 1998:70). The only educational institution subsidized by the British colonial government was a small school founded by A.D.F. Pahud, a Swiss from Lausanne, father of the later Governor-General C.F. Pahud (1856-61); its aim was to teach "in the first instance Dutch and afterwards English and French grammars". This school, which had 30 pupils by the end of 1815, proved to be so unprofitable that Pahud migrated to the Netherlands in 1818 (J. A. van der Chijs, 1902, *Het middelbaar schoolonderwijs te Batavia gedurende de eerste helft van de 19e eeuw, volgens officieele bescheiden*, Batavia: Kolff., p. 3-7 in Groeneboer, 1998:71). Raffles definitely had a low attitude toward Malay spoken in the East Indies and in a speech given to the Batavian Society of Arts and Sciences in April 1813, he stated:

> Essential to notice with regard to our future proceedings is the necessity of encouraging and attaining a more general knowledge of the Javanese language. Hitherto the communication with inhabitants of the country has been chiefly through illiterate Interpreters, or when direct, through the medium of a barbarous dialect of Malays, confounded and confused by the introduction of Portuguese and Dutch. Without a thorough knowledge of this language, it is impossible to form any accurate idea of the modes of thinking or acting among the people of this country.
> (T.S. Raffles, 1814, "A discourse delivered at a meeting of the Society of Arts and Sciences in Batavia, on the twenty-fourth day of April 1813, being the anniversary of the Institution", *Verhandelingen van het Bataviaasch Genootschap van Kunsten en Wetenschappen 7*, pp. 13-14, in Groeneboer, 1998:70).

With the intervention of the British short occupation (1811-1816) and the occupation of Napoleon in the Netherlands, the East Indies was then under direct control of the Netherlands and became one of the Netherlands' official and formal empires. The direct control takeover only caused more sufferings to the East Indies peasants. The natives' education was totally neglected. The nineteenth century was crowded with slave trade and export in the Cultivation System, large plantations and forced cultivation system to enhance the Dutch income through international trade system. Besides spices, two other significant resources in the East Indies were exploited by the Dutch. The first was petroleum, and for this reason, the Royal Dutch Company was established in the Netherlands Indies in 1883. This company was first simply known as 'de Koninklijke' but then merged with the British capital and became The Shell Transport and Trading Company in 1907 or was simply called the Royal Dutch Shell (Ricklefs, 1981:195). In 1920, Shell was producing about 85% of the total oil production in Indonesia. The second product was rubber. By 1930, Indonesia was producing nearly half the world's rubber supply which was the result of the Cultivation System previously imposed by the Dutch colonizer.

During the *Cultuurstelsel,* Dutch imperialism reached its height and they acquired high incomes from their colonies. On the contrary, the quality of life in the East Indies life was getting poorer and poorer, as famine was widespread. This misery became a great debate among the conservatives and liberals in the centre of the Empire. This was followed by further protests in the heart of the Empire as they urged for better treatments for the people of the East Indies. During the Cultivation Steel, the colonial government introduced a new form of trade system which was imported from the European 'laissez-faire' principle of economy. The introduction of the tax had made the government regulated the system of land administration. The officers in the East Indies distributed the land to the landowners and the peasants were supposed to rent the lands in the hope that the peasants would produce much more crops and could pay the necessarily imposed tax. The intricate effect was that most of the landowners were those who feudally had connections with the local kingdoms and the Chinese settlers who had powerful hold on the local trade and economy. The system of the liberal economic in the East Indies led to the expulsion of the poor peasants from their lands and finally made them paupers. They had become the wholly subject of the arbitrariness of foreign capitalism. Such views were shared by the Governor-general Van de Capellen who said:

> "Measures, that if seen at three thousand miles distance apparently are liberal, here prove to be highly illiberal in their effect. I must assume that in the Netherlands Liberalism is understood to be the protection of European landowners at the expense of the native population, and that the interests of the latter are completely disregarded to give a few speculators and adventures their chance to succeed in their schemes, then I must declare myself to be an ultra anti-Liberal" (Vlekke, 1943:275).

Van de Capellen was among the governor-general who understood the urgent needs for a better education for Indonesians. He saw that the Dutch colonial policy did it utmost to improve the material supply from Indonesians in the international trade, but continued to underestimate the people's educational and political needs. The urge to educate the colony was at its height. For this purpose, they founded a new department in the government, that of "Agriculture, Arts and Education". Unfortunately this plan was executed only to address the elite in the East Indies and to fulfil the betterment of the Agriculture to be exploited further by its imperial ruler. With the arrival of the western education system, there appeared to be a discrepancy with the existing local education, the one which was in the hands of the Muslim religious teachers and Hindu-Buddhist religious teachers. The two later education systems were mostly confined within the religious contents and heavily imposed the teaching of Arabic and Sanskrit. Before the execution of the Ethical Policy, western-type of education for the indigenous East Indies was primarily left to the Christian missionaries (at first mainly in the Moluccas and Timor, and from the 1830s also in Minahasa, North Sulawesi), the non-Christian populations were completely ignored.

Foreign languages introduced in the Dutch colonial education system and schools run by missionaries were Dutch and other European languages such as German, French and English. The teaching of four European languages was often problematical for the Dutch sytem of education, as what happened in Europe influenced the way the Dutch imposed its foreign language policy. As the previous three main religions in the archipelago taught their languages through *padepokan* and *pesantren*, the Dutch language policy was applied through church services and colonial government schools. The Dutch and other European languages were only introduced to the elite of the noble ranks (*raja* and *bangsawan*), the Chinese people and indigenous people who had converted to Christianity (Groeneboer, 1998: 27). Western education type was formally introduced to indigenous Indonesians at the beginning of the twentieth century in the introduction of the Dutch Ethical Policy which was urged by many Dutch liberal movements. Although the Ethical Policy had its root in humanitarian concerns, this policy was also initiated by some economical interests. During the liberal period (1870-1900), the Dutch industry began to see Indonesia as a potential market. Thus, the standard of this potential market had to be uplifted in through so that it could provide Indonesian cheap labours in the modern market. The former slaves' position in the eighteenth century Europe was simply formulated in another word, "labours", a concept which was alien to the indigenous. To create obedient labours, the colonial government needed to elevate their education, especially to support the economic exploitations.

In 1899 C. Th. Van Deventer published an article in the Dutch journal *de Gids*, "*Een eereschuld*" (*A Debt of Honor*), in which he urged the Netherlands government to pay the debts of all the wealth they had exploited from Indonesia by promoting the education for the indigenous. Only after his death in 1915, the Netherlands set the Ethical Policy in three schemes: education, irrigation and emigration under Queen Wilhelmina's reign (1890-1948). There were two different approaches as to how to execute the education system in Indonesia. The first approach was the "elitist" which was supported by the well-known Snouck Hurgronje and J.H. Abendanon. This view departed from the assumption of providing a more European-style education in the Dutch language for westernised Indonesian elites which then would execute most of the official duties in the East Indies. Both further expanded the view that "our rule will have to justify itself on the basis of lifting the natives up to a higher level of civilization in line with their innate capacity" (Vickers, 2005:21-22). The second approach favoured more basic and practical education in vernacular languages for the lower classes. Snouck Hurgronje then advocated a bold policy of education that "The Indonesian is imploring us to give them instruction; by granting their wish we shall secure their loyalty for an unlimited time" (Vlekke, 1943:330). One of its policies was imposing the natives to learn Dutch as a gateway to the West and learning other European languages as regular subjects, i.e. German, French and English, which will be introduced in the junior high school.

The language of the European was first introduced in the elite education called MULO-*Meer Uitgebreid Lager Onderwijs* (Advanced Elementary Education/Junior High School) in 1914. This was designed for the noble rank Indonesians, Chinese and Europeans who had finished their respective primary schools (HIS & ELS). In 1937, MULO which served as a follow-up to the Native School Second Class introduced foreign languages to the Indigenous East Indies, their local language was used as the medium of instruction, and Dutch was taught in addition to English and Malay. According to Koeswandono (78 years old, a MULO graduate) and Dwitjahjo (80 years old, a MULO graduate), MULO students had to learn Dutch everyday, English—a compulsory subject—three to four times a week, and they still had to choose either German or French, and either Javanese or Malay (Sadtono, 1997:4-5). In independent Chinese schools in Indonesia, English was the favourable foreign language to be taught due to its usefulness in business transactions shortly before the Second World War. The MULO graduates could speak, read and write good English (Mistar, 2005:73). French was then abolished from the curriculum of ELS-*Europesche Lagereschool* (European Primary School) when Napoleon conquered the Dutch. French was then replaced by English. This signalled the strong hold of the Dutch, English and German languages. The German language was then also banned short after the German occupation in the Netherlands.

The teaching of Dutch and English became prominent by the end of the World War II. The teaching of Dutch was, however, then banished by the two prominent factors, namely the occupations of the Japanese in Indonesia and the rejection of Indonesian independence fighters and/or nationalists, as it was considered as the colonizers' language. The year 1945 signalled the victory of English as the only foreign language accepted in indigenous schools. At that time the teaching of English was considered to be successful due to the small number of the students as it apparently only addressed the noble rank and the indigenous who converted to Christian.

The introduction of the four European languages to indigenous Indonesians gained many supports from larger scale whether in the Netherlands or its Empire. This policy however was not accompanied with active steps from the colonial government. In the 1930 census, the literacy rate for adult Indonesians throughout the archipelago was only 7.4 percent. This was very poor compared with the educational programme of the United States in the Philippines, where by 1939 over a quarter of the population could speak English (Ricklefs, 1981:203). In the former Southeast Asian British colonies of Malaysia and Singapore, no less than one-third of the total population of 23 million now speak English (Crystal, 1997:57-60). Although previous data only shown the literacy rate and language policy, but they also reflected how much emphasis was placed on education in general in the colonial empire. The British in India, Malaysia and Singapore, the US in the Philippine, and the French in Indochina had spent two to three times much more than the Dutch in Indonesia on Education (Nieuwenhuis 1923a: 202; Kelly 1978: 102, 119-20 quoted by Groeneboer, 1998:11). In spite of its material gains exploited from Indonesia, the Dutch never had any serious commitment to the welfare of the Indigenous East Indies as the public education policies in the East Indies merely addressed the indigenous elites. UNESCO found that in 1947, the illiteracy rate in British India was 88 percent, 40 percent in the Philippines, 80 percent in Vietnam, and a startling 95 percent in the Dutch East Indies (Indonesia). A possible reason was that the pragmatic language policy was always dictated by practical, economic and financial considerations. This colonial attitude demonstrated vividly that in practice, welfare was subordinate to the economic interests of the colonizers.

4. The Dawn of the English Language Teaching (ELT) & the Role of America in the New Indonesia (1942-1965)

With the turmoil of the World War II, the Japanese with the support from their Central Axis (Germany, Italy, Turkey, and Japan) ousted the Dutch in 1942. The governor-general of the East Indies was seeking help from its Allies. During the Second World War many criticisms were directed to the Dutch language policy by its Allies—England, Australia, and America. They saw that the Dutch policy hindered rather than promoted the spread of Dutch and other European languages. They also had to accept that less than two percent of the population could communicate in Dutch at the end of colonial period. This had triggered another policy which had been contemplated by the Dutch Minister of Colonies, H.J. van Mook to the East Indies Department of Education while he was in exile in Brisbane:

> A common language is the surest measure for spreading culture and loyalty. The British always encourage the speaking of English in their dominion and colonies. We have not done this in the Netherlands East Indies. Let us do it after the war.
> (*Rijks Instituut voor Oorlogs Documentatie—Indische Collectie*, Amsterdam (National Institut for War Documentation—East Indies Collection), C 050294 quoted by Groeneboer in the Introduction, 1998:1)

However, Mook could never realise this as the teaching of Dutch, English, Germany, and French was banned in the entire archipelago by the new colonizer. The new colonizer, Japan, preferred to be called as the "Old Brother" of South East Asia. Within this disguise they conquered Indonesia. Books and other materials written in Dutch and other European languages were burnt. Bahasa Indonesia was then inaugurated as the language of instructions at schools. From 1942 until 1945 during Japanese occupation, no formal schools taught any of the European languages, although this was still carried out clandestinely. Bahasa Indonesia gained a more powerful position in uniting different etnicithies in Indonesia. On 17 August 1945 Soekarno proclaimed the Independence of the Republic of Indonesia and the 1945 Constitution proclaimed that Bahasa Indonesia was the language of the state in Chapter XV, article 36. This had ousted the dream of the Dutch to reclaim Indonesia by its new language policy after the World War II.

The birth of a nation, independent Indonesia, at the end of World War II was followed by further contesting efforts from the outside world to re-claim Indonesia whether through political, educational, cultural or economic colonization. The multiethnic religious state continued struggling from within and from the outside. Many compromises had to be taken by the new nation in facing the coming of the global era. One of the hurdles faced by the new nation was the burden of the debts imposed by the former Dutch colony to Indonesia. When the United States brokered the final settlement of the Revolution, it sacrificed the new nation's interests for its own purposes. The US insisted that Indonesians accept a deal, that is, they had to take over the Dutch debts of US$ 1,723 million plus interest. The US wanted to protect the economic rebuilding of Europe that established in the Marshall Plan and to create the North Atlantic Treaty Organization as the basis of their campaign against communism (Vickers, 2005: 133). Instead of the Dutch compensating Indonesians who had been exploited for almost 350 years, Indonesians had to compensate the Dutch, based on the fiction that the Indies had been an autonomous entity, and not part of the Netherlands (Kahin, 1952:443). It was scandalously arranged as the trade-off in liberating Indonesia from the total re-invasion of the Dutch military and its ally between 1945 until 1950. Indonesia was faced with a great misery during its struggle either from the financial exploitation of the debts and the re-invasion from the Dutch until 1949 when the Dutch finally accepted the independent state of Indonesia. The economic colonization in the young Indonesia nation has been succinctly summed up by an Australian historian, Ricklefs as follows:

> In the economy generally non-Indonesian interests remained important. Shell and the American companies Stanvac and Caltex were strong in the oil industry, and most inter-island shipping was in the hands of the Dutch KPM line. Banking was dominated by Dutch, British and Chinese interests, and Chinese also controlled much of the rural credit. It was clear to informed observers that Indonesians were not independent economically, a fact which was to contribute to the radicalism of the late 1950s (Ricklefs, 1981:291).

Despite becoming the contesting field in the economic sector, the education sector also suffered the same struggling foreign forces which strove to penetrate their foothold within the curriculum formation of the newly fresh Indonesian education system. The new government led by Sukarno regime gave priority to foster education sector. The number of elementary school entrants had increased from 1.7 million to 2.5 million between 1953 and 1960 although 60 percent were then dropped out before completing the school. By 1961 the adult literacy rate had been 56.7 percent for those over the age of ten compared to the poor rate of the Dutch Ethical Policy on Education reform in 1930 which had been merely 7.4%. Many schools were set up and teachers were enforced in in-training service to meet the demands of the school entrants. The onset of the Dutch Ethical Policy in 1930 had heralded the nationalist schools which were called as 'wild schools' by the Dutch. In these classes nationalist teachers rejected to teach History of the Netherlands and promoted History of the People of Indonesia as an effective way to counter and read against the colonial ruler. Curricular reform had provided a different perspective in cultivating indigenous-modern school system. The notable influence of western-modern teaching was the book of Karl Marx which was introduced by a German teacher and then absorbed by the first Indonesian President Sukarno when he attended a school in Surabaya. Marxist influences among Indonesian independent insurgents were strong. One of emerging political leaders Sutan Sahrir even married a Dutch Marxist, Maria Duchateau who supported Sutan defiance of the Dutch authority. He denounced the inferiority complex of Indonesian people under the Dutch colonization. Many of their movements were joined by other young insurgents from the Islamic fronts. One notable figure was Haji Ahmad Dahlan who then established Muhammadiyah. Muhammadiyah, as the leading national 'modernist' social Islamic organization, had branches throughout the country and has approximately 30 million followers today. Founded in 1912, Muhammadiyah has been establishing mosques, prayer houses, clinics, orphanages, poorhouses, schools, public libraries, and universities. Muhammadiyah was being set up to meet the educational gap in the Islamic-indigenous Indonesia in the Dutch colonial era. Muhammadiyah envied the way the Dutch provided schools only for the Christian-Indonesians. He then adopted the system of western modern schools while providing the pupils with Islamic teachings. From 1913 until 1918 Dahlan promulgated five elementary schools, *Hooge School Muhammadiyah* for the junior high school in 1919. He then altered the name, *Kweek School Muhammadiyah* and in 1930 he separated schools for boys as *Mu'allimin* and for girls *Mu'allimat*. The focus on Muhammadiyah modern Islamic schools will be explored in the next chapter.

Although they were obviously in an ambivalent position in projecting the Dutch as sources of knowledge as well as oppressions, they were able to raise indigenous sense of independence as shown in their willingness to become teachers of those "wild schools" and be willing to do it voluntarily. Such schools were so widespread and the Dutch's suspicion was not able to suppress their influences among the indigenous. The schools however could not abandon the teaching of European languages within the paradox of the educational system. From the onset of the Ethical Policy Muhammadijah modern Islamic education combining western and Islamic teachings were prevalent until today. The former Dutch universities in Indonesia were altered into state-owned universities and those of Islamic universities are mostly run by Muhammadiyah. Almost all of the schools and universities in Indonesia then adopted the teaching of English as the sole significant foreign language.

Four years after Indonesia's independence, English Departments were also started to be founded at university level. Table 2 shows that the first English Department was established in a private nationalist-initiative university in Jakarta called Universitas Nasional Jakarta in 1949. Table 1 shows that a state-owned University of North Sumatera followed the step in 1952. In the beginning of October 1954, the famous English Department of IKIP Malang (now Universitas Negeri Malang) was established followed by Politeknik Negeri Manado in the same year. Other state-owned universities such as Universitas Syiah Kuala Banda Aceh established English Department in 1961, Universitas Sriwijaya Palembang and IKIP Jogjakarta (now Universitas Negeri Yogyakarta) in 1964 and Universitas Diponegoro Central Java in 1965. During the three-and-half-year of the Japanese colonialism (1942-1945) and during the Sukarno era (1945-1965), there were approximately seven state-owned universities which established English Departments. Despite supports from the government, the propagation of establishing English Departments was mostly led by Christian and Catholic missionaries who then established Universities in several Christian-Catholic social enclaves in Indonesia, such as Universitas Katolik Indonesia

Atmajaya Jakarta in 1961, Universitas Kristen Satya Wacana Salatiga in 1962, Universitas Kristen Petra Surabaya in 1963, Universitas Kristen Tomohon Sulawesi in 1964, as well as Universitas Katolik Sanata Darma Jogjakarta and Universitas Klabat Manado North Sulawesi in 1965. The only modern Islamic institution which established English Department was Muhammadijah, i.e. Universitas Muhammadiyah Dr Hamka (formerly IKIP Muhammadiyah Jakarta) Jakarta in 1958. More focus on the English Departments in Muhammadiyah Universities will be explored in the next Chapter.

English Departments were established mainly by the government (Table 1) and private initiatives in which Christian, Catholic and Muhammadiyah religious institution (Table 2) played central roles in the propagation. There were four Christian Universities that established their forerunner English Departments. The first Christian university was Universitas Kristen Satyawacana (UKSW) that was located on the Highland of Salatiga Central Java, and it was established on November 30, 1957 by 10 Church Synods from Java, Sumatera, Kalimantan, Sulawesi, Maluku, Irian Jaya (now Papua), Bali, Nusa Tenggara Barat and Nusa Tenggara Timur. Satya Wacana was drawn from Sanskrit, meaning "faithful to the Word of God". The English Department was established four years after the university was founded on May 17th, 1962. Secondly, Universitas Kristen Petra (UKP) Surabaya East Java, was established by PPPK Petra (Petra Christian Education and Teaching Association) which is a Christian union established on April 12th, 1951 with the purpose to provide education from the level of kindergarten to senior high schools. On September 21st, 1960, the committee of University Establishment Planning Preparation was formed with the duty to establish universities which were consisted of mainly Christian-converted Chinese Indonesian; drg Tan Tjiaw Yong, Gouw Loe Liong, drg Tan Gie Djien, Tjoa Siok Tjoen, Lie Ping Lioe and Kwee Djien Kian. The first department founded was Faculty of Letters and the English Department was initiated on May 21st, 1963. The third was Universitas Kristen Tomohon. Tomohon was one of the towns in Minahasa, North Sulawesi. Tomohon was renowned as a Christian town since the Dutch reign. Many Dutch missionaries lived there and opened schools and clinics. The earlier clinic, now called Rumah Sakit Umum Gunung Maria which is now the biggest hospital in North Sulawesi, was established on February 11th, 1930, by Marianheuvel Ziekenhuis. One of the famous universities being established was Universitas Kristen Indonesia Tomohon (UNKIT) by GMIM (Gereja Masehi Injili di Minahasa). The English Department was established on the 19th of October 1964. The fourth Christian university was Universitas Kristen Klabat (UNKLAB). It was established on October 7th, 1965, by Gereja Masehi Advent Hari Ketujuh Uni Kawasan Timur Indonesia through Yayasan Universitas Klabat. The English Department was established on the 7th October

1965, exactly the same year as the establishment of the university which offered two year-programme of Theology and English Education.

The second initiatives were taken by Catholic missionaries who built two prominent Catholic universities, i.e. Atmajaya and Sanata Dharma. The first was Universitas Katolik Indonesia Atmajaya in Jakarta which was established on June 1st, 1960, by Yayasan Atma Jaya in which Cardinals in Java and young Catholic intellectuals met to establish the foundation in June 1950. Most of them were Catholic-converted Chinese Indonesian; Ir JP Cho, Ir Lo Siang Hien-Ginting, Drs Goei Tjong Tik, IJ Kasimo, JB Legiman SH, Drs FX Seda, Pang Lay Kim, Tan Bian Seng, Anton M Moeljono, St Munadjat Danusaputro, JE Tan, Ben Mang-Reng Say. Atma Jaya stemmed from a Sanskrit word, meaning the glory of soul. The English Department was established in the faculty of Education on June 1st, 1961. The second university was Universitas Katolik Sanata Darma in Yogyakarta. In 1955 Catholic Priests of the Order of the Society of Jesus Central Java and other Catholics intellectuals decided to establish a teacher's training college. With the support from the Congretio de Propaganda Fide, Father Kester, the Superior Jesuit Missionaries, united the diploma courses in Education under de Britto Foundation in Yogyakarta and in English under the Loyola Foundation in Semarang into a higher learning institution called PTPG Sanata Dharma on October 20, 1955. English department was established among other three departments of Education, History and Natural Science. Sanata Dharma is a Sanskrit phrase, means "the true dedication" or "the real service", the dedication and the service have been devoted to the nation and the church (Pro Patria et Eclessia).

Besides propagated by Christian-Catholics missionaries, the indigenous nationalist and modern Islamist also played a significant role. The first English Department in Indonesia was established on October 15th, 1949, in the second oldest university in Indonesia, Universitas Nasional (UNAS) Jakarta by prominent western-educated indigenous nationalist: R Teguh Suhardjo Sastrosuwignyo, Sutan Takdir Alisyahbana, Soedjono Hardjosoediro, Prof Sarwono Prawirohardjo, Prajitno Soewondo, Hazil, Kwari Katjabrata, Dr Djoehana, RM Soebagjo, Adam Bachtiar, Ny Noegroho, Drs Adam Bachtiar, Dr Bahder Djohan, Dr Leimena, Ir Abd Karm, Prof Dr Soetomo Tjokronegoro, Ali Budiharjo Poerwodarminto, Soetikno, Ir TH A Resink, Dr Soemitro Djojohadikusumo, Noegroho, Soejatmiko, HB Jassin, Mochtar Avin, L Damais, A Djoehana, Nona Boediardjo and Nona Roekmini Singgih. The establishment of the university was aimed to cater graduated senior high schools (Dutch MULO) who did not want to enter into Dutch colonial *Universiteit van Indonesie/Universiteit van Nederlands-Indie* established in 1946 which then transformed by the government into state-owned university called Universitas Indonesia (UI) in February 2nd,1950, when the Dutch handed the university to the new Indonesian government. The first faculty of letter was actually established by the Dutch in 1920 in which several Dutch intellectuals and western-educated indigenous nationalists worked together to initiate *Faculteit der Letteren en Wijsbegeerte* in the House of Rechts Hogesschool which could only be realized twenty years later in December 4th, 1940. Instead of Dutch and other European languages, Bahasa Indonesia was opted to be the first language department at the university to cultivate the nationalist spirit in achieving the independence, as well as three other departments, namely Social Sciences, History, and Science on Nations. In 1942, the Japan colonizer came and established their own education institutions in the university, and surprisingly did not ban the Faculty of Letters while banning the teaching of Dutch and other European languages. In 1954 Dutch and Chinese Language Departments were established. English Department was established later on.

The modern Islamic organization, Persyarikatan Muhammadijah, which founded Universitas Muhammadiyah Prof Dr Hamka (UHAMKA) on 25 Rabiul Awal 1377 H/18 November 1957 in Jakarta, also established an English Deparment. UHAMKA was formerly known as IKIP Muhammadiyah Jakarta or PTPG (Perguruan Tinggi Pendidikan Guru). The founders were Arso Sastroatmodjo and HS Projokusumo. Similar to the Christian and Catholics universities which were based on the teachings of the Bible as well as Pancasila and UUD 1945, UHAMKA as a modern Islamic university, was also based on Islamic teachings (Al Quran and As-Sunnah) as well as Pancasila and UUD 1945 (the Constitution of Indonesia).

**Table 1:
English Departments established by
State-Owned Universities (1942-1965)**

Year of Establishment	State-Owned Universities
1952	Universitas Sumatera Utara
1954	IKIP Malang, now Universitas Negeri Malang, East Java[1]
	Politeknik Negeri Manado
1961	Universitas Syiah Kuala Banda Aceh
1964	IKIP Yogyakarta, now Universitas Negeri Yogyakarta[2]
	Universitas Sriwijaya, Palembang
1965	Universitas Diponegoro, Semarang, Central Java
Total	**7 English Departments in State-Owned Universities**

Sources: Direktorat Jenderal Pendidikan Tinggi, 2005, *Rekapitulasi Perguruan Tinggi dan Program Studi*, Jakarta: Dirjen Dikti; and Majelis Pendidikan Tinggi Penelitian dan Pengembangan Pinpinan Pusat Muhammadiyah, 2006, *Direktori Perguruan Tinggi Muhammadiyah (PTM): Profil Universitas, Sekolah Tinggi, Politeknik, dan Akademi Muhammadiyah se-Indonesia*, Yogyakarta: Diktilitbang Muhammadiyah, Pp.: 1-56.

1 *Keputusan Presiden Republik Indonesia Nomor 93 Tahun 1999 tentang Perubahan Institut Keguruan dan Ilmu Pendidikan (IKIP) menjadi Universitas* (Edict of President RI No 93, 1999 about the change of IKIP [Institute for Teacher Training and Education] into University), Pp: 1-2.

Table 2:
English Departments established by Private-Initiatives Universities (1942-1965)

Year of Establishment	Private-Initiatives Universities
1949	Universitas Nasional Jakarta
1958	Universitas Muhammadiyah Dr Hamka, Jakarta
1961	Universitas Katolik Indonesian Atmajaya, Jakarta
1962	Universitas Kristen Satya Wacana, Salatiga , Central Java
1963	Universitas Kristen Petra, Surabaya, East Java
1964	Universitas Kristen Indonesia, Tomohon, North Sulawesi
1965	Universitas Katolik Sanata Darma, Yogyakarta
1965	Universitas Kristen Klabat, Manado
Total	**8 English Departments in Private-Initiatives Universities**

Sources: Direktorat Jenderal Pendidikan Tinggi, 2005, Rekapitulasi Perguruan Tinggi dan Program Studi, Jakarta: Dirjen Dikti; and Majelis Pendidikan Tinggi Penelitian dan Pengembangan Pinpinan Pusat Muhammadiyah, 2006, Direktori Perguruan Tinggi Muhammadiyah (PTM): Profil Universitas, Sekolah Tinggi, Politeknik, dan Akademi Muhammadiyah se-Indonesia, Yogyakarta: Diktilitbang Muhammadiyah, Pp.: 1-56.

The success of establishing the English Departments in Indonesian universities instead of other Departments of European languages was partly due to the programme initiated by America through the Ford Foundation. In the beginning of Soekarno's period, the position of Sukarno (and Indonesia) was between the capitalist pole and the communist pole. The year 1950, however, witnessed the raising of Indonesian Communist Party (PKI). Sukarno's relationships with many Western countries grew apart and he even promulgated anti-western sentiments. From 1950 until 1965 Indonesians had to face several tensions because of the struggle of two opposing foreign influences, and to bear the consequences as well. The U.S government regarded the Sukarno regime to be left wing with his ultra-nationalist visions on education. Sadtono and Mistar reported that the teaching of English language had to be terminated due to pressures from the communists (Mistar, 2005:72-73; Sadtono, 1997:10). Thomas et al states that "for political protection, Mr. Soenardjo Haditjaroko, director of the Foreign Language Institute had to state publicly that teachers should not compel their students to study English outside classroom, though privately he fully supported such activity" (Thomas et al, 1968:316). The result of the anti-western policy made the English language programme declined in educational system in Indonesia.

Nonetheless, the Ford Foundation launched an effort to make Indonesia a modernized country in 1954 with field projects from MIT and Cornell countering the communist influences. The US power through the Ford foundation had launched the establishment of English as the most important foreign language to be taught at universities and schools. Despite the rising influences of the English language after the World War II, English teaching programme in Indonesia had been supported explicitly by the US. After the Americans took control of the Philippines in 1900, the American language policy rejected the Indigenous Languages and English was immediately introduced as the language of instructions in all schools (Groeneboer, 1998:5-6). The choice of English was therefore clearly motivated by cultural imperialism of the US, but also by the tempo in which the imperialistic aspirations had to be realized in education (Groeneboer, 1998:5-6). The campaign of English language teaching in Indonesia occupied a central place in the policy developed by the US to counteract the influences of communism during the cold war.

FKIP Universitas Airlangga Malang (altered presently as IKIP Malang, and then UNM—Universitas Negeri Malang) set a project in August 1960, The English Language Teacher Training Project (ELTTP), in which the Ford Foundation backed up the project by sending American professors to teach there, as well as providing them with financial and technical assistance. The programme was to promulgate the core of English language teachers who would serve as the basis of ELT in Indonesia. They were sent to America to study and get overseas degree:

> No wonder that those who went to the US could get their master and doctoral degrees without too much difficulty. A number of ELTTP graduates now hold high positions in different parts of Indonesia, four are currently Rectors (Dr Muhammad Diah, UNRI Rector, Drs Agus Kafiar MA, Uncen Rector, Dr Moh Ansyar, IKIP Padang Retor, Dr Nuril Huda, IKIP Malang Rector (Sadtono, 1997:11).

They were becoming prominent people in the education system in Indonesia. It was reported that the two prominent professors in charge of the programme were pure linguists who had never been to Indonesia, so their program was arcane, unrelated to the needs of TEFL (Teaching English as Foreign Language) in Indonesia. The Ford sent a new American professor who had sufficient knowledge on TEFL to improve the situation. Ford further assisted the development of English syllabi, instructional materials, and manuals for secondary schools which then published in 1956 (Thomas, 1968). The dawn of English language teaching in Indonesia was developed under the auspices of the US. Despite the alien factor, English language has played the major role after the World War II and the arrival of communication wave. Indonesia could not deny and escape its powerful influences in the international arena. This has drawn Indonesia's decision to maintain the teaching of English in the formal school which had been stamped by the Dutch junior high school system. Until 1980s, German and French were still taught in senior high schools as optional subjects. The world-wide-web internet wave of the 1980s has witnessed the emergence of English as the International language.

5. Suharto Regime: English Language Teaching (ELT) Gaining its Stronghold (1965-1998)

The 1965 revolution started with the brutal massacre of about 1 millions the PKI members, left-wing sympathisers and many other citizens. Curriculum developments at schools were filled with negative images of the PKI and communism. School textbooks were designed from the perspectives of Suharto regime, and this was also a product of the Cold War. Education was under strict regulations from the Government, who installed education curricula at all levels. During Suharto's reign, High Javanese language gained its political weight compared to other languages. After several years of decline, English foothold was gaining its power in Indonesia. The former Ford programme was continued in the era of Suharto who advocated "openness" to his "New Order" Indonesia to replace the Marxian insurgency. Despite exercising constant and close supervision to the Leftist movements, Suharto regime also suppressed the political insurgency from the Islamic groups which was preferably called as Right wing. Islam in Indonesia was however never been a single narrative. Suharto's frame of political action was on how to maintain and play those two poles in a beneficial position for his advantage. The two poles were always being contested opposite to the western capitalistic values. In the era of Sukarno, the teaching of Dutch was terminated. And in 1990s facing the end of Suharto reign and the arrival of the internet, German and French were not taught in Indonesian senior high schools anymore. Suharto's regime advocated the literacy of foreign languages as its main prerequisite. English then played the most dominant roles among other western languages such as German and French. In the last years of Suharto's reign, Indonesia issued Law No 2 Year 1989 about National Education System which enforced the English language as one of the obligatory subjects for Elementary Education in Chapter IX, Kurikulum, Verse 39, Point 3, Article m (*Undang-Undang Republik Indonesia Nomor 2 Tahun 1989 tentang Sistem Pendidikan Nasional*, Pp. 1-4):

The content of elementary educational curriculum should contain (minimally) the following subjects:

a. Pendidikan Pancasila (Pancasila Education);
b. Pendidikan Agama (Religious Study);
c. Pendidikan Kewarganegaraan (Civic Education);

d. Bahasa Indonesia;
e. Membaca dan Menulis (Reading and Writing);
f. Matematika (termasuk berhitung);
g. Pengantar Sains dan Teknologi (Introduction on Science and Technology);
h. Ilmu Bumi (Geography);
i. Sejarah Nasional dan Sejarah Umum (National History and General History);
j. Kerajinan Tangan dan Kesenian (Art);
k. Pendidikan Jasmani dan Kesehatan (Sport);
l. Menggambar (drawing); serta
m. Bahasa Inggris (English Language)

The previous apparent attitude toward English as the only foreign language that should be taught in elementary level was changed in 2003 of post-Suharto era—precisely during the presidency of Megawati Soekarnoputri, a well-known daughter of the former first President Sukarno. Sukarno was popular for his insistence on including national identity as a discourse in education. During his daughter's presidency, attitudes toward English were more neutral compared with those during Suharto period. Indonesia issued a similar law on education system, Law No 20 Year 2003 about National Education System which did not mention any foreign language, even English as a compulsory subject. Such a policy was also not issued for elementary education. In this law, the use of the language of instruction, that is Bahasa Indonesia, was clearly stated, and foreign language (Bahasa Asing) subject was also supported but not mentioning "Bahasa Inggris" in the Law of Republic of Indonesia No 20 Year 2003 about National Education System, Chapter VII, Bahasa Pengantar (Language Instruction), Verse 33, Point 1-3, Article (3) (*Undang-Undang Republik Indonesia Nomor 20 Tahun 2003 tentang Sistem Pendidikan Nasional*, Pp. 1-46):

> Bahasa Pengantar (Language of Instruction)
> Pasal 33
> (1). Bahasa Indonesia sebagai Bahasa Negara menjadi bahasa pengantar dalam pendidikan nasional (Bahasa Indonesia as state language is the language of instruction in the national education).
> (2). Bahasa daerah dapat digunakan sebagai bahasa pengantar dalam tahap awal pendidikan apabila diperlukan dalam penyampaian pengetahuan dan/atau ketrampilan tertentu (Local dialects could be used as medium of instruction in the introductory level if necessary).
> (3). Bahasa asing dapat digunakan sebagai bahasa pengantar pada satuan pendidikan tertentu untuk mendukung kemampuan berbahasa asing peserta didik (***Foreign language*** could be used as medium of instruction in particular subjects to support learners' competency).

The previous Law 20, 2003, also stated that the curriculum contained in the elementary and high education level only mention Bahasa Asing/Foreign Language as one of the obligatory subjects instead of "English language" as stated in the previous Law 2, 1989 during Suharto's presidency (*Undang-Undang Republik Indonesia Nomor 20 Tahun 2003 tentang Sistem Pendidikan Nasional*, Pp. 1-46). The apparent attitude towards English during Suharto's presidency culminated in the statement issued by the Government Regulation No 55 Year 1998 about Basic/Elementary Education about the Change of Government Regulation No 28 Year 1990 about Basic/Elementary Education. Chapter 14 a of this Regulation states:

> (1). Bahasa pengantar dalam pendidikan dasar adalah Bahasa Indonesia (Language of Instruction in the basic education is Bahasa Indonesia).
> (2). Bahasa Daerah dapat digunakan sebagai bahasa pengantar dalam tahap awal pendidikan dan sejauh diperlukan dalam penyampaian pengetahuan dan/atau keterampilan tertentu (Local Dialects could be used as medium of instruction in the introductory level when it is necessary to deliver particular sciences and/or skills.).
> (3). Bahasa Inggris dapat digunakan sebagai bahasa pengantar sejauh diperlukan dalam penyampaian pengetahuan dan/atau keterampilan tertentu (***English language*** could be used as medium of instruction when it is necessary to deliver particular sciences and/or skills).
> (*Peraturan Pemerintah Republik Indonesia Nomor 55 Tahun 1998 tentang Perubahan atas Peraturan Pemerintah Nomor 28 Tahun 1990 Tentang Pendidikan Dasar*).

The support of the Suharto's regime for English language was different in senior high school level and high education level. He only issued regulations which mentioned "Foreign Languages" instead of "English language" (*Peraturan Pemerintah Republik Indonesia Nomor 56 Tahun 1998 tentang Perubahan atas Peraturan Pemerintah Nomor 29 Tahun 1990 Tentang Pendidikan Menengah*; *Peraturan Pemerintah Republik Indonesia Nomor 57 Tahun 1998 tentang Perubahan atas Peraturan Pemerintah Nomor 30 Tahun 1990 Tentang Pendidikan Tinggi*; and *Peraturan Pemerintah Republik Indonesia Nomor 60 Tahun 1999 tentang Pendidikan Tinggi*. In the practical level, however, English language was becoming an obligatory subject. The former edicts show the clear support Suharto had toward English language teaching. During the formation of the New Order, Bahasa Indonesia was challenged by the advocacy of teaching English throughout Indonesia to adopt liberal free market in which Suharto regime adhered. The teaching of English as a foreign language, however, posed by insurmountable obstacles due to Indonesian high illiteracy rate, lack of English teachers and suitable teaching materials. The boom of capitalism during Suharto era, however, had supported the infrastructural support to the schools and universities. The hard-factors however had not been accompanied by a good soft-factor such as the curriculum. The Curriculum in Indonesia tended to copy directly from the US. When the communicative approach was introduced in the US, the curriculum in Indonesia was advocating it as well. The development of English curriculum in Indonesia was never independent. Its position was strongly influenced by what happened outside Indonesia. In other words, the legacy of teaching English in Indonesia was never in Indonesians' hand. The curriculum makers anyhow supported such perspective inasmuch as to support their own legacy of the teaching of English and the making of the curriculum being applied in universities and schools. Such legacy was then taken over by the Ministry of Education who played the main role of establishing the legacy of teaching English for Indonesians.

In 1968 an English Language Project was set up by the Ministry of Education which consisted of two sub-projects. The English Teachers Upgrading Project (ETUP) to improve the junior high school teachers and the English Materials Development Project (EMDP) to prepare materials for the senior high school (Djojosoekarto, 1973:17-27). This core project then developed further the dissemination of a number of projects on in-service training and materials development. In 1985, as a follow-up to the former project being supported by many of the US universities in the scholarship schema, the PKG Approach (*Pemantapan Kerja Guru*—strengthening teachers works) in ELT at the secondary school was launched which was funded by loan from the World Bank and UNDP. Further assistant was under the schema provided by Ford Foundation and Ministry of Education to build Standard Training Course (STC) in Jogjakarta Central Java and Bukittinggi West Sumatera. STC was a successful project in which many qualified English teachers were produced. After the decline of English teaching under the threat of the Communist Party during the Sukarno era, English teaching in the Suharto era was strongly supported by the US government scheme through its Ford Foundation. The popularity of TOEFL compared to IELTS in Indonesia also became a strong indicator of the American English influence in the development of ELT in Indonesia.

Table 3:
English Departments established by State-Owned Universities (1965-1998)

Year of Establishment	State-Owned Universities
1966	Universitas Gajah Mada, Yogyakarta, Java
1969	Universitas Tanjung Pura, Pontianak, Kalimantan
1976	Universitas Sebelas Maret, Surakarta, Central Java
	IKIP Malang, now Universitas Negeri Malang, East Java
1978	Universitas Mulawarman, Kalimantan
1981	Universitas Tadulako, Palu
1982	Universitas Bengkulu, Sumatera
1983	Universitas Jember, East Java
	Universitas Andalas, Padang
1984	Universitas Nusa Cendana, Kupang
	Universitas Sam Ratulangi, Manado
	Universitas Negeri Medan
	Universitas Palangka Raya
	Universitas Riau, Pekanbaru
1990	Universitas Terbuka, Jakarta
1993	Universitas Jambi
1996	Universitas Pattimura, Ambon
	Universitas Padjadjaran, Bandung
	Universitas Lambung Mangkurat, Banjarmasin
	Universitas Negeri Gorontalo, Gorontalo
	Universitas Indonesia, Jakarta
	Universitas Cendrawasih, Jayapura
	Universitas Haluoleo, Kendari
	Universitas Negeri Makasar
	Universitas Mataram
	Universitas Pendidikan Ganesha, Singaraja
	Universitas Negeri Padang
	Universitas Negeri Semarang
	Sekolah Tinggi Seni Surakarta-STSI, Central Java
Total	**29 English Departments in State-Owned Universities**

Sources: Direktorat Jenderal Pendidikan Tinggi, 2005, Rekapitulasi Perguruan Tinggi dan Program Studi, Jakarta: Dirjen Dikti; and Majelis Pendidikan Tinggi Penelitian dan Pengembangan Pinpinan Pusat Muhammadiyah, 2006, Direktori Perguruan Tinggi

Muhammadiyah (PTM): Profil Universitas, Sekolah Tinggi, Politeknik, dan Akademi Muhammadiyah se-Indonesia, Yogyakarta: Diktilitbang Muhammadiyah, Pp.: 1-5.

Table 4:
English Departments established by Private-Initiatives Universities (1965-1998)

Year of Establishment	Private-Initiatives Universities
1967	Universitas Sarjana Wiyata Taman Siswa, Yogyakarta
1970	Universitas Simalungun, Medan
1971	Universitas Muhammadiyah Palu
1976	Universitas Muhammadiyah Sumatera Utara
1979	Universitas Tidar Magelang, Central Java
1980	Universitas Islam As-Syafiyah, Jakarta
1981	Universitas Wijaya Kusuma, Surabaya
	Universitas Balikpapan
1982	Universitas Jabal Ghafur, Medan
	Universitas Pakuan, Bogor, West Java
	Universitas Advent Indonesia
	Universitas Muria Kudus, Central Java
	Universitas Mahasaraswati, Denpasar, Bali
	Universitas Islam Riau, Pekanbaru
	Universitas Indraprasta PGRI, Jakarta
1983	Universitas Muhammadiyah Tapanuli Selatan
1984	Universitas Abulyatama Aceh
	Universitas Muhammadiyah Surakarta, Central Java
	Universitas Muhammadiyah Ahmad Dahlan, Yogyakarta
	Universitas Muhammadiyah Surabaya, East Java
	Universitas Dr Soetomo, Surabaya
	Universitas Warmadewa, Bali
	Universitas Katolik Widya Mandira, Kupang
	Universitas Lancang Kuning, Padang
	Universitas Mahaputra Muhammad Yamin, Solok
	Universitas Siliwangi, Tasikmalaya
1985	Universitas Serambi Mekkah, Aceh
	Universitas Wiralodra, Bandung, West Java
1986	Universitas PGRI Palembang
	Universitas Universitas Darma Persada
	Universitas Kristen Cipta Wacana, Surabaya, East Java
	Universitas 17.08.1945 Surabaya, East Java
	Universitas Ibn Khaldun, Bogor
1987	Universitas Gajayana, Malang, East Java
	Universitas Sisingamangaraja XII, Medan

	Universitas Nadlatul Wathan
	Universitas Muslim Makasar
	Universitas Satria Makasar
	Universitas Sawerigading, Makasar
	Universitas Muhammadiyah Palu
	Universitas Muhammadiyah Malang
1988	Universitas Sintuwu Maroso, Sulawesi Tenggara
1989	Universitas Batanghari, Jambi
	Universitas Muhammadiyah Jakarta
	Universitas Muhammadiyah Jember
1990	Universitas Islam Jember, East Java
	Universitas Darma Agung, Medan
	Universitas Sisingamangaraja XII, Tapanuli Utara
1991	Universitas Samudra Langsa
	Universitas Muhammadiyah Bengkulu
1992	Universitas Dayanu Ikhsanuddin, Makasar
	Universitas Kristen Indonesia Toraja
	Universitas Muhammadiyah Mataram
1993	Universitas Islam Nusantara, Bandung
	Universitas Kristen Maranatha, Bandung
	Universitas Panca Sakti, Tegal, Central Java
	Universitas Islam Kadiri, East Java
	Universitas Muhammadiyah Ponorogo, East Java
	Universitas Muhammadiyah Pontianak
	Universitas Muhammadiyah Makasar
1994	Universitas Muhammadiyah Palu
	Universitas Muhammadiyah Palembang
1995	Universitas 45 Makasar
	Universitas Muhammadiyah Purwokerto
1996	Universitas Muslim Nusantara, Medan
	Universitas PGRI Kupang
	Universitas Nusantara Manado
	Universitas Islam Darul Ulum, Surabaya
	Universitas Muhammadiyah Ahmad Dahlan, Yogyakarta
	Universitas Widyatama, Bandung
	Universitas Gunadarma, Jakarta
1997	Universitas Kanjuruhan, Malang, East Java
	Universitas PGRI Adi Buana, Surabaya
	Universitas Muhammadiyah Bengkulu
1998	Universitas Graha Nusantara, Padangsidempuan
	Universitas Pasundan, Bandung
	Universitas Galuh, Ciamis, West Java
	Universitas Katolik Widya Mandala, Surabaya
	Universitas Wijaya Putra, Surabaya
Total	**77 English Departments in Private-Initiatives Universities**

Sources: Direktorat Jenderal Pendidikan Tinggi, 2005, Rekapitulasi erguruan tinggi dan Program Studi, Jakarta: Dirjen Dikti; and Majelis Pendidikan inggi Penelitian dan Pengembangan Pinpinan Pusat Muhammadiyah, 2006, irektori Perguruan Tinggi

Muhammadiyah (PTM): Profil Universitas, Sekolah Tinggi, Politeknik, dan Akademi Muhammadiyah se-Indonesia, Yogyakarta: Diktilitbang Muhammadiyah, Pp.: 1-56.

While only 15 English Departments established during the Sukarno era (Tables 1 & 2), Tables 3 and 4 show that the Suharto regime left remarkable footprints of establishing seven times more, with around 106 English Departments throughout Indonesia in which 29 English Departments by state-owned universities and 77 English Departments by private initiatives, especially those established by Christian-Catholic missionaries and modern Islamic institutions, most notably by Persyarikatan Muhammadiyah. Muhammadiyah has established one fifth of all private initiatives, 14 Muhammadiyah universities and Christian-Catholics initiatives have established around one tenth of all Indonesian private universities. And the rest of the seventy percent were initiated by other traditional Islamic institutions such as NU, Hindu-Buddhist religious institutions, and other indigenous nationalist and local institutions. During the Suharto regime, more than fifty percent of the English Departments that were established by the government and private initiatives played seminal role in disseminating the emergence of teaching English at Indonesian universities.

During the Suharto era and after his fall, the number of private universities has been growing rapidly and it is necessary to coordinate each university under one Koordinasi Perguruan Tinggi Swasta/Kopertis (Private High Education Coordinator). The total number of the English Departments in Indonesia until 2006 is 121, and the numbers of the English Departments in each Kopertis are as follows: Kopertis Wilayah I (Medan, North Sumatera) has around 12 English Departments; Kopertis Wilayah II (Palembang, Sumatera) has 4; Kopertis III (Jakarta) has 8; Kopertis Wilayah IV (Bandung, West Java) has 18; Kopertis Wilayah V (Yogyakarta) has 14; Kopertis Wilayah VI (Semarang, Central Java) has 11; Kopertis Wilayah VII (Surabaya, East Java) has 22; Kopertis Wilayah VIII (Denpasar, Bali) has 7; Kopertis Wilayah IX (Makasar, South Sulawesi) has 15; Kopertis Wilayah X (Padang, West Sumatera) has 4; Kopertis Wilayah XI (Banjarmasin, Kalimantan) has 3; and finally Kopertis Wilayah XII (Ambon, Maluku) has 3. From the previous distribution of English departments in each province in Indonesia, it is clear that the development of teaching English in Java is fostered more than the outer Islands. Of 121 English Departments at private universities, more than half of these are located in Java and less than half are in the outer Islands of Java. The discrepancy of the distribution of English Departments has hindered the development of English language especially in the eastern part of Indonesia as it apparently only has one twelfth of the number of all English Departments. The policy of stressing the development in Java during the Dutch reign was continually adopted during the Suharto regime, although he had started the program of decentralization in 1992, the progress of the outer Islands still faced many obstacles. From 1992 onward around half of the total number of the entire English Departments was established. The growing number of English departments was also supported by the government's attitude toward English language post-Suharto era. During Abdurrahman Wahid (Gus Dur) presidency in 2000, he advocated the Minister of Education, Yahya A. Muhaimin, being also Muhammadiyah elite leaders, to issue edicts on the regulation of core curriculum in Indonesian universities. The edict stated that English language teaching could become part of institutional curriculum of particular faculties outside of English Department:

> (2) In the MPK group, institutionally, could be Bahasa Indonesia, **Bahasa Inggris (English Language)**, Ilmu Budaya Dasar, Ilmu Sosial Dasar, Ilmu Alamiah Dasar, Filsafat Ilmu, Olah Raga dan sebagainya. (*Keputusan Menteri Pendidikan Nasional No 232/U/2000 tentang Pedoman Penyusunan Kurikulum Pendidikan Tinggi dan Penilaian Hasil Belajar Mahasiswa, Chapter IV, Verse 10*).

Contrary to the Sukarno era, the result of pro-western policy and favourably political situation to free market economy in Suharto era made the English language program increased in priority scale in the educational policy. Post-Suharto era witnesses the apparent support from the government toward English language teaching. Even outside of the government policy, formal education schema, informal language courses grew like mushrooms from 1980s onward. English language informal courses were found innumerable in Indonesia nowadays. During the Suharto era, English language teaching whether in formal or informal education was gaining its stronghold.

6. The Brief sketch of the development of National English Syllabus

As early as 1950, when a foreign language to be chosen for the schools curriculum nationwide (either Dutch or English), the policy makers in Indonesia were well aware that English could serve a very important role as a tool in the development of the country, both for international relations and scientific-technological advancement. English was chosen over Dutch despite the fact that the Dutch had colonized Indonesia for three and a half centuries. As is very well recorded in the Indonesian history, the official status of English in the country has been "the first foreign language" and the political stance of Indonesia's government is quite firm: "English is not and will never be a social language nor the second official language in Indonesia" (Sadtono, 1997:7).

With English being given this status, the objective of English language teaching (ELT) in Indonesia is to equip students with a working knowledge of the language. While this instructional objective may appear self-explanatory, in the context of formal schooling, the notion of "working knowledge in English" has been approached in different ways throughout the history of ELT in

Indonesia. For instance, in the 1975 English syllabus, while the final goal of teaching was said to be the development of communicative competence in English, the actual English teaching focused almost exclusively on the mastery of linguistic patterns without giving proper attention to its use in communicative situations.

Quite predictably, the mismatch between the goal of ELT and how it was taught led to the disappointment of both ELT theorists and practitioners. In the 1984 Syllabus, which served to correct the 1975 syllabus, the notion of "working knowledge in English" was then approached by restoring the true goal of English teaching, that is, "meaningfulness and communicative functions" (Ministry of Education and Culture 1986 and 1987 cited in Huda, 1999). In actual classroom practices, however, the notion of "communicative competence" was misinterpreted and taught by most teachers as "oral skills". This misunderstanding, in turn, caused controversies among English teachers and experts.

Building on the lessons learned from these two failed attempts, current ELT in Indonesia adopts communicative language principles under 1994 English Syllabus, which brings to the forefront the notion of "meaningfulness approach". Huda (1999) has interpreted this approach in two ways: 1) meaning-based instruction, and 2) meaningful instruction. Meaning-based instruction starts from the notion of language as a means to express and understand meaning. As meaning is determined by language scope and is also defined by social contexts. ELT should be targeted to develop students' ability to understand and express meaning in the context of language used for communicative purposes. Language learning is meaningful if students learn expressions at the discourse level as opposed to isolated words. To this end, the presentation of learning materials must be in the context of specific situations because meaning changes in different contexts.

The second interpretation of the "meaningfulness approach" is that instruction should be meaningful to the learners. Language instruction is meaningful if it is relevant to the learner's needs and demands. The relevance of English instruction to the needs of the learners as a group is ensured when what is being taught to—and engaged by—the learners is somehow related to what they think is important and useful. To this end, the selection and presentation of learning materials should be made with references to what is generally of interest to the learners (horizontal relevance) and/or what is likely to be needed by the learners in the near future (vertical relevance). To make the whole learning activity authentic, all language components and linguistic macro skills should be integrated, and treatment of any linguistic aspect or skill is to be made in the context of the whole discourse.

While, at the theoretical level, the goals seem reasonably clear, remaining at issue here is how classroom teachers as front-line players can translate the ideas as originally conceived by the syllabus designers. The issue of the teachers' ability to translate principles into classroom practices becomes important because it is the classroom teachers who will determine what happens—and does not happen—in the classroom. Another important issue is the kind and focus of the tests administered to assess the relative success of the instructions. The test format and syllabus are crucial because we have learnt from research and experience that grade is important to both teachers and students. That is to say, tests, as research has established, will drive instructions. The biggest challenge then is to empower classroom teachers so that they are productively involved in the design of course syllabi and assessment instruments.

7. Conclusion

The previous brief sketch of foreign language teaching in Indonesia raises the spectre of the dominant roles of the Dutch colonization in introducing the English language in Indonesian educational system as early as the twentieth century, before the World War II broke (See Diagram 2). The role of Bahasa Indonesia was gained through two main movements, the anti-Dutch movement which led to the Sovereignty of Indonesia as a state and through the banning of Dutch and other European teaching by the Japanese colonizer. This was further supported by the sense of nationalism in the era of Sukarno. The power of Bahasa Indonesia, which was formerly only spoken by seven percent of Indonesians in Riau Sumatera, was enhanced by its position as a constant melting pot of other languages. Languages such as Sanskrit, Arabic, Portuegese, Dutch, and English have taken part in developing the vocabularies in the Indonesian language. Latin transliteration system being introduced by the Portuguese was then adopted into the formation of the Low-Malaya language into Bahasa Indonesia. Javanese which was spoken by the majority of Indonesians was not adopted. Instead, it was the Low-Malay which already served as a lingua franca of many ethnicities, which was adopted as the national language. Bahasa Indonesia increasingly played a significant role encouraging the sense of nationalism and in the discourse of identity in Indonesia. To most of Indonesian people, their first languages were their respective dialects, and the second language was Bahasa Indonesia, and their foreign language was most likely English.

The development of English language teaching has been up and down. First it was introduced by the private initiatives of English short interregnum (1811-1816) and then by the colonial Dutch government in the onset of the Ethical Policy in the 1930s. The education policy, however, was an elitist one in which the schools only accepted noble ranks, Chinese people and those who were converted to Christiany. The teaching of four European languages, Dutch,

The Cultural Politics of Teaching English in Indonesia

Foreign Languages : Sanskrit, Arabic, Portuguese, Dutch, English, German, French
Indigenous Languages: High Malay, Low Malay, Javanese, and other 200 dialects from 300 ethnics
Melting Pot/Transformation: Bahasa Indonesia
Affirmed Foreign Lang.: English Language

Transforming the Fabric of Foreign Languages: Bahasa Indonesia

Propagator/Ruler Mission/ Economic & Political Pursues	Indian Hinduism Spice trade	Persian-Indian Islam Spice Trade	Portuguese Catholics Spice & Natural Sources Imperial Expansion	Dutch Christian	Britain Christian	Dutch Ethical Policy Dutch, English, German, French	French & German were banned due to Napoleon & Germany invasions
Languages Indonesia	Sanskrit	Arabic	Portuguese	Dutch	*British English*	The Rise of Bahasa Indonesia	Support on Dutch, English, Bahasa
Interregnum	7th AD	12th AD	16th AD	1602 (17th AD)	1811-1815	1901-1942	
Educational Institution	Padepokan Traditional	Pesantren Traditional	Private Initiatives from Missionary Western-Modern Schools		Pahud's School of English Grammar	Colonial Govt Schools: MULO (Junior High Schools)	
Persyarikatan Muhammadiyah						Private Initiatives of Western Modern Schools:: 1. Christian/Catholics Missionary Schools 2. Nationalist Indigenous Schools 3. Modern Islamic Schools: ***Persyarikatan Muhammadiyah 1912-1923: 207 Muhammadiyah Western Schools***	

The Legacy of American English & Persyarikatan Muhammadiyah's Participation

Propagator/Ruler Aims	Japan Asia-Pacific War	Sukarno's Post Independent The Rise of Indonesian Identity	Suharto's New Order Economic Expansion	Post-Suharto (Habibie, Gus Dur, Megawati, SBY) Transformation
Languages	Japanese Bhs Indonesia	Bahasa Indonesia Foreign languages were discouraged	Bahasa Indonesia *American English*	Bahasa Indonesia *American English*
Interregnum	1942-1945	1945-1965	1966-1998	1999-2005
Educational Institution/ Eng. Depts.	Dutch was banned	Dutch schools transformed into state-owned Schools: State-Owned Uni: 7 Eng. Depts. Private Initiatives: 8 Eng. Depts. 1952-1965: Unsu, UNY, Pol Manado, Unsyiah, UNY, Unsri, Undip Christian Missionary 1962-1965: UKSW, UKP, UKIT, UKK Catholics Missionary 1961-1965: Atmajaya, Sanata Darma	establishing and developing Universities State-Owned: 29 Eng. Depts. Private Initiatives: 77 Eng. Depts.	State-Owned: 40 Eng. Depts. Private Initiatives: 121 Eng. Depts.
Persyarikatan Muhammadiyah		***Persyarikatan Muhammadiyah 1958:1 Eng. Dept. in UHAMKA***	***Muhammadiyah: 20 Eng. Depts.***	***Muhammadiyah: 21 Eng. Depts.***

German, French, and English could only be accessed by the upper classes. The popular education was then advocated by two main other institutions, the nationalist and the modern Islamist which proposed by Ahmad Dahlan in Muhammadiyah. The two types of considered "wild schools" (by the Dutch) were barely copied the Dutch (Western) education system with additional Islamic teaching for Muhammadiyah. Almost all of the education system which is now prevailed in Indonesia was formerly adopted from the Dutch system. Muhammadiyah schools and universities also adopted the teaching of English in their curriculum. Although English language teaching declined during the Japanese colonial era and Sukarno era, it was then gained a stronghold during Suharto era when he adopted free market system into Indonesian economy through its apparent policy toward the adoption of English as the only foreign language to be taught in schools and universities.

The major support of the teaching of English in Indonesia was the followings: (1) Government positive attitude toward English language due to the adoption of capitalistic economy; (2) private initiatives in which (a) western-educated nationalist indigeneous actors; (b) Christian as well as Catholic missionaries; and (c) modern Islamic institution, i.e. Persyarikatan Muhammadiyah played significant roles in propagating the education to the neglected-indigeneous; (3) and finally the support from the US via the Ford Foundation which promulgated the soft core of the English department curriculum and in-service training for teachers of English. Although the Dutch colonial government support to the education during the Ethical Policy was considered small, the impact of creating western-educated indigenous nationalists and modern Islamist elite was influential in creating their own ideological education institution which then spread over Indonesia and touched into a more popular ground on the mass education level. The private initiatives from the nationalists and religious missionaries were then continued after Indonesian gained its Independence. During the Japanese and Sukarno reigns, English teaching was not so enhanced due to the anti-western policies by both political actors. During Sukarno's reign, however, the US had once helped in designing the syllabus of English teaching via the Ford Foundation in the hope that in the course of the Cold War, the more left Indonesian president would not adopt communism into the new state. The first seed disseminated through in-service training for English teachers and material developments were imported with the paradigm of the American English. Almost all of Indonesian universities used TOEFL test rather than IELTS for testing at University levels. American English has painted the color of Indonesian English nowadays since the policy adopted by Suharto was in accordance with the US in the post cold-war era. Not having been colonized by the British, Indonesia adopted the American English rather than the British English adopted in Malaysia. The stronghold of the English language in Malaysia was dated formerly, before the World War II when the British Colonizer spent much of its financial effort to educate the Empire. Compared to Indonesia, the Dutch spent the least among the European colonizer in South East Asia. This resulted in the double jeopardies in the formative era of education in Indonesia where most of the people were not literate. The fosterization of education was gaining its height during Suharto's reign when he adopted capitilistic policy in developing the country. English became the sole choice to challenge the global power from the 1980s onward. From the onset of 1980s, the teaching of English as a Foreign Language (TEFL) recapitulated overnight and spread in Indonesia. The quality of it, however, is still under way.

Chapter III
English as a Means of *Dakwah*: A Survey on the History of English Departments in the Indonesian Muhammadiyah Universities (1958-2005)

1. Introduction

As the Dutch colonial government in Indonesia was entering the twentieth century, it had to create groups of local people who could help the state manage itself and its population. Thus the ethical policy was launched to educate some of these people. That brought an influx of modernity into the lives and minds of several Indonesians, and created news aspirations. These aspirations spawned the initiatives to create civil associations—social, educational, and religious—that was to build schools and published newspapers to fulfil the desire to bring education and progress to the people. This development in turn nurtured national consciousness that would later give birth to the Indonesian independence movement (Abdullah 1999, p. 8).

The mushrooming of civil organizations followed the influx of ideas from both the West and the East. From the West, the fledging Indonesian intellectual communities learned about new political ideas and modern sciences; from the East, especially the Middle East, they learned about Islamic reformist movements and ideas about how to free Islam from the shackles of both ancient traditions and the colonial rules (Maarif, 1985:52-79). A central issue was whether to fight colonialism through confrontational political struggles or through cultural struggles. In Indonesia, the intellectuals were divided into different ideological groups: those who liked to apply Western ideas on Indonesian soil; those who liked to combine Western and native traditions; those who liked to combine Western and Islamic ideas; and those who preferred to maintain the existing combination of Islam and native traditions (Scherer, 1975). Intellectuals also debated the appropriate strategies for dealing with colonialism.

These contending ideas constituted the ideological context in which Ahmad Dahlan founded Muhammadiyah. Muhammadiyah is an Indonesian Islamic social organization well known for providing education and health services. Structurally, Muhammadiyah's organization consists of *Pengurus Pusat* (national office, or PP), *Pengurus Wilayah* (provincial offices, or PW), *Pengurus Daerah* (district offices on the kabupaten level, or PD), *Pengurus Cabang* (branch offices on the kecamatan level, or PC), and *Pengurus Ranting* (sub-branch offices on the desa level, or PR). The administrative units below the state in Indonesia are *Propinsi* (province), *Kabupaten* (district), *Kecamatan* (sub-district), and *Desa* (village). Delegates from offices around the country from all levels, representing millions of Muhammadiyah's supporters, attend its quinquennial national conference (*Muktamar*). The conference elects a new chair of the national office and ratifies national policies and programmes.

Muhammadiyah also functions as an umbrella for its "autonomous organizations", such as Aisyiyah (Muhammadiyah Women Movement), Nasyiatul Aisyiyah (Muhammadiyah Young Women Movement), as well as Pemuda Muhammadiyah (Muhammadiyah Young Men Movement).

Muhammadiyah views these activities as the best way for propagating Islam, empowering the *ummah* and improving the social conditions of Muslims. Muhammadiyah was established in Jogjakarta in 1912, in the decade that saw the emergence of civil associations and political organizations in Indonesian at a national scale. Some observers have seen the decade, therefore, as the first flowering of the civil society in Indonesia and the beginning of the nationalist movement in Indonesia (Abdullah, 1999:4-6). Ideologically, Dahlan was one of those who opted for a combination of Western and Islamic reformist ideas as the basis for his activities. His concerns with poverty and backwardness of the people of the Netherlands East Indies, the majority of whom belonged to the Islamic *ummah*, led him to the fields of education and health. Within the politically restrictive colonial environment, Dahlan adopted a by-and-large co-operative, though not wholly uncritical, attitude towards the colonial government (Suminto, 1985:36-37 & 193-98). This co-operative attitude became the basic policy for Muhammadiyah throughout its history.

This chapter will examine the historical evolution of the educational institutions exercised by Muhammadiyah in standing between traditionalists and western modernists paradigms towards the propagation of Islam in Indonesia. The Dutch introduction of the ethical politics had created a new class of educated indigenous, including Muslim educated elites which then established Muhammadiyah. Muhammadiyah was established to encounter the traditionalists' perspectives towards the propagation of Islam. Muhammadiyah rejected blind surrender to the *madzab* followers as well as uncritical embrace to particular interpretations produced by the *ulema*. Besides rejecting their authorities, Muhammadiyah reformed the prevalent stagnant Islamic educational institutions that were famously spread throughout Indonesian which were known as *madrasa*. Muhammadiyah saw that *madrasa* merely became the subtext of the religious and political authorities possessed by the ulema and jurists. Muhammadiyah believed that this was the source of Muslim backwardness in the face of the powerful Western civilization.

To access the western scientific tradition, Muhammadiyah have been willing to support the process of teaching and learning of several European languages. First it was the Dutch before World War II, and second it was the English language during the reign of Soeharto which was then embraced openly and consciously by Muhammadiyah in the rapid changing global era. The rest of the chapter will be devoted to inquiring the history of English Departments in the Indonesian Muhammadiyah universities from 1958 until 2005.

2. *Madrasa* as the Encounter from Traditionalists

In Islam, the Quran, considered as the core of knowledge, is the major power or force to legitimize, produce, and operate the truth in society. The tradition of learning in Islam was first propagated in Central Arabia in the form of traditional religious schools of higher learning called *madrasa* (literally, "place of study", plural *madaris*), that was first emerged during the ninth century as a major center of organized learning (Pedersen & Makdisi, 1960:123-27). The *madrasa* gradually became the source through which all forms of knowledge were legitimized. Its curricula consisted of the Quran, traditions of the prophet Muhammad (*hadith*), jurisprudence (*fiqh*), and the Arabic language. All forms of knowledge not patronized by *madaris* and not part of Islamic learning, such as philosophy, chemistry, astronomy, and mathematics, were pursued privately and to some extent secretly, under the guise of other subjects, as the traditions or medicines. In the *madaris* the objective of education was the achievement of the bliss (*sa'ada*) in the hereafter. Inasmuch as religious knowledge was concerned, to achieve *sa'ada*, the curriculum was confined solely to religious and linguistic studies (Pedersen & Makdisi, 1960:123-24). If other subjects had to be mastered to facilitate the acquisition of this religious knowledge, they were merely auxiliary. Such subjects included grammar, rhetoric, logic, and philosophy (Pedersen & Makdisi, 1960:123-24). The acceptance of the Arabic language and literature in the *madrasa* system, for instance, was based on the idea that linguistic studies would help in understanding the Quran. Similarly, knowledge above that was minimally required to meet daily social and economic needs was considered dangerous. Subjects such as astronomy, medicines, or mathematics that exceeded religiously justifiable needs were seen as unnecessary (Pedersen & Makdisi, 1960:1123-24).

The previous paradigm was developed mostly by traditionalists. Its apex reached when Al-Ghazzali (died AD 1111) and his successors systematically elaborated on the scope and nature of Islamic pedagogical knowledge based on epistemological dichotomies. The first division was between the revealed (*wahy*) and the acquired (*iktisabi*) knowledge. Revealed knowledge was sacred and given to the chosen few, namely, prophets. As a priori knowledge, it was to be transmitted as revealed without any rationalization or other forms of "manipulation". Transcendent and absolute, it should be accepted without question. Acquired knowledge included transmitted traditions (*naqli*) and rational knowledge (*'aqli*). These two categories were further divided into the good or desirable (*mahmud*) and the condemned or undesirable (*madmum*). The latter, which included philosophy and ancient sciences, was excluded from the curriculum. *Mahmud* included religiously approved knowledge, such as medicines, logics (with certain restrictions), and mathematics. However, these were also divided into necessary and excessive (Pedersen & Makdisi, 1960:118). Approved forms of knowledge were to be acquired only to the extent that they were necessary for survival, while research and inquiry should be forsaken. According to Al-Ghazzali, “One must forbid men to look for those mysteries and must turn them to the pronouncements of religious law, where there is sufficient proof for the believers to be content with” (Pedersen & Makdisi, 1960:1123-24). This rigid framings and classifications of knowledge based on religious law and dogma inevitably gave jurists and traditionalists (*muhdith*) final authorities in religious and worldly matters. Religious scholars became self-appointed interpreters and guardians of religious knowledge. People were to follow without questioning (*taqlid*) in all matters, and these scholars condemned all other forms of knowledge as well as inquiry and research. Even independent study of the Quran and traditions was forbidden. Hujwari (died ca. 1077) argued, for example, that “knowledge is obligatory only in as far as is requisite for acting righteously. God condemns those who learn useless knowledge” (Pedersen & Makdisi, 1960:1123-24). In short, *madrasa* learning was confined to the transmission of traditions and dogmas, and was hostile to research and scientific inquiry. This had far-reaching cultural and intellectual consequences for Islamic civilization. Orthodox Islam developed an ethos of conformism and respect for authorities which meant scholarship tended to be stagnate (Hurst, 1983:1539-40). Thus, pedagogical discourse produced by the *madrasa* became an effective device for social control, and resulted in an educational stagnation that still persists nowadays. Educational knowledge became increasingly irrelevant to changing socioeconomics realities and to new expectations and aspirations among Muslims. In other words, outside the *madrasa* everything was changing and inside everything remained static.

3. *Madrasa* and the Encounter with Modernity

Muslims encountered modernity through colonialism, which stripped their political power and brought about structural, normative, and attitudinal changes for both individuals and society. Modernization stands in opposition to traditionalism, with values such as individualism, secularism, rationalism, and consumerism that threaten traditional systems. As modern institutions replaced traditional ones—which had protected and passed on enduring values and knowledge—the locus of power to control and legitimize change shifted. The result has been profound changes in the normative, psychological, and material aspects of Muslims’ lives (Eisenstadt, 1973:25).

In the Indonesian islands, the Dutch adopted policies that made it difficult for the indigenous institutions to grow, and undercut the power base of colonized people. The traditional *madrasa* resisted change and became anachronistic in the modern world. Islamic education is a mere shadow of its past. The modernization of education in the empire has led to its complete transformation. During the Dutch, the concept of education fundamentally changed as secular education became a necessary qualification for jobs. The colonial bureaucracy opened new employment opportunities and required different types of qualifications than those offered by *madaris*. After an initial resistance, Muslim began to accept and participate in the new secular educational system because of its wider accessibility and economic utility. However, opposition to modern education by traditional Muslims continued. Colonizations also changed the objectives of education in *madaris* from achieving the bliss in the hereafter and providing government bureaucrat to defending the faith against colonial infiltration.

In the postcolonial era, the traditionalists continued to believe that Western secular education promotes immorality, and anti-Islamic or sometimes Christian ideas, and continued to oppose and modify it. They proposed that Muslims wrapped up in the ancient glory, preferred Islamic rather than a secular liberal education. The Indonesian Muslims became hostile to Dutch rule and alienated from Western education due to racial policy Dutch applied of only allowing aristocrats and those Christians-converted indigenous in accessing the schools. Despite the previous theological and psychological change experienced by Indonesian Muslim with the arrival of Western modern education incepted by the Dutch during Politics of Ethics, limited economic growth under the Dutch colonial government created uneven development, which diminished the opportunities of Muslims in Western education.

As the basic principle of colonial education was for the higher class, it was expected that the upper classes, in their turn, would provide education for the lower classes, with education thereby permeating down from the above. The government's continuous meritocratic policy of elite recruitment for colonial administrative and technical services implicitly, if not explicitly, legitimized the prevailing inequalities. In other words, Western liberal education created an unfavourable condition in a pluralistic society with regards to the distribution of opportunities. Therefore, only a small segment of the population, that is, the upper-classes who lived around the feodal local kingdoms, continued to benefit from Western education. Indeed, to the members of this stratum, the Dutch rule had given opportunities for their career, wealth, and influence, as well as possibility to broaden their intellectual horizons through Western connections. Therefore, as a group, they remained loyal to the colonial state. A colonial education system based on inequal opportunities widened the social and intellectual gaps between Muslims and the upper-caste feodal aristocrats as well as Christian-converted indigenous, in particular, in a country where the mother tongue was different from any of the European languages. These inequal conditions and opportunities led to the exclusion of Muslims from the Western education.

4. Muhammadiyah Establishing Modern Islamic Schools & Universities (1912-2005)

Muhammadiyah was established to promote modern Islamic education during the Dutch reign in Indonesia. Muhammadiyah became one of the influential and significant Indonesian Islamic modernist organizations which reformed the traditional Islamic education, *madrasa* traditional system. Although Muhammadiyah was not the first organization, its influences and its stronghold throughout Indonesia was lasted until now. The birth and development of Islamic modernism in Indonesia was influenced by the awareness of the Muslim society of their backwardness which was triggered by the western imperialism and its progress in the science. Through this, it was expected that Islam would be able to avoid the danger of *taqlid* which had become the major characteristics of the traditionalist *madrasa* and the *madzab* followers, and thus liberate the Muslims from accepting anything without reservation and further investigation. This was directed to open the door of *ijtihad* in Islam, meaning the right for individual interpretation of anything connected to the Faith through a process of intellectual exercise at its utmost degree. Individual opinion (*fatwa*) on certain cases or issues, or any particular rule of law (*hukum*) could be exercised by any man, called *mujtahidin* (singular, *mujtahid*). Previously, *fatwa* became the mere privilege of the traditionalist ulema. The new *mujtahidin*, reformer, could be any man who exercise his rationality at its utmost, were fighting against the disease of anti-intellectualism who would champion Islam as compatible with the modern world which aimed at the challenges posed by the surge of Western intellectual, cultural, political invasion. Several *mujtahidin* in Indonesia had promoted their *ijtihad* through mission (*dakwah*) and education by establishing modern Islamic education which combined secular subjects and religious teachings in its curriculum in which a more reformed and western modern style of schools was introduced and applied into the traditional system of *pesantren* Islamic schools (*madaris* traditional system). European languages, Dutch, German, French and English were also introduced in the modern Islamic senior high school during the Dutch reign.

The first Islamic modern school was established in Padang Sumatera by Haji Ahmad in 1909 (Djaja, 1951:296; Noer, 1963:51&59). The name of the school was *Adabijah School* which offered both religious and secular subjects in the curriculum for both boys and girls and which then finally subsidized by the Dutch colonial government in 1915. Adabijah School adapted completely the Dutch colonial elementary school, HIS. By 1916 the school had seven teachers, of which two were European, four Indonesian with teaching certificates from Western schools. It shows clearly how western-oriented was Adabijah School, while consequently, still maintained its Islamic teachings. The second Islamic modern school in Sumatera was Dinijah School at Padang Pandjang Sumatera which was established in 1915 by Zainuddin Labai El-

Junusi (1890-1924), in which he was to introduce a radical departure from the prevalent "*pesantren* system". By 1922 he was able to spread his school system to about 15 schools in Minangkabau Sumatera (Djaja, 1951:323-330).

In Java, the first Islamic modern school was established in Batavia (now Jakarta) in 1906. The Dutch prototype elementary school was called *Djamijat Chair School* which offered secular subjects such as arithmetic, history (Islamic History), and geography. The Arabic which was used in the traditional pesantren school was substituted with Malay (Bahasa Indonesia). Djamijat Chair Islamic Organization was criticized by the dominancy of the Arab-descendant members. Two of its prominent members were Sheikh Surkati which later founded *al-Irsjad* and Ahmad Dahlan which later founded *Muhammadijah*. In 1913 Sheikh Surkati (Sudanese) established his own organization, *Djamijat al-Islam wal Ersjat al-Arabia* which was commonly known as *al-Irsjad*. Besides establishing organization, his followers later also established al-Irsjad modern Islamic schools.

The vast spread of modern Islamic schools throughout Indonesia was mainly led by *Muhammadijah* Islamic modern organization which was founded in Jogjakarta by Kijai Hadji Amad Dahlan (indigenous Indonesian, Javanese) in 1912 which will become the focus of this research. One of the famous teachings of Ahmad Dahlan was: "Be progressive Ulama" (*"Jadilah Ulama yang berkemadjuan"*), meaning Ulama who followed the progress of the modern world, and who had to be knowledgeable and familiar with worldly matters (secular subjects) as well as the sciences of religion (Wiriosukarto, 1962:58). Dahlan's first inner logic of Islamic modernism was to return to the purely orthodox teachings of the Faith; and the second side of the inner logic which proved that Islam was compatible with the modern world. He never wrote his *ijtihad* in any serious and seminal books. Any available record of him was offered by organizations and activities that he established. As a true pragmatist he was to liberalize Islam as he had liberalized *Muhammadijah* to accept everything which he thought was beneficial, provided that it was not in contradiction with the true Faith, or deviating from it.

In Article II of the Statute of the Establishment of Muhammadijah it was aimed to (a) The spreading of Muslim religious teaching among the native people in the Residency of Jogjakarta and; (b) The promotion of religious life among its members. And in Article III of the Statute stated that to achieve the previous goal, several steps were taken as follows:

a. To establish and maintain good support of educational institutions, where besides common ***(secular) subjects*** the principles of Muslim religious teachings would also be given.
b. To hold meetings among its members and interested persons, where topics from Muslim religious teachings would be discussed.

c. To establish and maintain good support of the prayer-houses (wakafs and mosques), where publics religious services would be held.
d. To publish and render support in publishing books, treatises, brochures, and newspapers, wherein the subjects from religious usages and holy teachings would be treated, shall, in each aforementioned case, as well as other means, never be in conflict with law of the land and with public order or good custom.

Paragraph (a) of the Article III clearly indicates the desire to become an agent of social change within the Muslim community by specifically mentioned its effort to introduce and offer secular or modern subjects besides religious teachings in the curriculum of its educational system. This overt non political position taken by Muhammadijah before the Dutch colonial government had eased Ahmad Dahlan to make friends with the nationalist indigenous and even Christians organizations. From his friendship with the Christians, most notably Reverend Baker, he got valuable inputs in establishing the school system that they employed in Muhammadijah schools. He copied *HIS met de Bibel* (HIS with the Bible) into *HIS met de Koran* (HIS with the Quran). He was even called as *Kijai Kristen* (Christian Kyai/Ulema) and *Kijai Modern* (Modern Kyai/Ulema). This incited rejection among the traditional ulemas who saw that Dahlan had polluted Islamic teachings with the western knowledge. He was then accused of being a fake ulema (*Kijai Palsu*). Most notable opposition was then held by many traditional ulemas in East Java who formed the Nahdlatul Ulama (NU) in 1942. Dahlan was not afraid of the attack from the rural-based Ulema and he continued his progressive movements in the Muslim community, mainly in the urban areas, by establishing the core infrastructure of Muhammadijah, namely:

a. Tabligh/Dakwah (religious propagation)
b. Education (Muhammadiyah schools and universities throughout Indonesia)
c. Aisyijah (the women's section of Muhammadijah)
d. Penolong Kesengsaraan Umum, PKU (Improving the People's Misery which then established many hospitals in Indonesia)
e. Hizbul Wathan (Boyscout)
f. Taman Pustaka (Publication and Library)
g. Bahagian Penolong Hadji (Department to assist pilgrimage to Mecca)

The seeds of Muhammadijah modern school in which both secular and religious subjects were to be included in the curriculum, were planted the year before Muhammadijah formally established a religious school at Kauman on the first of December 1911 with 29 youngsters, and it increased to 62 pupils in 1912. The colonial government, consequently, responded generously to Muslim aspirations. It revised its earlier position that Muslims were indifferent to Western secular liberal education because they were anti-Dutch and wrapped up in the glory of the bygone days of Islam. On 12 June 1912, Muhammadijah received its first subsidy from the Dutch colonial government although the amount was far less compared to those which were received by the Christian schools conducted by Christian missionaries in Indonesia. A Dutch language course was introduced afterwards in *HIS mit de Koran*. Muhammadijah schools since then were developed like mushrooms throughout Java and Madura. Table 1 shows the rapid expansion of the Muhammadijah school system. Around 316 schools were already operated in the whole Java and Madura, of which 207 were categorized under the Western Schools System. Of particular importance was the introduction of the European foreign language, that is Dutch as obligatory, and English, German and French as regular subjects in Senior High Schools, those are the MULO/Normal HIK and Kweekschools. Before the break of world war II, the amount of Muhammadijah schools were far less behind those run by the colonial government and other private schools, notably those run by the Christian missionaries.

Table 1. Muhammadiyah schools in Java and Madura in 1932

Type of School	**West Java**	**Central Java**	**East Java**	**Madura**	**Total**
Western School System					
Volksschool	8	88	2	0	98
Standard School	1	23	2	2	28
Schakel	0	17	5	1	23
H.I.S. (Elementary School)	7	32	10	1	50
MULO/Noormal H.I.K (Senior High School)	1	2	1	0	4
Kweekschool	1	3	0	0	4
	18	165	20	4	**207**
Religious Schools					
Dinijah	2	59	12	4	77
Wustha	1	9	1	0	11
	3	68	13	4	**88**

Other Schools					
Aisyijah/Meisje school	2	6	0	0	8
Jatimschool (Schoolf for Orphans)	0	7	0	0	7
Bustanuf Athfal (Kindergarten)	1	1	0	0	2
Others	0	4	0	0	4
Grand Total	**24**	**251**	**33**	**8**	**316**

Sources: *Pemandangan Alam Islam dan Muhammadijah* 1932-1933, Jogjakarta, Hoofdbestuur Muhammadijah, n.d., pp. 118-128.

Besides quantity problem, Muhammadijah schools exposed to the quality matters as well. In spite of lack of financial support, Muhammadijah also lacks of qualified teachers who will support the infrastructure of all Muhammadijah schools throughout Java and Madura. Before the World War II, Muhammadijah mainly concentrated in establishing secondary schools. In 1934, Muhammadijah established a Senior High School (AMS-Algemeene Middelbare School) in Djakarta, while the plan to establish Muhammadijah University was also expressed in 1936 (Alfian, nd:310). This plan, however, was never realized before the Independence of Indonesia. The positive attitude taken by Muhammadijah towards modernism had probably had a far greater impact on the Muslim community as a whole than its very small tangible achievements.

Table 2.
Muhammadiyah Educational Institutions in Indonesia (2005)

Level of Educational Institutions	Total
Pre-School & Elementary Schools	
Busthanul Athfal (TK ABA—Taman Kanak-kanak Aisyiyah Busthanul Athfal)	3.370
Koran Education (Taman Pendidikan Al Quran)	3.015
Elementary School (Sekolah Dasar Muhammadiyah)	1.128
Madrasah Diniyah/Ibtidaiyyah	1.768
Total	**9.281**
Secondary Schools	
Junior High School (SLTP Muhammadiyah)	1.179
Madrasah Tsanawiyah	534

Senior High School (SMU Muhammadiyah)	509
Special Schools (Sekolah Menengah Kejuruan Muhammadiyah)	249
Madrasah Aliyah	171
Total	**2.642**
High Educations	
Universities	36
High Education	74
Academy	52
Polytechnic	4
Total	**166**
Grand Total	**12.089**

Sources: Report from Majelis Diktilitbang PP Muhammadiyah on Muktamar Muhammadiyah 45, Malang, East Java.

Until 2005, the number of Muhammadiyah schools has rapidly increased as follows (see Tabel 2 for detail): 3.370 TK *Busthanul Athfal*/ Kindergarten, 3.015 Koran education (TPA-Taman Pendidikan Al Qur'an), 1.128 elementary schools, 1.768 *Madrasah Diniyah/Ibtidaiyyah*, 1.179 Junior High School (SLTP Muhammadiyah), 534 *Madrasah Tsanawiyah*/junior high schools, 509 senior high schools (SMU Muhammadiyah), 249 specialised schools (Sekolah Kejuruan Muhammadiyah), 171 Madrasah Aliyah. Besides schools, Muhammadiyah began establishing higher education institutions since 1958. By 2005, Muhammadiyah has established 36 universities, 74 high schools institutions, 52 academies, 4 polytechnics. Muhammadiyah expanded its educational institutions especially throughout the Muslim social enclaves in the outer islands outside Java, such as Aceh, West Sumatera, West and South Kalimantan, Central and South Sulawesi, West Nusa Tenggara as well. Approaching the 21st century, the number of Muhammadiyah educational institutions is far beyond other private ones. The quantity of Muhammadiyah educational institutions, however, is not accompanied by a proper standard of education. Of 166 PTM (Perguruan Tinggi Muhammadiyah/Muhammadiyah High Schools) with 666 study programs, solely 410 got the accreditation from the Education Department (*Badan Akreditasi Nasional* [BAN], 2000). The rest—the 256 of them—have not achieved the standard set by the government. This fact illustrates the lack of proper quality Muhammadiyah educational institutions have compared with the private ones.

The positive attitude taken by Muhammadiyah towards Western education system was proved by its commitment in elaborating western type of schools and higher education. Tables 1 & 2 show that Muhammadiyah is still combining the traditional type of *madrasa* and western schools. The most historical moment Muhammadiyah made was when it conducted its Muktamar in 1959 in Pekalongan, Central Java. There was a dispute within the Muhammdiyah policy committees whether to establish higher education in a "university" form such in the West or "madrasa" form such as in Central Arabia. A faction represented by Kyai Haji Mas Mansyur preferred the "madrasa" form for the higher institutions, such as *Zawiyah* (traditional *madrasa*) in North Africa which he visited formerly. Another faction represented by Mulyadi Joyonegoro (the Minister of Social Affair at Soekarno's era) proposed that Muhammadiyah established a "university" form similar to the one in the western countries. After a serious debate between the two factions, "university" was applied to all Muhammadiyah higher institution. The prototype of the university Muhammadiyah embraced was totally similar to what is now employed in the western countries. Though the template Muhammadiyah employed is similar with the western educational system, the content of the curriculum is different. Muhammadiyah adds "Islamic and Muhammadiyah" teachings to all its educational institutions.

5. The History of the English Departments in Muhammadiyah Universities (1958-2005)

Despite the positive attitude of Muhammadiyah towards the teaching of secular subjects, Muhammadiyah is adaptive as well to the arrival of English as a global language. This positive attitude is especially taken due to the high quality standard owned by western education which undeniably supported by the vessel of monolingual English and other European languages. From 1912-1923, Muhammadiyah had introduced Dutch and other European languages such as English, French and German to its 207 Muhammadiyah Western Schools. Only after 1958 Muhammadiyah decided to establish its first English Department in Universitas Muhammadiyah Dr Hamka (UHAMKA). Due to President Soekarno's policy of accentuating national identity and rejecting the western-imported identity, the development of English department at his reign (1945-1965) was very low compared to the reign of President Soeharto. His policy was departed from the danger Indonesian Independence had to face regarding Dutch re-invasion to Indonesian in 1949. Dutch's reinvasion highly influenced the educational policy takers in pushing forward program on studying European languages in the Indonesian universities. Soekarno's presidency could merely produced 7 English departments run by state-owned universities (UNSU, UNY, Pol Manado, UNSYIAH, UNSRI, UNDIP), 4 English Departments established by Christian missionaries (UKSW, UKP, UKIT, UKK) and 2 English

Departments run by Catholic missionaries (Atmajaya & Sanata Dharma), as well as 1 English Departments developed by Muhammadiyah (UHAMKA). Only after Soeharto's reign (1966-1998) did English departments grow like mushrooms. Soeharto's presidency had established 29 English Departments by State-Owned universities, 77 by private initiatives as well as 20 by Muhammadiyah. Soeharto's free market economic policy had fostered the need of Indonesians to learn English. This step was followed by Muhammadiyah's adaptive educational policy in incepting English Departments in almost all Muhammadiyah universities.

Muhammadiyah policy on English, since Indonesian independence, was highly influenced by the policy of the Indonesian government. The teaching of Dutch, English, French and German was still prevalent before the World War II broke. Only after Indonesia got its Independence had Muhammadiyah had to resort to the policy set by Soekarno. The teaching of Arabic is still introduced from 1912 until now. The teaching of European languages in Muhammadiyah schools, however, experienced a significant backlash during Soekarno's presidency. After 1965 when Soeharto took the reign, Muhammadiyah schools began introducing English in its schools. Other European languages were not taught. Soeharto's economic think tank that was graduated from the US had played significant roles in shaping the face of educational policy. American English was chosen as the only foreign language learned in schools. TOEFL is chosen by Muhammadiyah in testing its students and future teachers. Until 2005 Muhammadiyah has already established 22 English Departments (see Tabel 3). In this study I am going to focus on the history of seven English departments, ranging from 2 in West Java, 2 in Central Java, 1 in East Java, 1 in West Nusa Tenggara, and 1 in South Sulawesi.

Table 3.
English Departments established by Persyarikatan Muhammadiyah (1958-2005)

Year of Establishment	**English Departments**
Soekarno Presidency (1945-1965)	
1958	Universitas Muhammadiyah Prof Dr Hamka, Jakarta (UHAMKA)
Total	**1 English Department**

Soeharto Presidency (1966-1998)

1976	Universitas Muhammadiyah Sumatera Utara
1983	Universitas Muhammadiyah Tapanuli Selatan
1984	Universitas Muhammadiyah Surakarta, Central Java (UMS) Universitas Muhammadiyah Ahmad Dahlan, Yogyakarta (UAD) Universitas Muhammadiyah Surabaya, East Java
1987	Universitas Muhammadiyah Palu Universitas Muhammadiyah Malang (UMM)
1989	Universitas Muhammadiyah Jakarta Universitas Muhammadiyah Jember
1991	Universitas Muhammadiyah Bengkulu
1992	Universitas Muhammadiyah Mataram (UMMat)
1993	Universitas Muhammadiyah Ponorogo, East Java Universitas Muhammadiyah Pontianak Universitas Muhammadiyah Makasar (UMMak)
1994	Universitas Muhammadiyah Palembang
1995	Universitas Muhammadiyah Purwokerto
Total	**16 English Departments**

Post-Soeharto Presidency (1998-2005)

1999	Universitas Muhammadiyah Pare-Pare Universitas Muhammadiyah Semarang
2001	Universitas Muhammadiyah Buton Universitas Muhammadiyah Gresik
2003	Universitas Muhammadiyah Sukabumi (UMMI)
Total	**5 English Departments**
Grand Total	**22 English Departments in Muhammadiyah Universities**

Sources: Direktorat Jenderal Pendidikan Tinggi, 2005, Rekapitulasi Perguruan Tinggi dan Program Studi, Jakarta: Dirjen Dikti; and Majelis Pendidikan Tinggi Penelitian dan Pengembangan Pinpinan Pusat Muhammadiyah, 2006, Direktori Perguruan Tinggi Muhammadiyah (PTM): Profil Universitas, Sekolah Tinggi, Politeknik, dan Akademi Muhammadiyah se-Indonesia, Yogyakarta: Diktilitbang Muhammadiyah, Pp.: 1-56.

a. The English Department, Universitas Muhammadiyah Prof Dr Hamka (1958)

Universitas Muhammadiyah Prof Dr Hamka (hereafter Uhamka) is located in several areas in Jakarta, such as Pasar Rebo, Klender and Matraman East of Jakarta. Uhamka was first developed on 18 November 1957 from IKIP Muhammadiyah Jakarta as Perguruan Tinggi Pendidikan Guru (PTPG), which aims to train future teachers. Organized and founded by Arso Sastroatmodjo, HS Prodjokusumo, Semangun, Asnawi, H Gozali Dunia, Doeraini and Soeroto Karto Soedarmo and with only 17 students applied to the university, PTPG was then transformed into faculty of teacher training (FKIP) which became the branch of Universitas Muhammadiyah Jakarta (UMJ). In 1965 FKIP UMJ was further transformed into an independence high institution named IKIP-MJ. With the instruction from Directorate General of High Education-Department of Education No 138/DIKTI/Kep/1997 on 30 May 1997, it was then transformed into university of HAMKA which was named after Prof Dr Haji Abdul Malik Karim Amrullah (Hamka). Hamka was a Muslim activist who wrote several Islamic novels, travelogues, and *dakwah* (propagation) newspapers. Persyarikatan Muhammadiyah and Hamka's family agreed to name the university after him. Uhamka was founded by Muhammadiyah with the following visions and missions. The visions of education: the university is the centre of intellectual, emotional and spiritual search. Its missions: (1). To develop an educational institution based on the principle of long-life education, research, as well as commitments to Islamic values. (2). To develop freedom of scientific thinking which guides by spirit of *tauhid* (Islamic monotheism). (3). To develop entrepreneurship in scientific knowledge and art. (4). To increase the quality and the quantity of serving the Ummah. (5). To make Uhamka the center for *dakwah* movement.

The English Department in Uhamka was founded in 1958 along with the Department of Indonesian language and literature. The curriculum was developed with the following visions and missions. The visions: to create students who are intellectually, emotionally and spiritually excellent in mastering the English language. The missions: (1). To establish education, training, research, and commitments to the society in the field of English education. (2). To develop freedom of scientific thinking in the field of English education. (3). To develop entrepreneurship in technology and art in the field of English education. (4). To make English department as a means of *dakwah* in empowering the *ummah* by using English education. (5). To develop English education as a means of sincerity to serve Allah SWT. (The historical sketch of Uhamka is taken from *Direktori Perguruan Tinggi Muhammadiyah* (pp. 37-39). The curriculum of English department is taken from *Kurikulum Program Studi Pendidikan Bahasa Inggris Uhamka 2006-2007*, p. 52.)

b. The English Department, Universitas Muhammadiyah Surakarta (1984)

Similar to Uhamka, Universitas Muhammadiyah Surakarta (hereafter UMS) was also first founded as one of the branches of Universitas Muhammadiyah Jakarta which is located in Surakarta, Central Java (quite far away from Jakarta). It was founded on 18 September 1958 with three departments: General Education, Economics, and Islamic Education. In 1965 it was separated from its center in Jakarta, and became an independent IKIP, a higher education which produced teachers for secondary schools. On 24 October 1981, with the initiatives from Drs. Haji Muhammad Djazman Alkindi, IKIP was then transformed into Universitas Muhammadiyah Surakarta which was legalized by Department of Education based on Ministry Edict No 0330/O/1981. UMS was founded by Persyarikatan Muhammadiyah with the following vision and missions. The vision: UMS as one of the filial institutions of Persyarikatan Muhammadiyah is an Islamic University directed to become the centre of excellence in developing scientific knowledge, technology and art which is in accordance to Islamic values and the demand from age (*Zeitgeist*) to fulfil the progressiveness. The missions: (1). to advance the scientific knowledge and technology. (2). To serve the *ummah* through education and research to build Indonesia as an advanced society.

The English department was established three years after its conversion into university. The curriculum was developed with the following visions and missions. The visions: The English Department is directed to be the center of excellence in learning English and developing human resources. By the center of excellence in learning English means that the existence of the English department and the role it plays are recognized, needed, and preferred by the wider community at various levels. By the centre of excellence in developing human resources means that the outputs the English department produces should be professional, critical, analytical, innovative, creative, independent, and competitive, in addition to having entrepreneurship, fighting spirit, and good conducts. The missions: the mission that the English department wants to accomplish is to advance the English language learning, to produce outputs, and to give services education, research, and community services. The objectives: (1). To conduct effective, efficient, well-planned learning. (2). To produce skilled, devoted, dedicated scholars. (The historical sketch of UMS is taken from *Direktori Perguruan Tinggi Muhammadiyah* (pp. 53-54). The curriculum of the English department is taken from *Kurikulum Program Studi*

Pendidikan Bahasa Inggris, Universitas Muhammadiyah Surakarta 2004-2005, p. 168).

c. The English Department, Universitas Muhammadiyah Ahmad Dahlan (1984)

Universitas Muhammadiyah Ahmad Dahlan (hereafter UAD) was the conversion from IKIP Muhammadiyah Yogyakarta which was established on 18 November 1960. The conversion into university form was legalized with the edict from department of education, SK Mendikbud RI, No. 102/O/1994. The conversion was initiated by Rector of UAD, Prof. Dr. Noeng Muhadjir, in *Milad* (anniversary) of IKIP on 18 November 1990. He saw that IKIP as teacher training was no longer adequate to contend graduate from secondary schools who wanted to pursue other departments. It was located near the central office of Persyarikatan Muhammadiyah in Yogyakarta and named after its founder, Kyai Haji Ahmad Dahlan. Its vision is as follows: to become advanced university in scientific knowledge, technology, and art in order to contribute to the building of Indonesia with the spirit of professionalism, dedication, and sincerity to the *ummah* which are founded on the moral and ethic of Islam. Its mission: to educate the life of the Indonesian *ummah* based on the Islamic moral and ethic.

The English department was established in 1984. Its vision is as follows: to teach English language in order to contribute to the building of Indonesia with the spirit of professionalism, dedication, and sincerity to the *ummah* which are founded on the moral and ethic of Islam. Its mission: to teach English for the life of the Indonesian *ummah* based on the Islamic moral and ethic. (The historical sketch of UAD is taken from *Direktori Perguruan Tinggi Muhammadiyah* (pp. 1-2). The curriculum of The English department is taken from *Kurikulum Program Studi Pendidikan Bahasa Inggris, Universitas Muhammadiyah Ahmad Dahlan 2000*).

d. The English department, Universitas Muhammadiyah Malang (1987)

Universitas Muhammadiyah Malang (hereafter UMM) was formerly the branch of Universitas Muhammadiyah Jakarta (UMJ) which was founded on September 1965, and which was legalized with the edict from directorate general of higher education, SK No. 68/B-Swt/P/1966, on 30 December 1966. On the first of July 1968, UMM was independent from UMJ. It is located in Malang, East Java. Its vision is to create UMM as the centre of excellence in the field of education, faith, and knowledge which are useful to the development of Indonesia in the present and in the future. Mission: to actualize the three duties of universities which are founded on the social conscience and Islamic values.

The English department was initiated in 1987. Its vision is to produce outputs in the field of teaching English who are useful for the development of Indonesia in the present and in the future. Missions: to actualize the teaching of English which are founded on the social conscience and Islamic values. (The historical sketch of UMM is taken from *Direktori Perguruan Tinggi Muhammadiyah* (pp. 21-23). The curriculum of The English department is taken from *Kurikulum Program Studi Pendidikan Bahasa Inggris, Universitas Muhammadiyah Malang*).

e. The English department, Universitas Muhammadiyah Mataram (1992)
Universitas Muhammadiyah Mataram (hereafter UMMat) was founded in 1980. It is located in Mataram, West Nusa Tenggara. Its vision is to create scholars who have good moral conducts, who can master and develop scientific knowledge and qualified cultural values which are correlated to the need of the development of Indonesia by maintaining the local wisdom and protecting the natural resources as *dakwah amar makruf nahi munkar* in establishing a pious community with the blessing from Allah SWT. Its mission is to develop the filial institution of Persyarikatan Muhammadiyah in the field of higher education which is implemented in the four duties of university in educating the Indonesian based on the *akidah* (theology) of Quran and Sunnah Rasulullah Muhammad SAW (the tradition of Prophet Muhammad).

The English department was established in 1992. Its vision is to teach English to the students in order to have good moral conduct, could master and develop scientific knowledge and qualified culture which are correlated to the need of the development of Indonesia by maintaining the local wisdom and protecting the natural resources as *dakwah amar makruf nahi munkar* in establishing pious community with the bless from Allah SWT. Its mission is to develop the teaching of English in educating the Indonesians based on the *akidah* (theology) of Quran and Sunnah Rasulullah Muhammad SAW (the tradition of Prophet Muhammad). (The historical sketch of UMMat is taken from *Direktori Perguruan Tinggi Muhammadiyah* (pp. 24-25). The curriculum of the English department is taken from *Kurikulum Program Studi Pendidikan Bahasa Inggris, Universitas Muhammadiyah Mataram 2005*).

f. The English department, Universitas Muhammadiyah Makasar (1993)
Universitas Muhammadiyah Makasar (hereafter UMMak) is located in Makasar, South Sulawesi. It was founded on 19 June 1963 as one of the branch of UMJ which was legalized by Notary Act No. 71 on 19 June 1963. Its founder was M.S. Daeng Mattinri, Drs. Abd. Matif Masri, Drs. Syahruddin Kaeng, Muh Daeng Patompo, Drs A Tajuddin Baso Rum, Drs Fachruddin AE as well as Drs Ahmad Dahla Maing. Its vision is to make UMMak as an Islamic university which is independent, credible as well as excellent. Its missions are as follows: (1). To increase the quality of *iman* (faith) and *taqwa* (piety). (2). To increase

the quality of teaching and learning. (3). To sow the innovative and competitive research. (4). To increase the quality of the life of the community.

The English department was initiated in 1993. The curriculum was developed with the following vision and mission. The vision: to create outputs mastering English who are highly competitive and Islamic. The missions: (1). To conduct teaching in English which is based on the development of knowledge in accordance to *iman* (faith) and *taqwa* (piety). (2). To increase the quality of teaching and learning based on the up-to-date curriculum and the need of the market. (3). To create an atmosphere of education which support students' creativity in learning, teaching, as well as research which are correlated to the department. Aims: (1). To prepare students to become scholars in English language teaching who are piety and have strong faith in Islam to create an Islamic society. (2). To prepare future teachers in English who are in accordance with the Islamic values. (3). To prepare professional teachers of English who are creative in developing and implementing the knowledge and become the ideal public figure among the society. (The historical sketch of UMMak is taken from *Direktori Perguruan Tinggi Muhammadiyah* (pp. 20-21). The curriculum of The English department is taken from *Kurikulum Program Studi Pendidikan Bahasa Inggris, Universitas Muhammadiyah Makasar 2004*).

g. The English department, Universitas Muhammadiyah Sukabumi (2003)

Universitas Muhammadiyah Sukabumi (hereafter UMMI) is located in Sukabumi, West Java. It was founded with the edict from the directorate general of higher education No. 81/D101/2003. Unlike other Muhammadiyah universities, as a new university its visions and missions are still not yet clear. It is even the youngest university Persyarikatan Muhammadiyah has. Its establishment was supported by the local government which donated its unused local office to Persyarikatan Muhammadiyah. With the support from the central office of Muhammadiyah and Sukabumi local government, UMMI got its campus at the centre of Sukabumi town. The vision of education: the university is the centre of intellectual, emotional and spiritual search. Its missions: (1). To develop an educational institution which based on the principle of long-life education, research, as well as commitment to the Islamic values. (2). To develop freedom of scientific thinking which guided by spirit of *tauhid* (Islamic monotheism). (3). To develop entrepreneurship in scientific knowledge and art. (4). To increase the quality and the quantity of serving the Ummah. (5). To make UMMI as center of *dakwah* movement.

The English Department in UMMI was founded in 2003. The curriculum was developed with the following vision and missions. Vision: to create students who are intellectually, emotionally and spiritually excellent in mastering English language. The missions: (1). To conduct education, training, research, and commitments to society in the field of English education. (2). To develop freedom of scientific thinking in the field of English education. (3). To develop entrepreneurship in technology and art in the field of English education. (4). To make the English department as a means of *dakwah* in empowering the *ummah* by using English education. (5). To develop English education as a means of sincerity to serve Allah SWT. (The historical sketch of UMMI is taken from *Direktori Perguruan Tinggi Muhammadiyah* (pp. 46-47). The curriculum of The English department is taken from *Kurikulum Program Studi Pendidikan Bahasa Inggris, Universitas Muhammadiyah Sukabumi 2006-2007*).

6. English as a Means of *Dakwah*

Muhammadiyah's pragmatist educational vision states that English is the only foreign language to be taught both in Muhammadiyah schools and universities. Even the role the English language plays is greater than Arabic seen from its educational policy. Persyarikatan Muhammadiyah (Muhammadiyah Foundation), however, saw English as a useful tool in spreading the *dakwah* through education. Within Muhammadiyah establishment statuta, Muhammadiyah institutional education serves as the subordinate to the higher aim the organization has, that is to spread the good work and eradicating the evil work (*amar ma'ruf nahi munkar*). In this case, education becomes the subtext of the ideological force Muhammadiyah propagates. Muhammadiyah is still consistent in applying the traditional type of *madrasa*, that is to reach the bliss of *sa'ada*, thereafter. This persistence, however, has been transformed by Muhammadiyah in different way compared to the old ideology. Muhammadiyah highlights the role to spread the bliss to other people. There is an apparent social empowerment which still persists at present. This decision creates paradoxical development in teaching and learning English, especially in teaching western literature, as implied in the curriculum. During my eight year-service in teaching English at Universitas Muhammadiyah Surakarta, I found that the students tended to bring with them a kind of cultural conflicts when apprehending other cultural norms. Compared to state-owned universities and Christian universities, students in Muhammadiyah tended to have less quality in literary subjects. Students' literary appreciations are limited due to Muhammadiyah's decision in making English as *dakwah* tools instead of a subject of literary and dialectical discussions. The previous histories and educational philosophy of the English departments in Muhammadiyah demonstrate vividly that one of the most important missions and visions of teaching English is to propagate the *ummah* and make English as *dakwah* tool.

The visions and missions of the curriculum in Muhammadiyah universities are connected with a willingness to use the global spread of English to further the spread of Islam. All see English language teaching (ELT) as a legitimate site for *dakwah* work. Islam brings a set of moral and spiritual values for discussions to the teaching of the English language. As a consequence, English language teaching is a highly Islamic political project which inevitably makes classrooms become cultural and political sites. Muhammadiyah saw that better access to English can be a better solution to global inequalities. Despite intercultural understanding, the acceptance of difference, witnessing, serving, and ministering, English teaching as a means of *dakwah* remains a project devoted to the promotion ('sharing') of a particular set of ideologies and beliefs based on supposedly external criteria (Allah, the Koran, and the *Ummah*) that give its validity.

7. Conclusion: the Limit of Islamic Education

Islamic education has assumed a new definition and received wider application by traditional Muslims during the last two decades. In 1977 an important meeting—the World Conference for Muslim Education—was held in Mecca, where a group of predominantly fundamentalist Muslims emphasized the need for education relevant to Islam's sociocultural values, relevance being seen in moral and eschatological terms (Engineer, 1978:86-95; Watts,1986:174). They argued that education could redirect and reshape the attitudes of Muslim children by shifting their orientations from Western to Islamic values. The role of Islam, defined in terms of its worldview and dogma, was seen as determining the objectives of education and influencing educational processes. This, they believed, could be achieved by rejecting current practices colored by Western cultures and ideologies. "For them, if there was a change it could only be for the worse, and the worse could only be cured, not by creating something new, but by renewing what had once existed" (Hourani, 1983:83). In short, these traditionalists viewed education as an important means of creating an Islamized society and an instrument for forging a new Islamic identity. With this in mind, they attempted to reformulate educational objectives, redesign curricula, and rewrite textbooks.

Recent Islamization efforts differ significantly from the revivalist movements of the early twentieth century. In the past, Islamic religious scholars and jurists clearly distinguished between religious and secular forms of knowledge as they attempted to revive traditional Islamic knowledge and ethics. The recent Islamization movement, by contrast, attempts to eliminate that dichotomy and reconstruct social discourse within the eschatological worldview of Islam. Islam thus becomes the legitimizing discourse for the production and regulation of knowledge. To transform various facets of Muslim society, Islamists coin terms such as Islamic education, Islamic economics, Islamic democracy, Islamic science, and so on.

For fundamentalists, educational discourse must be based on religious knowledge. Since it is infallible divine knowledge, it is an instrument in the selection and validation of pedagogical knowledge. A.R.S. Abdullah, a traditionalist writer, states, "the superiority of revealed knowledge is due to the fact that it is derived from the truth (*Haqq*) while some other types of knowledge are based on speculation (*zann*) or desires (*hawa*)" (Abdullah, nd:83). For the traditionalists, a strong link exists between education and theology. Education is not an enterprise of free inquiry and research but an extension of theological learning.

Tibawi also believes that the Quran and the collected traditions of Muhammad comprise the essential knowledge upon which to build an education system. "The single fundamental fact that determines the concept, dictates the content, governs the evolution of the philosophy of Muslim education, is the belief that God's final message to mankind was revealed in its entirety through Mohammed and is enshrined in the Quran" (Tibawi, 1957:78-89).

To traditional Muslims, the ethical implications of the scientific mode of thought are a sensitive issue: "Modern science is guided by no moral values but naked materialism and arrogance. The whole branch of knowledge and its application is contaminated by the same evil" (Jameelah, 1983:8). Furthermore, knowledge "divorced from faith is not only partial knowledge, it can even be described as a kind of new ignorance" (Hussain & Ashraf, 1979). Traditionalist Muslims permit subjects such as science, technology, mathematics, and history only if they pass the "test of validity and effectiveness in fostering a deeper awareness of the Divine Presence in the Universe" (Hussain & Ashraf, 1979). Traditionalists also believe that humans have divinely fixed destiny and role on earth. Therefore, they require moral teachings and religious upbringing since they are young. Since traditionalists believe education must be based on ethical and religious foundations, only jurists are qualified to develop Islamic educational systems (See Diagram 3).

In a fundamentalist discourse, science is an ideological tool by which Western civilization extends its hegemony over Muslim societies. Hence, the transformation of Western scientific discourse was the major issue debated at the 1977 World Conference on Muslim Education in Mecca. The basic problem identified by the participants—mostly traditionalist Muslims—was that no applied or social sciences were drawn from religion. In Islamic societies, originality, innovation, and change were never upheld as intrinsic values. The ideal of Islamic culture was not mechanical evolutionary progress but the permanent immutable transcendent divinely revealed moral, theological, and spiritual values of the Quran and Sunnah.

The fundamentalists advocated that all subjects must reflect Islamic beliefs and values as shown in the curricula of the seven English departments that were previously discussed. This implies a change in objectives, curricula content, pedagogy, and other aspects. Because all textbooks were perceived as being imbued with the ethical values of Western writers, traditionalists argued that Islamic sciences must be distinct and foster Islamic values. In other words,

Diagram 3

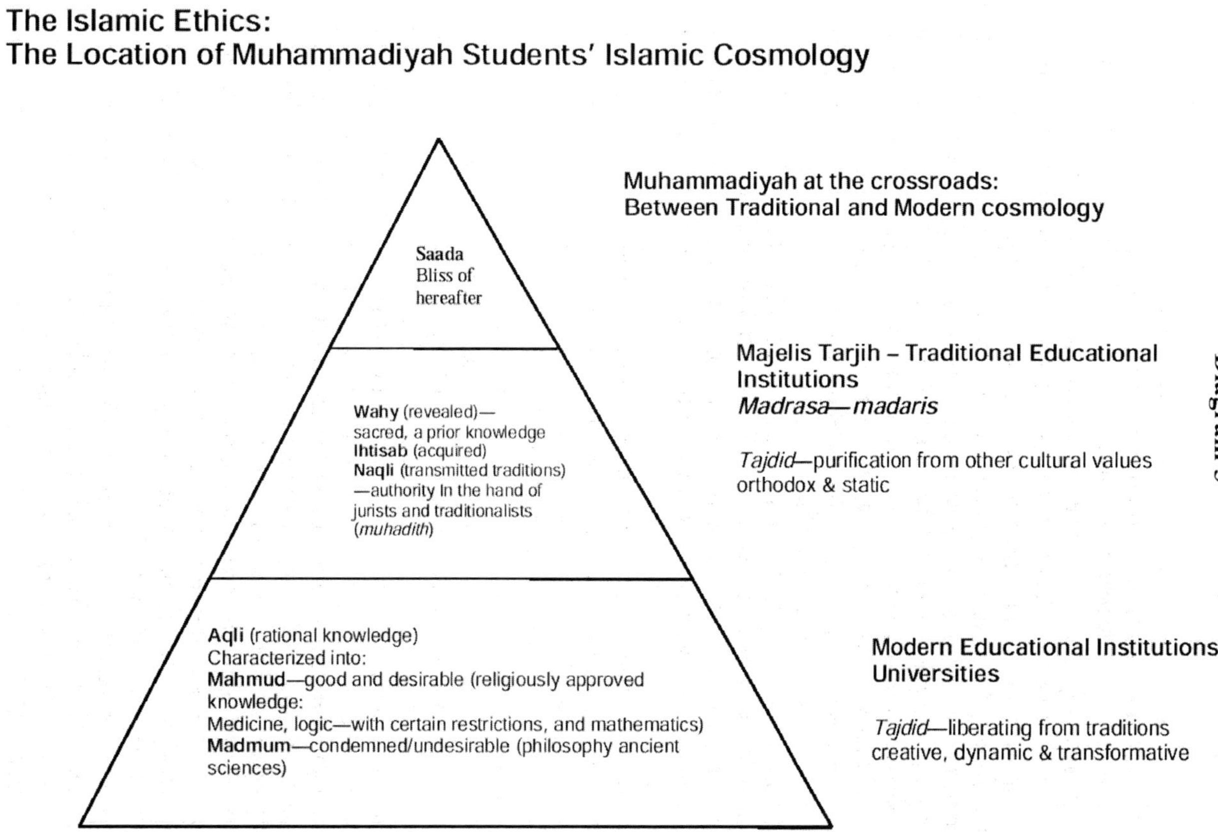
The Islamic Ethics:
The Location of Muhammadiyah Students' Islamic Cosmology
Saada
Bliss of
hereafter
Wahy (revealed)—
sacred, a prior knowledge
Ihtisab (acquired)
Naqli (transmitted traditions)
—authority in the hand of
jurists and traditionalists
(muhadith)
Aqli (rational knowledge)
Characterized into:
Mahmud—good and desirable (religiously approved
knowledge:
Medicine, logic—with certain restrictions, and mathematics)
Madmum—condemned/undesirable (philosophy ancient
sciences)
Muhammadiyah at the crossroads:
Between Traditional and Modern cosmology
Majelis Tarjih – Traditional Educational
Institutions
Madrasa—madaris
Tajdid—purification from other cultural values
orthodox & static
Modern Educational Institutions
Universities
Tajdid—liberating from traditions
creative, dynamic & transformative

western sciences have a secular character that can be changed by infusing Islamic values into them. They proposed that "Muslim writers should write books on the basis of Islamic ethics and assimilate that which is in conformity with Islam and reject the rest" (Sageb, 1981:48-9). Fundamentalist writers now contend that because Western sciences are taught without any mention of Allah or Muhammad they are the sources of straying from the truth (*gumrahi*). Specifically, reflections on the nature of modern education and customs immediately reveal their contradictions with the natures of Islamic education and customs. For the fundamentalists, it is necessary to exorcise the evil (secular) spirit from Western science and Islamize it. They assume that these applied and social sciences were developed in Islam, were thrown into the background during the colonial period, and must be revived in present times. Yet that assumption ignores the historical fact that the Muslim clergies—like clergies in many other religious traditions—had earlier opposed science and philosophy.

The total assimilation of all subjects into an Islamic moral and religious frameworks, especially to propagate the dakwah as shown in the previous discussions concerning curricula, means that they are all to be judged on their moral outcome and are to go through a process of scrutiny and censorship before being accepted in so-called Islamic polity. As a result of this understanding, science at all levels is taught conservatively with critical and analytical methodology absent. Scientific knowledge develops critical thinking and avoids the uncritical acceptance of traditional answers to human inquiry. Science challenges the validity and relevance of all discourse of knowledge, because nothing is accepted as permanent and sacred. Unlike theology, science permits the critical comparison of competing theories and frameworks. While the mark of a scientific theory is that it is testable, religious knowledge is empirically untestable and demands unquestioning acceptance and practice.

The Islamization of knowledge is then followed by the Islamization of laws in Indonesia. The implementation of *Sharia* laws in 53 regions in Indonesia has resulted in the oppression of vulnerable groups in Indonesian society, especially women and religious minorities. The *ulamas*, the military, and elites all benefited from Islamization in those regions. In addition, the legitimization of traditional elites show that Islamic ideology has failed to provide the promised equality and social justice. The *ulamas* never reach a consensus as to what constituted an Islamic educational, economic, or political system, or how it could be implemented. Nevertheless, Islamic discourse has given a tremendous power to the *ulamas*. The emphasis on ideological education has intensified cultural and religious differences, resulting in cultural clashes and resentments of other cultures.

PART II
MAINSTREAMING GENDER THROUGH POSTCOLONIAL MUSLIM WOMEN WRITERS

Chapter IV
Muhammadiyah Students' Quest for Islamic Identity: The Call for Universal Brotherhood (*Ummah*) and the Return to Total Islam (*Kaffah*)

1. Introduction

Chapter IV is an investigation into the inner cosmological constructions of young Muhammadiyah followers. This chapter provides a basis for the further examination of how students read and engage with Western literature discussed in later chapters. An understanding of students' own cosmological constructs can be traced, among other ways, through their reading and interpretation of new Islamist writings that have flowered in Indonesia in the post-Suharto era. Some of this literature has been produced by writers associated with Muhammadiyah's own 'young writers' circle. These literary works reveal a range of cosmological perspectives informed by both general Islamic precepts as well as by historical and current debates within Muhammadiyah on Islam. Written in the Indonesian language, the Islamic expressions found in such literary works provide an important insight into the current range of perceptions, experiences and constructions of Islamic cosmology. Amongst young Indonesian Muslims and within Muhammadiyah itself. Muhammadiyah students' love of reading such literature also says a great deal about how Islam is perceived within day-to-day class-room interactions. The cosmological orientation of Muhammadiyah students is similar in orientation to that of the 'new Islamism', and contrasts with earlier forms of Islamism—or 'old Islamism'—as established by the founders of Muhammadiyah. Two Islamic notions in particular energize the current new, that of Ummah (Muslim brotherhood or the community of Muslim 'brothers' and 'sisters') and Kaffah (total adherence to the laws of Islam).

This Chapter considers in some detail the recent focus on Ummah and Kaffah in new-Islamist writings as well as the influence of these writings on the cosmological orientation of contemporary Muhammadiyah students. Indonesian new Islamist organizations are first analyzed before I discuss some of the works of literature associated with the new Islamists. The idea of an ideal Ummah and the manifestation of total Islam, or Kaffah, conclude this Chapter. Before discussing the emergence of new-Islamist movements in Indonesia, however, I would like to clarify how I am using the term 'Islamism' in order to avoid the term being rendered as 'fundamentalism' in a pejorative sense.

Gabriel Almond *et al.* provide one of the most widely-cited definitions of fundamentalism. They describe the term as: "*Discernable religious militancy by which self-styled 'true-believers' attempt to arrest the erosion of religious identity, fortify the borders of religious community, and create viable alternatives to secular institutions and behaviours*". The previous definition highlights the following points: firstly, *religious militancy* stresses that the movement is religiously motivated and geared to achieving religious ends. Secondly, the notion of *self-styled 'true-believers'* refers to the typical characterization of fundamentalists, that is, as believing whole-heartedly that their vision of religion is the only true and correct interpretation. Their mission of *arresting the erosion of religious identity* refers to their goal to re-establish and protect the traditional values of their religion, which entails *creating viable alternatives to secular institutions and behaviours*, that are perceived as threatening such values. In particular, the threat of secularism needs to be countered not by escaping modern life, but by creating parallel institutions and behaviours so that believers can live in a modern world safe from secular erosions.

Some scholars regard the term fundamentalist as the best option amongst other synonyms such as 'orthodox', 'conservative', or 'militant'. For example, Marty and Appleby (1991:vii-xiii) argue that the term fundamentalist best conveys the idea of "institutionalised religions' reactions against secularism", and best captures the phenomena of religious resurgences noted across cultures by scholars, journalists and politicians. It is, however, a highly problematic term when applied to Muslims. Firstly, the word fundamentalism in this context is used more as a pejorative instead of descriptive term. Reference to fundamentalism and fundamentalists are part of the stock-in-trade language of international commentators and journalist, wishing to undermine the legitimacy of certain groups. Secondly, this negative usage has led some to equate 'fundamentalism' with 'extremism' even 'terrorism'. Thirdly, its historical origin within American Protestantism has led some to assume that this early 20th century movement is the template for all fundamentalist movements, encourage non-specialists to make facile generalizations (Appleby & Sivan, 2003:14-15). Finally, it ought to be noted that the people in question, the so-called Muslim fundamentalists, reject the designation of the term and its continued use therefore tends to hinder efforts to build constructive cross-cultural engagement and communication, as well as inhibit further serious research.

An alternative term, derived from a traditional Muslim term, is "*Salafism*", which literary means "early generations". This term therefore implies a project of reclaiming, reanimating and imitating the life-styles and values of an earlier generation of Muslims—particularly that of the 7th-9th century. In looking to follow the way of life of an earlier generation of Muslims, Salafists usually emphasize the literary interpretations of the Qur'an and the *Hadith* and the adoption of Islam as total way of life, governing the life and day-to-day activities of Muslims from ritual to trade, from politics to sexuality. The rigidity of their religious interpretations affects not only their attitude toward social life, but also towards social change. Salafists they tend to reject innovations which are not in line with Islamic way of life. However, again, recent popular discourse has shifted the meaning of Salafism into a kind of derogatory term. More and more writings on the topic refer to Salafism from a radical perspective, as if Salafism equals to fanaticism and radicalism.

Another synonym is *Islamism,* which is used to refer to a variety of Islamic groups that emphasize the ideological and political aspect of Islam. The word '*Islamisme*' was first coined by the French philosopher, Voltaire, as a substitute for the problematic term '*Mahometisme*', used at that time to refer to the religion of the Arabs. Islamism was adopted into English in the 1900-edition of *The Oxford English Dictionary* but later fell into disuse as the Arabic word '*Islam*' became widespread. The term 'Islamism', however, became ubiquitous among scholars and journalists when the discussion of political Islam became a major topic in international politics after the collapse of the former Soviet Union (Kramer, 1996). At present, Islamism refers more specifically to certain forms of religious interpretation organization and movement amongst Muslims, which emphasize the ideological and political aspect of their identity, combined with strong belief of the uniqueness and superiority of Islam vis-à-vis other political ideologies. To sum up, in the context of this thesis, the term new Islamism is intended to convey a number of the meanings noted above. Firstly, it is used to accommodate the deeply anti-secular meaning contained in the term fundamentalism. Secondly, the term 'new Islamism' shares the emphasis found within Salafism that Islam offers a total way of life. Finally, the term refers to an understanding of Islam as a distinct modern civilization, which is the antinomy of Western secular modernism and global capitalism.

New Islamism is shaped foremostly by the search for Islamic identity in the course of globalization. Democracy and freedom of expression are partly responsible for the promulgation of the discourse of 'new Islamism' as one of the non-linear and non-monolithic Islamic identities which are interpreted differently by Muslims worldwide. Freedom of expression facilitates their adherence to and profession of new Islamism. The term has become one of the more dominant and widely-accepted interpretations of Islam in Indonesia, although there is no uniform or unified interpretation of new Islamism. It represents a field or a discourse of practices and meanings rather than a single, identifiable set of principles and actions. On the one hand, reference to new Islamism offers Muslims the possibility of critical inquiry and grants them relative freedom in reviewing and rethinking the so-called the grand-narrative of Islam. On the other hand, new Islamism has established its own set of prevalent and dominant interpretations, which can be narrow and lacking in self-critique. To take just one example, the distinction between *Darul Islam* (the house of Islam) and *Darul Harb* (the house of war) has been interpreted by some new Islamists to differentiate between Muslims from non-Muslims—where non-Muslims are associated with a threatening and alien outside world of *Darul Harb.* The division into "us" and "them" leads to the rejection of any values created by the non-Muslim Other. The way to purify Islam is, then, a two-fold purification of Islam, that is, both from local cultural values which are non- or pre-Islamic, and from global values which are seen as representative of the West.

The prominent Egyptian revivalist and member of the Muslim Brotherhood, Sayyid Qutb, expressed this sentiment when he declared that "the decline of Muslim civilization is the result of the deviation in Muslim life from the guidance of God as promulgated in the Qur'an and Hadith (the Prophetic tradition). It is because of the Muslim rebellion against the sovereignty of God that they suffer from humiliation and backwardness. Deviation from Islamic identity is here defined as deviance from scripturalism. In line with scripturalist thinking, the more you are close to the literal meaning of Islamic sources, the more you are holding the truth. Such thinkers as Sayyib Qutb refer to themselves as both "revivalist" of Islam as well as conservatives, as they seek to "conserve" the values of Islam in the face of the alien. For many followers of revivalist Islam, societal and personal advancement follows from the individual's total adherence to Islam, as articulated in the Islamic notion of Kaffah (here translated as the uncritical embrace of the scripturalist interpretation of the Quran and Hadith). The literal interpretation of the holy texts in this version denies the historical and geographical context in which Islam was first established. Consequently, anything Arab is equated with Islam. The universal value of Islam as *rahmatan lil alamin* (blessing on the universe and humanity) that provides Muslims a sense of critical engagement with the outside world is ignored. In this way, one of the core Islamic values—one that acknowledges a universal conscience shared by other religions and other cultural values—is ignored. This is the same value that demands an engaged and critical attitude of Muslims in their efforts to renew and revisit Islam, in the light of contemporary social and cultural contexts, both in Indonesia and elsewhere.

2. Contextualizing New Islamism in Indonesia: Propagating Islam *Kaffah* and *Ummah*

Indonesians refer to their country as *tanah air* (land-and-water) *Nusantara*, a geographical term covering the region lying between the Pacific and the Indian Oceans, as well as between the Asian and Australian continents. The name *Nusantara* also invokes a history of regional and international political and cultural influence in this part of the world. It is useful, therefore, to understand the history and the dynamics of Islam in Indonesia in the context of the dynamics of regional and international politics.

Introduced by traders and wandering mystics from Gujarat South of India, Islam gained a foothold in the coastal regions of Sumatra, Northern Java, and Kalimantan between the twelfth and fifteenth centuries. Some historians argued that Islam had not penetrated into the hinterlands of the archipelago until the arrival of the westerners, especially the British in present day Peninsular Malaysia (George, 1980:19-20). The way that Islam was spread in Indonesia, that is, peacefully without coercive state power but through the activities of mystics-wanderers (*Sufis*) and traders, has influenced the basic characteristics of Indonesian Islam. For centuries, Islam in the country was well known for its eclecticism, its flexibility to adapt to and adopt local cultures. Pejoratively it has been called syncretistic Islam. The Javanese Sultan Agung Hanyokrokusumo (1613-1645) represents this flexible approach to the introduction of Islam. Famous for his approach which simultaneously localized Islam while Islamizing local cultures, his most successful project was blending the Islamic lunar calendar with local Javanese cosmology. The names of Arabic/Javanese lunar months are as follows: Muharram/Suro, Safar/Sapar, Rabiul Awal/Mulud, Rabiul Akhir/ Bakda Mulud, Jumadil Ula/Jumadil Awal, Jumadil Thani/Jumadil Akhir, Rajab/ Rejeb, Sha'ban/Ruwah, Ramadhan/Poso, Syawal/Sawal, Dhulqodah/Selo, Dzulhijjah/Besar.

During the colonial era, Muslims played an important role in fighting western invaders—ranging from Aceh in northern Sumatra, Demak and Mataram in Central Java, to Makasar in South Sulawesi. Islam, however, did not become a political ideology until the 19th century, under the influence of the puritanical doctrine of Muhammad bin Abdul Wahab (1703-1792) and the "Pan Islam" movement campaigned by the Muslim reformer Jamaluddin al-Afghani (1838-1897), whose teachings were brought by returning pilgrims from Mecca (*Hajj*). The first instance of Islamism in Indonesia occurred in Western Sumatra from 1821-1823. Known as the *Padri* Movement and informed by the teachings of Muhammad bin Abdul Wahab, this movement launched a staunch campaign to purify Islam from impure local cultural debris, as well as waged a political and military war against the colonial Dutch (Ricklefs, 2001:182-4).

The original teachings of Ibnu Abdul Wahab were more theological than political, focusing on a strict monotheism (*tauhid*) and uncompromising rejection of practices associated with (1) spiritual mediums and those who claimed to intercede between God and people's prayers or good deeds (*tawassul*), (2) polytheism (*syirik*) and (3) heresy (*bid'ah*). His teachings sought to strip off any local elements from Islam (Al-Yassiny in Esposito, 1995:307-8). This doctrine is also known as *Salafiah*, meaning to practice "original and pure" Islam after the examples of the early Muslim generations (Davidson, 1998:50). The doctrine also emphasized the totality in observing Islam (*Kaffah*) after the Qur'anic term (II: 208) "O you who believe! Enter perfectly into Islam" (Esposito, 1984:60-4). The followers of *Salafi* believe that Islam is not merely a set of rituals but rather a complete way of life, and that the Prophet Muhammad was not just a religious leader but also a perfect example of human nature and right living (*Uswatun Hasanah*). Muslims, the Salafists argued, should follow every example of the Prophet Muhammad in every aspect of life, from ritual practices to social ethics, from sexuality to economic entrepreneurships, because he was the "walking Qur'an."

The Pan-Islam doctrines of Al-Afghani were more political from the start and reflected Al-Afghani's resentment at witnessing the decline of the Islamic empire and the consolidation of European power over Muslim lands during his lifetime. In his reflections, he concluded that the decline of Muslim power was due to Muslims' abandonment of the true teachings of Islam. In order to revive Islamic glory, Al-Afghani urged Muslims to return to the original doctrines of Islam (the Qur'an and *Sunnah* or the Prophetic Traditions). Facing the threats of western power that occupied Muslim lands, Al-Afghani campaigned the concept of *Ummah* or universal brotherhood directed against western military, political, economic and missionary penetrations (Davidson, 1998:87-8).

The term *Ummah* (literally "people or group of people") is repeatedly mentioned in the Qur'an, and originally had plural connotations: some referred to people in general, some referred to religious groupings, some even referred to misguided people. The Prophet Muhammad mentioned *Ummah* sometimes in reference to his religious followers, but sometimes also to refer to his lineage descendants (Sutton & Vertigans, 2005:97-9). Only after the death of the Prophet Muhammad did the concept of *Ummah* evolve into a specific legal-political term. Early generations of Muslims applied the term to refer to the Muslim community as a religious-political entity for two purposes: firstly, to unite different Muslim communities under the one leadership, and secondly to differentiate these communities from non-Muslim communities. The latter use of the term subsequently produced two other famous religious-political concepts, that of *Darul Islam* or the abode of Islam and *Darul Harb* or the abode of war. Legally, the *Ummah* refers to Muslim communities as a moral entity with a high moral authority. Muslim scholars refer to a *Hadith* in which the Prophet said: "my *Ummah* would never agree on an error". This means that a collective consensus has a very high status in Islam, which comparable to Latin saying *vox populi vox Dei* (Khadduri, 1995:51-4).

Early 20th century Indonesia was characterized by several nationalist and Islamist currents. This development was an outcome of a greater emphasis on mass-education, which formed part of the Ethical Policy introduced during the late Dutch colonial era, and the influence of Wahabism and Pan-Islam, which were introduced by Indonesian scholars and pilgrims on their return from the Middle East. Several of these early nationalist and Islamist currents continued to be an influence in Post-Colonial Indonesia, as in the case of Muhammadiyah. What characterized most of these social modernist movements was their commitment to combine Islamic teachings within a modern orientation. In the field of society and education, one can see this in the organizational growth of Muhammadiyah. Currently Muhammadiyah has around 25 millions members and more than 12.000 educational institutions ranging from elementary schools to universities, and hundreds of hospitals, medical clinics and orphanages (see the official website www.muhammadiyah.or.id). Those organizations with more explicit political objectives also tried to pursue Islamic politics but within a modern system of representational democracy. An example here is the political party Masyumi, which stands for *Majelis Syuro Muslimin Indonesia* or The Consultancy Council of Indonesian Muslims. Founded in 1943 during Japanese occupation, Masyumi won 20.9% of the national vote in the 1955 general election, before the party was banned in 1960 because of the involvement of many of its leaders in a revolt in Sumatra against the central government (Ricklefs, 2001:255-321). Armed movements in various parts of Indonesia have also drawn on Islamist doctrines in their attempt to establish an Islamic state. One such example is DI/TII, which stands for Darul Islam Indonesia/Tentara Islam Indonesia or The Islamic State of Indonesia/Islamic Army of Indonesia. DI/TII waged a military revolt against the central government from 1951-1962. This armed struggle represented a highly complex movement, which combined intra-military conflicts, regionalism, economics conflicts as well as religiously-defined objectives.

The heat of international politics during the Cold War era also had a significant impact on Indonesian Muslims. Three movements across the Islamic world in particular inspired a new generation of Islamists in Indonesia. The first was the Egyptian Muslim Brotherhood (*Ikhwanul Muslimin*), founded by Hasan al-Banna (1906-1949) in 1923, which was successful in mobilizing popular support among Muslims because of its ideological vividness and organizational effectiveness. Echoing Salafist doctrines, Al-Banna taught that Muslim should organize themselves into a solid group in order to revive Islamic glory through gradual methods, such as education and persuasion through *Da'wah*. After the death of al-Banna, the ideology of the Muslim Brotherhood shifted under the influence of Sayyid Qutb (1909-1966) in favour of a greater emphasis on the doctrine of *Jihad* and military action (Davidson, 1998:130-42). The second movement informing Indonesian Muslims was *Hizbut Tahrir Al-Islamy* founded in Jerusalem by Taqiuddin an-Nabhani (1909-1977), who campaigned for the return of the Islamic caliphate as a more ideal political system for Muslims than either a capitalist democracy or socialism (Eickelman & Piscatori, 1996:139). The third movement was the fierce and successful *Jihad* in Afghanistan against the Soviet invasion. The success of the Mujahidin in Afghanistan revitalised the idea of Islam as a powerful political and military force (Zahab & Roy, 2004: 12-8).

Despite the repressive measures against Muslim political aspirations during the New-Order period (1966-1998), these wider political dynamics from across the Islamic world were reflected in the activities of Indonesian Muslims. The Egyptian Muslim Brotherhood inspired the formation of *Gerakan Tarbiyah* (The Islamic Student Movement) which flourished especially among secular universities. The very name of the movement inferred that it adopted the method of Hassan Al-Banna instead of Sayyid Qutb. After the collapse of the New Order regime, the Tarbiyah movement evolved into the Prosperous Justice Party (PKS) which has introduced Islamism into democratic politics. The party is popularly recognized as the campaigner of Islamic politics and for its strong anti-corruption stance (van Bruenessen, 2003:).

The Hizbut Tahrir first asserted its influence on Indonesian cultural politics in the form of Hizbut Tahrir Indonesia (HTI), which was founded at the end of 1980s by Abdurrahman Al Baghdadi from Australia (Collins, 2004:8-9). Today HTI sees itself as a political party with a mission is to re-establish a global Islamic caliphate that will govern Muslims across the world. The followers of HTI perceive the Indonesian state to be a non-Islamic state, and view Indonesia's Muslims as currently living in the *Darul Harb* or the abode of war (HTI official website http://hizbut-tahrir.or.id)

Meanwhile, the *jihad* in Afghanistan produced Indonesia branches of groups established in Afghanistan, such as *Laskar Jihad* (Jihad Militia) and *Majelis Mujahidin Indonesia* (MMI or The Indonesian Council of Mujahidin). These militant groups have such a preference for furthering their religious aspirations through military conflict and armed attacks. Laskar Jihad, for example, has not just promoted an Islamic state and Islamic laws in Indonesia, but also waged wars against Christians in eastern Indonesia. MMI was founded by Abdullah Sungkar and is now led by Abu Bakar Baasyir; these two men are both suspected leaders of the infamous *Jama'ah Islamiyah* (van Bruinessen, nd:19-21).

Similar to earlier generations of Islamists, the topics of total-Islam (*Kaffah*) and universal brotherhood (*Ummah*) are prominent among new Islamist movements. New Islamists are as firm as their predecessors in believing that Islam is a complete way of life that should be pursued and fought for by Muslims. At this point two different strands emerge on how this should be achieved: some Islamists prefer *Dakwah* or persuasion through education, while the other prefer *Jihad* which while not necessarily implying violence, does imply a tougher approach to achieving these objectives. One difference is the challenged faced by new Islamists in relation to globalisation of non-Islamic cultures. While the old Islamists tried to remove impure local cultural elements from Islam, new Islamists face the threat posed to Islam of global cultural invasion.

The idea of *Ummah* remains a major project for new Islamists, and to some extent this aspect of Islamic identity has been enhanced by the acceleration of rapid communication technologies such as the internet, which have transformed the world into a borderless space. Indonesian new Islamists are today very concerned about what is going on among their 'brothers' overseas, for example in Palestine and Bosnia, while may not so sensitive towards the misery are experienced by non-Muslim Indonesians, for example, in Papua,

North Sulawesi and North Sumatera (which are largely Christian enclaves). The dichotomy of "us" and "them" implied in the dichotomy of *Darul Islam* and *Darul Harb* is also prevalent. In fact this sense of us and them has taken on new dimensions, namely an anti-semitic sentiment. Such a sentiment, however, means in this context that Jews are not seen as an ethnic group but rather as a religious group—that Judaism is the antinomy of Islam which in many cases also applies to Christianity. Despite such anti-Jewish sentiment, anti-western sentiment has emerged as one of the strongest currents in new Islamist writing, particularly in terms of a perceived threat of cultural homogenization (or westernization) through globalization.

Anti-western sentiments are often expressed as anti-America sentiment, and has resulted in 'sweepings' of Americans in several Indonesia urban areas such as in Jakarta and Yogyakarta. The banning of the US porn magazine, *Playboy*, in the mid of 2006, is another example of such anti-American sentiment. This can be seen by the fact that local porn-magazines were allowed to publish freely despite the ban on *Playboy*. Islamists have also been vocal in their rejection of and protest against so-called western cultural values found in secular literature, which are said to harm Muslims' morality. The *Gerakan Tarbiyah* (the Islamic Student Movement) has been active in many secular universities throughout Indonesia in resisting what they see as a morally degraded global world. Muslims are encouraged to strengthen their Muslim identity in order to resist the onslaught of a homogenized global culture. This resistance has become a significant strategy in formulating an alternative identity, one which embraces Islam as offering an alternative global perspective.

The new Islamism therefore involves a strategic essentialism as part of its response and a resistance to a more homogenized global world. This can be seen in the reliance on Islamic symbolism as a means of establishing an essential Islam and Islamic identity. Referring to fellow Muslims as *Ummah* and Muslim women as *Muslimah*, and the inauguration of different Islamic fashion styles such as head-veiling, are aspects of this promotion of symbolic referents within new Islamist discourses. The day-to-day life of contemporary Indonesian Muslims has been strongly and vividly coloured by such Islamic symbolism. This has likewise transformed the way many new Islamist authors approach their writing, with *Islam Kaffah* becoming the ultimate goal and ultimate expression of their *dakwah* (mission).

3. Situating Literary Resistance: The Emergence of New-Islamist Literature

The emergence of the new Islamist writers in post-Suharto Indonesia can be traced to the establishment of the *Forum Lingkar Pena* (Pen Circle Forum, hereafter FLP). FLP was founded on 22 February 1997 by Helvy Tiana Rosa, Asma Nadia, Muthmainah, and other *Tarbiyah* activists involved in the Ukhuwah

Islamiyah mosque at the University of Indonesia, Jakarta. Their vision was to develop Indonesians' love of reading and writing as well as to build a network of qualified writers throughout Indonesia (Rosa, 2002:2). FLP is a financially self-sufficient organisation, which this enables it to have freedom of expression. The first founders of FLP, who were mostly women, agreed that writing was one of the processes which could enlighten the *Ummah* (Rosa, 2002:2). Helvy further qualified clarified this position in her statement given on the fifth anniversary of FLP in 2002. She said that that FLP membership is basically inclusive and non-Muslim members were welcome although in reality most members are Muslim (Rosa, 2002:2). At that time, there were only 30 members of FLP but since 2002 membership has grown to 5000—of whom 70 percent are women—and with members coming from both inside Indonesia and abroad (Syahidah, 2005). Since its establishment in 1997, FLP has published more than 200 books which range from serious texts, to adult fiction and children stories. FLP also runs its own publishing house—Lingkar Pena Publishing House—while maintaining commercial relations with many other Islamic publishing houses such as Mizan, Syaamil and Pustaka Ummat in Bandung; Gunung Agung, Gramedia, Zikrul Hakim, Ghalia, Senayan Abadi and Cakrawala in Jakarta; Darussalam in Jogjakarta; Fastabiq Media in Semarang; and Era Intermedia and D & D Publishing House in Surakarta. One remarkable *dakwah* (missionary) activity initiated by FLP was the donation of royalties from all FLP Islamic books to Palestinian children through MER-C (Rosa, 2002).

Most of the books published by FLP echoe Islamic themes (Rosa, 2002:3). Practically, FLP was designed with a particular Islamic and humanitarian mission, that is, to actively and critically counter literary texts containing hedonistic, bourgeois, pornographic and secular messages. One of Indonesia's leading Indonesian poets, Taufik Ismail, has called FLP "a gift from God to Indonesia", while *Tempo* has referred to FLP as a 'factory of writers'. FLP's propagation of Islamic themes in literary works is regarded as in competition with 'the existence of secular literary works'; as well as acting as beneficial stabilizing force in the Indonesian literary world (Rahman, 2003). *Republika* online wrote that FLP has brought about a new phenomena in contemporary religious texts, creating a new genre in Indonesian literature. The birth of FLP has been heralded by many Muslim activists as the start of a new springtime of Islamic literature in Indonesia and the organization has been hailed as one of Indonesia's most significant contemporary *dakwah* (mission) literary movement.

Helvy Tiana Rosa is one of the notable writers associated with this new Islamist literary movement. Both the founder of FLP as well as its present leader, Helvy Tiana Rosa (HTR) was born on April 2, 1970 in Medan, Sumatera. In 1995 she finished her studies in the Arabic Department, Faculty of Letters at the University of Indonesia. Since 1997, she has published 30 books which are mainly collections of Islamic short stories, novels and essays. Her collection of short stories, *Jaring-Jaring Merah* was awarded the Pena Award in 2002, and her short story, *Lelaki Kabut dan Boneka,* was also awarded Best Short Story by the Indonesian literary magazine, *Horison* (1990-2000). Several of her works have been translated into English, Japanese, French and Arabic. As well as being the head of the FLP, Helvy is also the chief editor and director of the popular mass Islamic magazine, *Annida*, which prints more than 100.000 copies per month. This Islamic fiction magazine also promotes membership to FLP and in 2003, around 3000 people applied for membership to FLP through *Annida* (Rosa, 2002:2).

Outside her writing activities, Helvy is involved in the new Islamist political arena as well, particularly the Prosperous Justice Party or PKS. In 2004, she was one of PKS's female legislature candidates for the city of Jakarta (Damanik, 2002:231-2). She was also one of the female candidates selected to represent the PKS in a publication profiling 150 of their female candidates and politicians (see Bidang Kewanitaan DPP PK Sejahtera, Jakarta: Misykat Publication, 2004:38).

Officially the Prosperous Justice Party (PKS) was founded in July 1998 by 52 young *dakwah* leaders between the ages of 20-40 years old, who were not associated with any established political figure or party from either the Old Order of Sukarno or the New Order of Suharto (Damanik, 2002:231-2). Formerly known as Partai Keadilan, or the Justice Party, the party changed its name to the Prosperity and Justice Party, or PKS, in 2003. Before the 2004 election, on December 15, 2003, SCTV, one of the private television channels in Indonesia, announced that PKS was the most favourite party in Indonesia. PKS has called itself the party of moral reform: "PKS has consistently campaigned for the urgent need for a greater morality. The party reiterates time and again that the present chaos in Indonesia is caused primarily by a lack of morality among the nation's leaders" (Mochtar, 2002). Besides its popularity, PKS is recognized as having the best record of any political party with regard to opposing corruption. In 2004, when its leader, Hidayat Nur Wahid, became the head of the Indonesian Parliament, he rejected the distribution of luxurious cars and houses because he considered such distribution as inducing corruption in the Indonesian government and parliament. PKS legislators have also become known for their refusal to engage in corruption that is widespread in provincial and district legislatures. PKS is based on the *Tarbiyah* network of "cells", where members meet for Quran reading and discussion. PKS is not interested in recruiting a mass membership but in attracting members who fully understand the party's message and the moral principles of Islam. That's why members of this party are referred to as 'party cadre'.

Although there is no formal organizational connection between FLP and PKS, both were established by new Islamists involved in Tarbiyah circles in the late 1990s. These organizations share similar characteristics which show the close connections between literary and political new Islamist movements. Both were founded by several *dakwah* leaders in secular campuses during the Suharto era, at a time when students were banned from taking part in Islamic political activities. As a result of this ban, new Islamist activists concentrated their energy in activities organized under the *Gerakan Tarbiyah* (or Islamic Student Movement), which after the fall of Suharto was transformed into a number of new Islamist groups, each with their own distinctive ideology and objectives: one direction was the formation of an Islamist political party, or PK/PKS; moving in another direction, Helvy established the Islamist literary movement or FLP. Despite the different foci of these two Tarbiyah movements (one literary and one political), they nevertheless share similar characteristics, such as a strong pan-Islamism and the propagation of an international 'brotherhood' of Muslims. In early 2006, for example, PKS sent around US$2 million to Palestine, in a gesture comparable to the FLP payment of royalities to Muslim 'brothers' in Palestine. A sign of mutual regard and working relations is the exposure given to several of Helvy's works and other FLP writers like Asma Nadia on several of PKS's national and international websites. (See for example, the link to the short story *Jaring-Jaring Merah* on PKS's Australia-New Zealand website: http://www.pks-anz.org/pkspedia/index.php?title=Helvy_Tiana_Rosa)

Most of Helvy's writing explicitly address Islamic themes. Several of her stories are set in places where Muslim enclaves are famously oppressed such as in Afghanistan, Moro, Myanmar, Liberia, Palestine, Azerbaijan, Aljazair, Kashmir, Chechnya, Bosnia Herzegovina, Kosovo, Rwanda, Somalia, Aceh, Maluku, Poso, and Sampit. In the literary production of Indonesian New Islamists, Palestine and Bosnia are commonly used to symbolize the experience of the oppressed Muslim living outside Indonesia. The representation of Muslim oppression through a symbolic reference to Palestine and Bosnia is frequently reiterated in the media and works as a mechanism to invoke the sympathy of Indonesian Muslim. Helvy in her own writings has documented her deep sympathy for the suffering experienced by Muslim women who are raped and tortured. Several of these Muslimahs are described in her short stories, such as *Jaring-Jaring Merah* (hereafter JJM), which is set in Aceh, *Maut di Kamp Loka* (hereafter MKL), which is set in Bosnia, and *Hingga Batu Bicara* (hereafter HBB), which is set in Palestine.

a. Jaring-Jaring Merah (The Red Net)

The 7th of August 1998 is a very meaningful date for the Acehnese because that is the date when the former Indonesian general, Wiranto, freed Aceh from the status of DOM. DOM stands for Daerah Operasi Militer, meaning Military Operation Area. As a military operation area under the command of General Wiranto, Acheh was subjected to a special operation called *Red Net Operation* from 1989 to 1998. The inspiration for Helvy's short story, the Red Net Operation (RNO) was a military operation designed to subdue and finally vanquish Aceh's independence movement, referred to as GAM (Gerakan Aceh Merdeka-Aceh Movement for Freedom) or earlier as GPK (Gerakan Pengacau Keamanan). The objective of GAM/GPK was to establish *Shariah Law* in a free-state of Aceh. Suharto, as is well-known, was a corrupt President who enriched his family and his associates through a variety of state monopolies and subsidies, and who constructed a strong, centralized national government that maintained political stability through the suppression of political dissent and regular use of military force. The decision to implement RNO was a purely political decision made by Suharto to devastate Aceh's independence movement. During this ten-year operation, the central Indonesian army was accused of committing gross violations of human rights. Crimes against humanity recorded during Red Net Operation are as follows: 871 died due to violence, 387 missing persons subsequently found dead, 550 missing persons, 368 cases of violation and intimidation, 120 burned houses, 102 raped victims (NGO HAM Aceh). These charges were substantiated by the discovery of mass graves in several places. The first place is Buket Tangkurak (literally, head skull hill) located at Seureuke, Jambo Jaye, North Aceh (60 km from Lhokseumawe) which became the setting of Helvy Tiana Rosa's short story, *Jaring-Jaring Merah (The Red Net)*. The second mass grave was found at Bukit Seuntang (5 km from the Medan-Lhokseumawe highway). Helvy wrote *Jaring-Jaring Merah* at the end of the military operation in Aceh and the downfall of the Suharto regime in 1998. In 2002, it received the Pena Award given by the Yayasan Forum Lingkar Pena (YFLP/FLP Foundation).

Helvy begins her story with the whirl of the cry of a desperate Acehnese Muslimah, Inong[3], who had been raped by a member of KOPASSUS (Komando Pasukan Khusus or Special Army Command). Not only is she raped, but also tortured and put in the so-called 'tortured-red nets'. The rest of her family are also tortured and finally shot in a mass killing of suspected defenders of the GPK's leader, Hasan Tiro. Inong is psychologically traumatized after the mass killings of the suspected GPK helpers.

> Alas, did those ugly dogs know that I saw seven to ten corpses floating in the river near my house? I saw Yunus Barong having his head cut and showed to the people in the villages. I saw people being shot in the yellow truck. Their blood shed everywhere. I saw my neighbour Rohani being ripped naked and raped by the red soldiers before they burnt her house. I saw when *Geuchik*[4] Harun was tied to a tree and shot several times until dead. I saw that all! Yes, all of them. And I saw as well when they slaughtered my family, without reason. (JJM, 1)[5]

---

[3] *Inong* is Aceh dialect means "young girl".
[4] *Geuchik* is *Kepala Desa* (Bahasa Indonesia), means "head of village".
[5] Author 's translat ion from Bahasa Indonesian

Inong and her family are actually innocent; hers is one of the many innocent families in Buket Tangkurak who became victims of the mass killings. When her family were threatened, Inong's parents had insisted that they were not members of GPK ("We are not GPK!, cried *Ma'e*[6]. "*Ulon hana teupheu sapheu*[7]", cried her father, JJM, 4). In her traumatized state, Inong begins to behave weirdly and people in her village call her insane. The heroine of the short story is a young woman who earnestly helps Inong recover from her trauma. Cut Dini is a fellow Acehnese, and a graduate from a university in Jakarta, where she had been a Tarbiyah activist associated with the university's mosque. In this story, Cut Dini helps Inong to forget her suffering through an Islamic therapy, such as reading the Koran and through prayer or *shalat*. Cut Dini also warns Inong that as a Muslimah, she should not go outside the house alone, without an appropriate companion.

> "Where were you *Inong*? I was looking for you all day. *Ureung-ureung*[8] found you near the road to *Buket Tangkurak* this *subuh*."
> I look at a face in a white *kherudoung*[9] in front of me. Cut Dini. Her soft hand is caressing my head.
> "I only had a walk. I did not disturb anyone," I answered her.
> "I know. You are a good girl. You wouldn't disturb anyone..., but don't go to that hill anymore or even to *rumoh geudong*. Dangerous. You are a Muslimah, anyhow. It is not good for you to go alone", said Cut Dini while giving me a glass of water. (JJM, 2)

Helvy chooses a "perfect Muslimah" as the heroine in her story. The perfect Muslimah described as complying with the values of *Islam kaffah* in which the use of Islamic symbols, such as wearing a head veil and not going out unchaperoned for Muslimah is strongly encouraged. Cut Dini is depicted as wearing a white *kherudoung* as she cures Inong. In addition to wearing a veil, Cut Dini is also described as performing shalat and reciting the Quran to calm Inong's soul.

> "Allah won't let them (go unpunished), Inong! (Allah) will not! You have to be normal, Inong! All are long-gone. The happenings of four years ago and this regime. Be strong, Inong! Be strong! *Laa haula walaa quwwata illa billah*[10]..." (JJM, 5)

---

[6] *Ma'e* is Aceh dialect, means "mother".

[7] *"Ulon hana teupheu sapheu"* means "I am only an ordinary man".

[8] *Ureung-ureung* is Aceh dialect for the Indonesian " *Orang-orang* " which means "people".

[9] *Kherudoung* is Aceh dialect for *Kerudung* in Indonesia. This refers to the *Jilbab*– which comes from the Arabic root word *jalaba* – meaning hed veil or headscarf.

[10] This is one of the expressions or *Kalimah Thoyibah* (good words) used in Islamic *dzikr* which means literary that "There is no power and no strength save in Allah".

b. Maut di Kamp Loka (the Death at Camp Loka)

> The name of the camp is Loka in Brcko town, one of many places in Bosnia whose function was transformed into a torture and killing camp. Now thousands of men and women are waiting for the next tragedy they have to face after they lost their families, houses and even their honour[11]! Yes, like me! (MKL, 1)

Evidence drawn from press reports, international relief agencies, refugees, and other sources of information indicate the extent to which ethnic Serbs were responsible for the vast majority of ethnic cleansing in Bosnia. The most brutal ethnic cleansing by Bosnian Serbs took place in 1992 and 1993 when some of the most notorious detention camps such as Prijedor, Brcko, and Foca became sites of atrocity against Muslims. In early 1992, Muslims constituted the majority of the inhabitants (56 percent) of the north-eastern city of Brcko (Bosnia Handout, 2005:1). There are no reliable estimates of how many Bosnians died as a result of Serbian ethnic cleansing, but information from refugees and press reports strongly suggest that they number in the tens of thousands (Bosnia Handout, 2005:3).

Brcko, one of the killing camps, is chosen as the setting of Helvy's *Maut di Kamp Loka*. The story narrates how many Bosnian Muslimahs have been raped, tortured, and finally killed.

> We were shocked! The door was pushed harshly from the outside. Several Serbian soldiers entered wildly. They dragged around ten *Muslimahs*. They struggled against the soldiers. In vain! (MKL, 2)

She employs another perfect Muslimah, Lizzeta, who was packed in the camp with other women. Two other Muslimah characters and friends of Lizzetta, Fathimah and Syikorvij are depicted by Helvy as striving to console other victims who have been raped and tortured by the Serbian's soldiers.

> "That is the first soldier who has ripped of my jilbab (head veil) and my Muslimah dress!" I said to Fathimah who held my hand. "He also cut my hair!" I said boldly. (MKL, 3)

In the face of death, they heal themselves and their victims with *dzikr* and *taushiyah*[12]. Afraid that the Serbians may burn them alive, they hold onto life through their love and faith in God.

---

[11] "Honour" refers to the lost of Muslimahs' virginity due to mass-rape.

[12] *Thaushiyah* is an Arabic word referring to the spreading of Islamic teaching in a small circle.

> "Allah..." I whispered to her ear. "Allah,...*laaa hauła wa laa quwwata illa billah*[13]....! Dzikir my sister....Allah...., mention Allah name as many as possible ...." (MKL, 2)

A strong incitement to hold on to Islam as their way of life and as saving them from their suffering is ubiquitously echoed. Although they may perish under the Serbians' hands in this "here and now", Lizzeta believes that a strong faith in Islam will save them in the world of "there and after". Committing suicide is not an honourable way if one hopes to enter into heaven.

> "If we are dead one by one..., I want that we all die with a strong faith. You see, Gernavic, one of our sisters who was traumatized in this camp, along with another two sisters, have committed suicide by choking their own throat, because they could not bear the Serbians' torture!" (MKL, 4)

Amongst the Muslimahs in the camp are some who have sold their bodies to Serbian soldiers in exchange for their freedom. This action is seen to undermine the other Muslimahs, who see that these other Muslimahs as mentally ill and not adhering to the true teachings of Islam.

> Not all of them want to hear (our preaching). Even among the Muslimahs who were already mentally ill and immoral had begged and prayed to the Serbians in the expense of their freedom. They had given their bodies to them and after that the Serbians killed them cruelly. Naudzubillah[14]! (MKL, 5)

The propagation of the true teachings of Islam is seen as the only redemption possible for the souls of these prisoners. For Lizzeta, death is a more honourable way to become a *Mujahidin fi sabilillah* (people who do jihad/struggle on the path of God) as she believes that death is not the end of life; it is merely the point of departure to see the *Rabbul 'Izzati* (the eternal, supreme Allah).

> We keep preaching and propagating Islam as a stronghold to other Muslimahs. Allah the Omnipotent and the Most Helpful. Strong faith and taqwa in Islam. For the Mujahidah fi sabilillah, death is nothing. We should not be afraid of the death. To be syahid in death is to fulfil our longing to meet the Ultimate Truth Rabbul 'Izzati! (MKL, 5)

Finally the women fight the Serbian soldiers together and succeed in escaping from the locked camp. The Serbian soldiers run after the women with tanks and they are shot and killed one-by-one. Lizzeta's body is flattened by a tank after she was shot in the leg. She felt, however, as if she were flying and experienced no pain in her body.

---

[13] Literally, "There is no power but God ".
[14] "Naudzubillah" means "May the Lord guard us from that deed".

> I run while creeping. Both of my legs have been shot by Serbians. It is very loud here. I keep creeping. From the back, at high velocity, a Serbian tank flattens my weak body. I don't feel anything! I feel light! Light! (MKL, 6)

The discourse of jihad is reiterated is this story when the heroine welcomes death as the front gate into the world of "there and after". For Lizzeta, striving to achieve the ideal of Islam Kaffah will allow her to reach Paradise and attain the ultimate Truth, God, the Allah.

c. *Hingga Batu Bicara* (*Until the Stones Speak*)

Palestine is the most famous and popular discourse in Indonesia on the oppression of Muslims, with Palestinians depicted as oppressed by the Israeli government. Tarbiyah movements in Indonesia have reiterated the misery of the Palestinians in particular to promote the bonds of universal Islamic brotherhood. Helvy's deep sympathy with the cause of the Palestinians can be seen in her depiction of the sufferings of the Palestinian Muslimah, the crazed Hanan, in front of Israeli soldiers.

> Yatom said, "I don't know who the girl is. Is she? Since I was stationed from Tel Aviv to the land where I was born, Jerusalem, exactly near Al-Aqsa and the Crying Wall, I saw her everyday.
> "One day I will ask her to go out with me! said David, a friend of mine who always proclaimed himself as the true *Lohemei Herut Israel*[15]." He grimed, showed his brown teeth. Just look!"
> Yes, after that we kill that crazy girl!" added Goldstein, my friend, with high pitch, while turning *Yediot Aharonot* news which he read. (HBB, 1)

In this story, Helvy employs the confrontation between Islam and Zionist Israel and draws into her story a Hadith from Bukhari Muslim that foresaw the future battle between Muslims and Jews, as well as the depiction of Zionist symbols such as Satanim/Harar.[16]

> "Rasullullah told before, *bannatii*[17]...., *kiamat*[18] will not come without our fight against them. Until... all the stones speak and tell us: Oo servant of Allah, the Jews are behind us! They won't be able to hide, my Son. Those stones and all Allah soldiers in this universe will help *Muslimin*. Rasullullah had confirmed..."
> (Hadith Rasullullah SAW[19] by Bukhari and Muslim, cited in the HBB)

---

[15] *Lohemei Herut Israel* means Fighters of Israeli freedom (HBB, Glossary).
[16] *Satanim/harar* refers to the ten programs of International Jewish Freemasonry, symbolized by Giant Octopus with ten legs, a snake with ten heads and a ghost with sharp steel-nail (HBB, Glossary).
[17] *"Bannatii"* means "my son" (HBB, Glossary).
[18] *Kiamat* is the Islamic version of judgement day.
[19] *Rasulullah SAW* means Muhammad as Messenger of God. *SAW* stands for *Sallalahu 'Alaihi wa Salam* , meaning "Peace be upon Him".

Helvy chooses Jerusalem as the setting for this story because Jerusalem is an important site to the three major monotheistic religions of Islam, Judaism, and Christianity. The Old City is surrounded by walls and it consists of four quarters: Muslim, Jewish, Christian and Armenian. The status of the city is hotly disputed. Since Israel's victory in the 1967, Israel has controlled Jerusalem and claimed sovereignty over it. Indonesia does not recognize Israeli sovereignty over some of the cities claimed by Israel and has decided not to have a diplomatic relationship with Israel. (When Abdurrahman Wahid was president of Indonesia (1999-2001), he tried to re-establish diplomatic relations with Israel. He, however, received a wave of mass criticism from many new Islamist movements in Indonesia, most notably from PKS and FLP, and diplomatic relations were not re-established.

Helvy's main character is Hanan, a mad girl who loves talking to stones. The other characters are Israeli soldiers, who confront this crazy girl, including David, Goldstein, and the narrator of the story, Yatom. Hanan believes that the stones will destroy Israeli soldiers. Everyday, she acts as if she were a general leading her soldiers, which in this case are stones. She arranges the stones in a neat position behind her before leading them to attack the soldiers. Her enemy often laughs at her silliness. One day the narrator, Yatom, dreams of being attacked and killed by Hanan's stone army. Until finally, in his dream, he remembers that his father seized Hanan's house and killed her parents when Yatom was a child. In his dream, he remembers his father's injunction that Yatom should protect and guard the Jewish land of Palestine, which was promised to the Jewish people by God. After his father advice, Yatom had become a soldier, a job he had held for five years at the time of the story.

> "Because this land has been promised to us and tomorrow it will be our home", said Dad while caressing his thick beard. "Yatom, whatever happens you have to be like me and fight for this land. Now mention the Satanim or harar!" He instructed me. (HBB, 3)

Helvy finishes HBB with Yatom's dreaming of being attacked by Hanan's stone soldiers. He then wakes up and sees that Hanan, the little girl, bringing a piece of stone in her small hand (HBB, 3).

JJM, MKL, and HBB have established Helvy's sympathy with the cause of pan-Islamism and the ideal of attaining a Muslim Brotherhood as the core of Ummah. Her vivid use of Islamic symbols such as the head veil, the Koran, *dzikir* and *thaushiyah* enhances the value of being Kaffah, as the profession of Islam as a complete and perfect faith. Her writing emphasizes the consolation offered by Islam in the face of harmful non-Islamic values, which erode the ties of Brotherhood. Her stories pave the way for her readers to better understand the rewards and value of pursuing a life in line a 'total Islam'. Her major characters are Muslimahs who are obedient to God and able to translate Islamic values in a total way into their daily life.

Her perfect Muslimah characters in fact succeed in saving the world. Although they may not be able to save themselves or others in the "here and now", they are ultimately successful in saving themselves and other in the "there and after" Cut Dini in JJM is a perfect and obedient Muslimah who wears a head veil and reads Koran to heal the tortured Inong. Lizzeta is a Bosnian Muslimah who performs *dzikir* to heal herself and her community as they face death. Hanan is a tortured girl, orphaned by the murder of her parents at the hands of Israeli soldiers in their seizure of Palestinian lands. Cut Dini, Lizzeta and Hanan exemplify perfect Muslimahs; they are indeed the ideal type of Muslimahs.

By presenting the suffering of other Muslims, Helvy's work summons the unity of all Muslims in a world which currently suffers from a detachment from true faith, i.e. Islam. Her stories ask readers to return to the true consolation of Islam and to revolt against the oppression of Muslim communities. The stories depict the suffering of Muslim, in a very strong and direct way, designed to incite sympathy. By conveying the suffering of other Muslims, Helvy's works stretch readers' empathy for their Muslim brothers/sisters. By giving greater insight into the sufferings of their Muslim Brothers, she is at the same time also spreading the seed of resistance, which becomes a strategic essentialism. This seed of empathy is the foundation on which to build a Muslim Brotherhood (*Ummah*). The primary message of her stories is that when the *Ummah* is achieved, the implementation of Islam will be as total as it is for her main characters. The main theme in the books is the dream of achieving an Islamic 'state' where all Muslims live happily together through their total adherence to Islam (*kaffah*). Helvy Tiana Rosa speaks to her readers as well as to her opponents through her works that the new Islamist movements are dreaming to have a strong worldwide Islamic Brotherhood (*Ummah*) and to implement a 'total Islam' (*kaffah*).

4. The Ideal Norm, *Darul Ummah*

The fall of the Suharto government has led to a more overt and growing criticism of secular society amongst new Islamist activists, including Muhammadiyah in the educational sector. New Islamist activists argue instead for a return to 'total Islam' (*kaffah*) through the implementation of Shariah law (*Shariah Islamiyah*) by the state. This demand by radical groups is a reaction to government corruption and what they see as the degraded level of moral values amongst most Indonesians. They are pessimistic about the chances of a secular, democratic state to improve the country. After the collapse of Indonesian economy in 1998, the concern to make Indonesia a better country has been raised by new Islamist political groups such as the Partai Keadilan Sejahtera

(PKS). Through its call for a strong Islamic Brotherhood (*Ummah*), it has campaigned strenuously for clean government and against corruption. During this period, Forum Lingkar Pena (FLP) has been concerned to correct what it sees as the degraded quality of reading materials available to the Indonesian Ummah through the establishment of its writing and publishing activities. Although—as noted above—there are no formal organizational ties between the PKS and FLP, most FLP members are PKS members at the same time. They also share similar characteristics as cadre movements, including their strong sense of pan-Islamic brotherhood manifested in their financial donations to Palestinian Muslims; a gesture which has its traces in Helvy's *Until the Stone Speak*. Both organization have attracted many middle class, educated Indonesians, including many young Muhammadiyah students, some of whom are not just attracted but also active in these new Islamist organizations.

There is evidence that these two Islamist movements have gained in popularity and influence over the past decade. PKS was successful in capturing votes in the 2004 general election as the most honest, clean and credible party. It continues to attract more and more electoral support, particularly from younger voters who see PKS as the most promising party for the next generation. FLP has been something of a phenomenon and has attracted many young Indonesian Muslims with a desire to read and to write from an Islamic perspective but who felt that they had no place in the existing establishment to express their views. FLP believes that secular-modern texts have degraded the morality of young Muslims and sets itself the task of saving the younger generation of Indonesian Muslims from the corruption of the secular and materialistic values evident in much literary. In pursuing this goal, FLP has given opportunities to new writers to publish their work and has established a distinguished new Islamist literary genre that confidently confronts and challenges the place of secular literary texts in Indonesia. .

Helvy Tiana Rosa's *Jaring-Jaring Merah, Maut di Kamp Loka* and *Hingga Batu Bicara* symbolize her struggle to explain to her readers the suffering of Muslim brothers and sisters both inside and outside Indonesia. Her stories promote the spirit of an Islamic Brotherhood amongst her readers and—most importantly—convey the message that salvation is found through adherence to a 'total Islam', through reference to Islamic practices, terms and symbols, such as *Kerudung, Muslimah, Qur'an, Dzikir* and *Thausiyah*. She teaches her readers through her major female characters what it means to be a perfect obedient Muslimah through their good Islamic moral conduct, such as wearing a head veil (for Muslim women), reading the *Qur'an*, observing *shalat* (prayer) five times a day; mentioning the name of Allah many times in one's heart (*dzikir* and, *thausiyah or* teaching correct moral conduct to other Muslim women. Besides teaching her readers on the virtues of good Muslim women (and to a lesser extent Muslim men), Helvy uses her writing to protest against the Israeli government in Palestine, against the Indonesian Army in Acehnese, and against ethnic cleansing in Bosnia. By drawing her readers into such experiences of suffering, Helvy summons the concept of Islamic Brotherhood (*Ummah*) and promotes the return to the 'total Islam' (*Kaffah*).

The achievement of a total adherence to Islam (Kaffah) is tied to the achievement of an "ideal *Ummah*" in the House of *Ummah* (*Darul Ummah*). The ideal norm of the Muslim community promoted by the new Islamists is thus opposed to what is seen as homogenized global world, in which the expressions of Muslim culture and community struggle to survive. Helvy's expression and use of Islamic symbols is the hallmark of this distinctive new Islamist literary genre. As with other new Islamist fiction writers, Helvy's writing seeks to express the unique identity and unity of Muslims from across the world, as part of her resistance to the advance of more secular and materialistic values.

The way these new-Islamists movements resist aspects of globalization, especially secularization and western values, is shared as well by many Muhammadiyah students. Their resistance to western secular values hinders and colours Muslim students' reading of Western works of literature. This finding is conspicuously real in the minds of contemporary Indonesian Muslim students. "An ideal Ummah is an ideal situation for Muslim life" said many Muhammadiyah students during the interviews. "And an ideal Ummah is an Ummah which implements Islam Kaffah" in the form of Sharia Law (detail of Sharia Ordinances in Indonesia will be discussed in Chapter V). As discussed in the next chapter, for many this resistance and rejection of non-Muslim non-Kaffah lifestyles entailed acute anti-western and anti-Jewish feelings, as well as a strident anti-secularism.

Chapter V
The Unquestioned Gender Lens in the Contemporary Indonesian Sharia-Ordinances: Female Students "should" wear the Headveil

1. Introduction

Muhammadiyah's views on the role and position of women are strongly influenced by a literalist reading of the Qu'ran and Hadith. Despite the fact that the Qu'ran and Hadith were only written down and codified sometime after the death of the Prophet Mohammed, they are nevertheless perceived as sacred texts, true for all time and all contexts, and the particular context which gave rise to verses downplayed. These texts have influenced the construction of an Islamic cosmology, including perceptions of the role of women in public life. One example of how these texts see the public role of women relates to leadership. According to one reading of these texts, a woman should not be the leader of the Islamic community (their *das sollen*). However, a woman is permitted to lead an Islamic community if the best leader available within a given situation is a woman (their *das sein*). This conception has resulted in the recent phenomenon of the Islamization of districts laws in Indonesia. In less then ten years—from the fall of Suharto in 1998 until the end of 2007—there has been a dramatic increase in the number of districts which have introduced Sharia ordinances. Approximately 63 districts, out of a total of 423 districts in Indonesia, have introduced Sharia ordinances, arguably denying women's rights and the rights of minority groups such as non-Muslim and other ethnic groups. While not the only organization involved in the promotion of Sharia in Indonesia, Muhammadiyah as the second largest Muslim organization in Indonesia continues to play an influential role here. And while within Muhammadiyah there is much internal debate on what the role and behaviour of women in public life should be, the dominant perspective on women within Muhammadiyah does seem to concur with many of the ideas objectified in various Sharia ordinances.

This Chapter discusses the contemporary Islamization of district laws in Indonesia in order to enrich our understanding of the contemporary situation of Muslim women there. Muhammadiyah is not only the second largest Muslim organization in Indonesia, but also represents the second largest enclave of Muslim women in Indonesia. It is therefore worthwhile investigating the educational atmosphere found within Muhammadiyah universities, particular as it relates to the normative role and behaviour of women. During my field research in mid 2007, I observed a new university ruling that all female Muhammadiayah students must wear the headveil. To my knowledge, this rule had not existed before the fall of Suharto in 1998. My recent interviews with students reveal how their construction of womanhood is strongly influenced by the phenomenon of Islamization of districts law.

This Chapter begins with a discussion of the former neglect of studies of Islam in Southeast Asia, before moving to consider the troubled relationship between Islam, democracy and gender justice. The Chapter then proceeds to address the Islamization of laws at the district level, including a discussion of how Indonesian women have resisted these laws. There is no monolithic ideology within the Indonesian Muslim community regarding these Sharia ordinances. And there is no unified Muslim voice which strongly supports or rejects these developments. Rather the gender lens is simply neglected and this is in spite of the non-segregative condition of Indonesian women. This Chapter ends with policy recommendations on how to tackle this problem from the perspective of Islamic education, specifically on gender issues.

2. Democracy, Yes. Gender, Not Yet

Until quite recently, there were few studies conducted on Islam in Southeast Asia by international Islamic scholars or Southeast Asian scholars. Robert Hefner describes this situation as the double marginalization of Southeast Asian Islam both in international Islamic studies as well as in Southeast Asian studies. For the former, this neglect was related to the relative historical lateness of Islam's flowering in Southeast Asia, making Southeast Asia among the last regions to join the caravan of Islamic civilization. Consequently, Islamic studies scholars were inclined to chose the older Islamic cultures and traditions of the Middle East, as they were assumed to be more authentically Islamic. Southeast Aisan, scholars, on the other hand, tended to view Islamic culture as just an outer veneer of more 'authentic' pre-Islamic cultures of characteristic of Southeast Asian societies (Heffner & Horvatich, 1997). That was an unfortunate situation given the fact that Muslims not only only constitute a considerable proportion of the population of Southeast Asia but that Indonesian Muslim make up a not insignificant proportion of all Muslims. What this double marginalization ignored was not only that Muslim political dynamics are very influential within the region but they are also influential within the global arena too.

Recent developments, however, have brought Southeast Asian Muslims into the spotlight of international media and scholarship, particular with respect to the question of democracy in the post-Suharto era. On the one hand, observers point to indications of democratic consolidation in Indonesia, especially after two successful elections in 2000 and 2005 during which Muslims played a pivotal role. This has led observers and analysts to see Indonesia as an example of a democratic Muslim country (Carter, 2004). Closer observations of the practice of democracy within Indonesia have further shown Muslims' capacity to exercise democracy not only at the procedural level, but also in terms of some basic elements of democracy, such as evidence of a pluralistic ideology (Ramage, 1996), growth of civil society and civil society institutions (Bush, 2002), and the development of social capital (Mujani, 2003). For some scholars, such developments in fact reflect Indonesian Muslims long historical involvement in the process of developing democracy (Heffner, 2000). On the other hand, several violent acts carried out by Muslim extremists have invited others to warn that Indonesia, and Southeast Asia in general, is a potential hotbed of global terrorism (Abuza, 2003). Some reports indicate an increasing tendency to use Islamic language and symbols to legitimize violence. For several years Muslim hardliners waged *Jihad* wars against Christians in the Indonesian cities of Ambon and Poso, resulting in thousands of casualties. There have also been several bomb attacks targetting Christians and westerners, including two bomb attacks on Bali, Indonesia's famous tourist island, in 2002 and 2005, and similar attacks on J.W Marriot Hotel and the Australian Embassy in Jakarta. Although the background to these terrorist attacks are very complicated—combining religious extremism, military and international interests (Jones, 2002)—they had the effect of daming the Muslim community in at least two ways. Firstly, these attacks and their representation in the media have given the wrong impression on the scale and influence of militant Muslims in Indonesia. Despite the picture given in the international media, such extremist groups are in fact only a very tiny segment of Indonesian Muslims. Secondly, and internal to the Muslim community, these attacks have set a very bad example, especially to youngsters, on the use of violence to achieve certain objects and interests.

This contradictory discussion of recent developments in Indonesia has reanimated the long-standing debate on Islam's compatibility with democracy. The debate has emerged at various times in the recent part in relation to political developments on the international stage. For example, some reports suggest Islam has a difficult relationship to democracy as it is predominantly Muslim countries which defy the global trend of democratization in the post Cold War period. According to the Freedom House Index of Political Rights, in the last three decades the number of democratized countries has increased from 40 countries (25%) in 1975 to 89 countries (46%) in 2006. The number of fully democratized countries within the Muslim world in 2006 was only 3, or 7% of the total number of 'fully democratized' countries in the world. A further 20 countries were characterized as 'partly free' (making up 43% of the total number of partly free countries), with a remaining 23 countries characterized as 'not free' (and accounting for 50% of all not free countries) (Freedom House, 2006).

Confronted by such facts, scholars vary in their conclusions about why Muslim lands seem democratically infertile. On the one hand, a number of experts consider the democracy's infertility in Muslim countries as directly caused by the structure of Islamic religion and culture. In short, although they differ in the detail, these scholars argue that Islam is basically incompatible with democratic values and practices. At least three different sets of arguments have been suggested to explain Islam's incompatibility to democracy.

First, Islam is seen to be an all-inclusive religion, regulating all aspects of the life of its followers. Islam, it is argued, knows no line between religion and other aspects of human life, and this lack of separation makes it impossible for a Muslim community to develop secular political systems, institutions or mechanisms, which are separate from religion. Lewis (2002:100) argues for example that in Islam political life is governed by religious dogma, which gives only limited space for rationality and other forms of human creativity. Islamic political culture, therefore, is very unlikely to nurture democracy in this view (Lewis, 2002:100). For Linz and Stephan (1996), the absence of secularisation processes in Islamic communities prevents the emergence of two basic institutions essential to democracy, i.e. nation-state and civil society. Muslim political identity is built upon a universal concept of *Ummah*, which divides the world into two irreconcilable realms: *Darul Islam* or the abode of Islam and *Darul Harb* or the abode of war. The notion of a universal Muslim community is incompatible with the concept of a nation-state, which is one of the most fundamental political institutions for modern democratic practice (Linz & Stephan, 1996). Moreover, the inclusion of all communal spheres within the sphere of religion makes it impossible for a civil society to emerge within Muslim communities. Whereas civil society requires an equality of civic interactions between citizens, the religious character of Islamic culture is clientalistic and hierarchical (Gellner, 1994:23-9).

A second perspective argues that the long history of confrontation between the Islamic world and the western world—from the crusades through to European colonialisms—has nurtured a virulent anti-western tendency in Islamic culture. This sentiment became even stronger after the abolishment of the last Islamic Caliphate and its impotence in the face of western modern development (Lewis, 2002:100). Anti-Western sentiments, furthermore, have made Muslims tend to reject products of western culture, including democracy (Huntington, 1997:112).

A third set of arguments proposes more political economy informed analyses, which emphasise structural factors accounting for the *underdevelopment* of democracy in Muslim societies. There are two main sets of arguments here. The first group of scholars argue that Muslim countries are not unique in their democratic underdevelopment. For them, anti-democratic sentiments are not found exclusively in Muslim societies, and therefore Islam should not be seen as the root cause. Instead scholars point to other factors—such as social, political economy, and geo-political factors (Fatah, 2004; Mujani, 2003). Another set of scholars argue further that Islam at heart values democratic principles, that it is a democratic religion, as seen in the principle of *shura* or consultation and *ijma* or consensus (Moussalli, 2001; Esposito & Tamimi, 2000). The previous thesis supports inclusively the idea of Muslim participation in the democratic arena provided by the state. If Muslim countries are not democratic than other factors, such as the failure of the state institutions and not Islamic cultural explanations, are therefore to blame.

Indonesian Muslim participation in the democratic arena is now contested with the arrival of the decentralization process in 423 districts since 1992. The most notable movement accompanying this process is the quest for Islamic identity in the rejuvenation of Sharia law, which is a codification of religiously endorsed laws drawn from a scriptual and symbolic interpretation of the Qu'ran and Hadith. One aspect of the process of Islamization of Law, popularly known as the formalization of Sharia in Indonesia, which has raised deep concerns among domestic as well as international communities, is the ratification of Sharia District Regulations inspired by Islamic teachings (known as *Perda Sharia* which stands for *Peraturan Daerah Sharia*). By February 2007 no less than 40 districts had ratified *Perda Sharia*. In general, these Shariah regulations are govern three aspects of public life, namely (1) the eradication of social ills or crimes, especially prostitutions and gambling; (2) enforcement of ritual observances among Muslims, such as reading the Qur'an, attending Friday congregations and fasting during Ramadhan; and (3) government of dress codes in the public sphere, which minimally designates that Muslim women wear the head veil.

These laws are controversial. Proponents argue that these laws are legitimate because they give people a sense of social and communal security which the state is unable to provide. Given that Islam is the religion and cultural system of majority, they argue, that it is only logical and democratic to take Islam as the common moral umbrella. Opponents however contend that although Islam is the religion of the majority, there are also non-Muslim Indonesians living in these districts who should not be subjected to Sharia laws. They argue that institutionally Indonesia is not an Islamic state, and that the ratification of *Perda Sharia* betrays the national (secular) consensus agreed upon by the founding fathers of the republic.

In addition, not all Muslims are agreeing with the introduction of Sharia laws, arguing that they represent only one among many interpretations (schools) of jurisprudence in Islam. Some argue that these laws represent a political rather than religious project, in that they deal more with intangible issues such as morality and preserving culture rather than with solving more concrete social problems such as poverty, unemployment and corruption. From a broader perspective, the *Perda Sharia* controversy is far from black and white. There are truths in the arguments of both the proponents and opponents. Firstly, as the majority in Indonesia, Muslims ought to have the right to express their identity according to their religion and cultural system. Secondly, the state has indeed proven incapable in many ways of providing social security to the people. Yet, people from other religious traditions also have an equal right to choose their own religious and cultural identities.

One notable backlash to the introduction of Sharia as part of an ongoing quest for identity amongst Muslims has been feminist protests against regulations dealing with issues of gender, sexuality and gender equality. Critics argue that proponents of the Perda Sharia fail to recognize the very unequal gender implications and biases inherent of these rules. The focus of most regulations pertain only to women's behaviour and dress, with the Perda Sharia in many cases merely governing the behaviour and dress of women in public. These laws thus impose an unfair burden on Muslim women, who are made to be the sole carriers of community morality. Perda Sharia embodies the feudal mores of female segregation, with women effectively segregated in public through the inforcement of dress codes, as well as by curfews introduced under the guise of 'protecting women'. Under Perda Sharia, women unaccompanied by a close male relative are banned from public spaces after 11pm at night. Men with political ambition have thus hijacked religion in order to gain political power both within their community in general and over women in particular through the ratification of Perda Sharia.

This Chapter will now address this dilemma, one that has produced significant fissures between different social enclaves in Indonesia. Special focus will be given to the objections raised by feminist activists who have criticized the formal legal material of *Perda Sharia* as being gender insensitive and unjust.

3. Situating Women's Resistance

The fall of Suharto and the economic crisis of 1998 ushered in a time of great social and political transition in Indonesia. One notable change has been the shift from a highly centralized political system to a more decentralized system, known in Indonesia as regional autonomy. Although decentralization had begun in 1992 under Suharto, it took a series of political and economic shocks to see this process rolled out across the country. During Suharto's reign, both Islamic political aspirations (or the "right wing") as well as communist political aspirations (or "the left wing") had been suppressed and blocked. The euphoria following Suharto's toppling saw a rapid growth in the number and range of political parties, including Islamist political parties, and their involvement in the decentralization process. Several strong Muslim enclaves have inaugurated their Islamic political aspiration through the ratification of *Peraturan Daerah Sharia*, or *Perda Sharia*, including Aceh, West Padang, Banten, Cianjur, Tangerang, Jombang, Bulukumba (South Sulawesi), and Sumbawa. The ratification of Perda (Peraturan Daerah/District Regulation) is based on Law No 10 (2004) on the Formulation of Laws and Law No 32 Year 2004 on District Government.

The previous law were used to draft and ratify new laws at the district level. The freedom being offered to many districts across Indonesia has resulted in a de-centralized approach to regulating and executing the many tasks with which Indonsia must tackle. This is a good starting point. This good news, however, is not followed by the inclusion of a gender perspective, including the centralized undertaking to gender mainstreaming as socialized at the national level by the Ministry for Women's Empowerment, in the drafting of regional and district laws. The national gender-mainstreaming policy is now disseminated by a range of minor actors, mostly led by women's NGOs, without much support from the government. The decentralization process has brought many additional perils for Indonesian women. The budget for reproduction health has being cut at the regional level and the amount is far less than the previous centralized government allocated. Besides this, the freedom that is offered to regional legislatures through the decentralization process has led to the objectification of womenhood in the ratification of several district regulations.

The fall of Soeharto and the 1998 economic crisis resulted not only in decentralization process but also the shift in the Indonesian perception of gender, with constructions varying across the spectrum from patriarchal to liberal perspectives. Women's bodies have been contested in the political arena at the national level as well as the regional or district levels. Quite recently in 2007, a draft bill of an anti-pornography law (RUU APP) was rejected by many women's NGOs. Their rejection was due to what they saw as the patriarchal perspective informing the bill. Within the bill, women's bodies are described as sources of temptation, which therefore require to be regulated. The beholders and spectators of pornography are left un-regulated. While many urban Islamist women organizations rallied on the street in support of the bill, the majority of Indonesia's urban-based women's NGO opposed the bill. This example of the clash and fissures among Indonesian women shows that there is competing gender constructions held even within related groups. Both groups claim to protect women's bodies, yet in very different ways. The Islamist NGOs' conception of womanhood is mainly dominated by scripturalist readings of holy texts, without critically re-reading the patriarchal construction of these interpretations. The latter group believes that the grand narratives of established traditions should be revisited and renewed in line with the changed historical context. A number of gendered political movements have emerged following the proposed anti-pornography bill and Perda Sharia. Those groups which are progressive in relation to gender are mostly led by urban-based NGO, specifically those in Jakarta. Such groups see that Indonesian women are increasingly well-educated and well-informed about their contractual rights with the state. They argue that women's agency in front of the state should also be used to promote gender mainstreaming policy. Women's individual agency is further claimed as part of the struggle over women's rights. These Jakarta-based women's NGOs, however, are too under-resourced and small in number in order to counteract the erosion of women's rights that has occured in the regions in line with decentralization.

Nevertheless, the drafting and ratification of several of the Perda Sharia have been closely monitored by many Jakarta-based women NGOs such as Komnas Perempuan, which specialized in monitoring these regulations' drafting and ratification, and Yayasan Jurnal Perempuan, which specialized in monitoring the districts' budget on women's needs from a gender-mainstreaming perspective. Many women's NGOs call for support to proceed with a judicial review of several *Perda Sharia*, which, in their perspective, erode and discriminate against women's rights.

In contrast to the spread of Perda Sharia, there have been only four district regulations which undeniably support women's rights. The National Commission on Violence against Women (Komisi Nasional Anti Kekerasan Terhadap Perempuan or 'KOMNAS Perempuan') has reported the following four regulations. The first is a set of regulations established to protect, advocate on behalf of, and support women who have been denied their rights as victims of violence. (Regulations by Desa Sido Urip, Kecamatan Kota Argamakmur, Kabupaten Bengkulu Utara No. 1 / 2005 Protection of Law to the Victims of Violence). The second district regulation comes from the same area as the first and states that victims of violence have the right to contact and to expect protection from local leaders if their rights are abused. (Regulations or SK Kepala Desa Sido Urip No. 2 /2005). The third example comes from the Province of West Java and guarantees the protection of women and children who are victims of violence. (Regulations or Peraturan Daerah Propinsi Jawa Timur No. 9/2005). The final example is a district level regulation from Sumbawa providing protection to migrant women workers. (Regulations or Peraturan Daerah Kabupetan Sumbawa No. 11/2003). Sumbawa is well known as the first and largest sources of migrant female workers, who travel abroad to work in Malaysia, Hongkong, Saudi Arabia, and other Middle East countries.

Contrast these four district regulations with the profileration of Sharia inspired regulations which violate women's rights as specified in the Pancasila and Constitution listed below. This list of 48 regulations was collected by KOMNAS Perempuan, which notes that all are inspired by literalist and scripturalist interpretations of the holy texts of the Qu'ran and Hadith.

List of District Regulations which violate women's rights and the existence of Pancasila and UUD 1945:

NO. TITLE OF REGULATIONS

1. Peraturan Daerah Kabupaten Bulukumba (Sulawesi Selatan) No. 04/ 2003 tentang Berpakaian Muslim dan Muslimah.Bulukumba District Regulation (South Sulawesi) No 04/2003 about Muslim/mah dressing.

2. Peraturan Daerah Kabupaten Enrekang (Sulawesi Selatan) No. 6/2005 tentang Busana Muslim.Enrekang District Regulation (South Sulawesi) No 6/2005 about Muslim/mah dressing.
3. Surat Edaran Bupati Cianjur No. 025/3643/Org & Surat Edaran No. 061.2/2896/Org. tentang Jam Kerja dan Anjuran Pemakaian Seragam Kerja (Muslim/Muslimah) pada Hari-hari Kerja.Letter of Bupati Cianjur (West Java) No 025/3643/Org & Setter No 061.2/2896/Org. about office hours and sugestion to wear Muslim/mah uniform in the weekdays.
4. Peraturan Daerah Solok (Sumatra Barat) No. 6/2002 tentang Wajib Berbusana Muslimah.Solok District Regulation (West Sumatera) No 6/2002 about the obligation to wear Muslim/mah dressing.
5. Instruksi Walikota Padang (Sumatra Barat) No. 0451.442/Binsos-III/2005 tentang Kewajiban Berbusana Muslimah.Instruction Letter from Madang City Mayor (West Sumatera) No 0451.442/Binsos-III/2005 about the obligation to wear Muslim/mah dressing.
6. Peraturan Daerah Kabupaten Maros (Sulawesi Selatan) No. 15,16,17/2005 tentang Buta Aksara Al Quran, Busana Muslim dan Pengelolaan Zakat.Maros District Regulation (South Sulawesi) No 15, 16, 17/2005 about Quranic illiteracy, Muslim/mah dressing and Zakat management.
7. Surat Edaran Bupati Garut tentang Pemakaian Busana Muslimah bagi Seluruh Karyawati Pemerintah Kabupaten Garut.Letter from Bupati Garut (West Java) about Muslim/mah dressing for all civil servants in Garut District.
8. Kabupaten Gowa yang mewajibakn pemakaian jilbab bagi karyawan pemerintah dan penambahan jam pelajaran agama Islam.Gowa District obliges all women civil servants to wear jilbab and join Islamic teachings after the works.
9. Surat Edaran Bupati Tasikmalaya No. 451/SE/04/SOS/2001 tentang Peningkatan Kualitas Ketakwaan dan Keimanan.Letter from Bupati Tasikmalaya No 451/SE/04/SOS/2001 about the Increasing of the quality of Taqwa and Iman (Faith).
10. Peraturan Daerah Takalar (Sulawesi Selatan) tentang Busana Muslim.Takalar District Regulation (South Sulawesi) about Muslim dressing.
11. Surat Edaran Bupati Indramayu Tentang Wajib Busana Muslimah dan Pandai Baca Al Quran.Letter from Bupati Indramayu about Muslim/mah dressing and Quranic Literacy.
12. Peraturan Daerah Propinsi Jawa Timur No. 2/2004 tentang Pelayanan Penempatan dan Perlindungan Tenaga Kerja Indonesia ke Luar Negeri.East Java Provincial Regulation No 2/2004 about the service, alocation, and protection on migrant workers abroad.

13. Peraturan Daerah Kabupaten Cianjur No. 15/2002 tentang Perlindungan Tenaga Kerja Indonesia Kabupaten Ciajur ke Luar Negeri.Cianjur District Regulation (West Java) No 15/2002 about the protection of migrant workers abroad.
14. Peraturan Daerah Kabupaten Kerawang No. 22/2001 tentang Retribusi Pelayanan Bidang Ketenagakerjaan.Kerawang District Regulation (West Java) No 22/2001 about retribution on the service to migrant workers abroad.
15. Peraturan Daerah Kabupaten Gorontalo No. 10/2003 Tentang Pencegahan Maksiat.Gorontalo District Regulation No 10/2003 about the banning and prevention of social illness.
16. Surat Edaran Bupati Pamekasan (Madura) No. 450/2002 tentang Pemberlakuan Syariat Islam.Bupati Pamekasan Letter (Madura) No 450/2002 about the ratification of Sharia Islam.
17. Surat Edaran Bupati Cianjur No. 551/2717/ASSDA.I September 2001 tentang Gerakan Aparatur Berakhlakul Karimah dan Masyarakat Marhamah.Letter from Bupati Cianjur No 551/27 17/ASSDA.I September 2001 about the movement of civil servant who have good Islamic moral conduct and Islamic civil society.
18. SK Bupati Cianjur No. 36/2001 Lembaran Daerah No. 34 tentang Pendirian Lembaga Pengkajian dan Pengembangan Syariat Islam.Letter from Bupati Cianjur No 36/2001 District Paper No 34 about the establishment of Sharia Islamic Center.
19. Peraturan Daerah Propinsi Sumatra Barat No. 11/2001 tentang Pemberantasan dan Pencegahan Maksiat.West Sumatera Provincial Regulation No 11/2001 about the banning and prevention of social illness.
20. Peraturan Daerah Padang Pariaman (Sumatra Barat) No. 2/2004 tentang Pencegahan, Penindakan dan Pemberantasan Maksiat.Padang Pariaman District Regulation (West Sumetara) No 2/2004 about the banning of social illness.
21. Peraturan Daerah Propinsi Nangroe Aceh Darussalam No. 5/2000 tentang Pelaksanaan Syariat Islam.Nanggroe Aceh Darussalam Provincial Regulation No 5/2000 about the application of Sharia Islam.
21. Qanun Propinsi NAD No. 13/2003 tentang Maisir (Perjudian)—Gambling
22. Qanun Propinsi NAD No. 14/2003 tentang Khalwat (Mesum)—Prostitution
23. Qanun Propinsi NAD No. 7/2004 tentang Zakat—Zakat Management
24. Surat Gubernur Propinsi Riau No. 003.1/UM/08.1 tentang Pembuatan Papan Nama Arab Melayu.Letter from Gubernur Riau No 003.1/UM/08.1 about the making of Arab Melayu name-holder.

25. Peraturan Daerah Bengkulu No. 24/2000 tentang Pelarangan Pelacuran.Bengkulu District Regulation No 24/2000 about the banning of prostitution.
26. Instruksi Walikota Bengkulu No. 3/2004 tentang Program Kegiatan Peningkatan Keimanan.Instruction from Bengkulu City Mayor No 3/ 2004 about the program to increase the Islamic faith.
27. Peraturan Daerah Kabupaten Tangerang (Banten) No. 8/2005 tentang Pemberantasan Pelacuran/Maksiat.Tangerang District Regulation (Banten) No 8/2005 about the banning of prostitution and social illness.
28. Peraturan Daerah Provinsi Sumatra Selatan No. 13/2002 tentang Pemberantasan Maksiat.South Sumatera Provincial Regulation No 13/ 2002 about the banning of prostitution and social illness.
29. Peraturan Daerah Kota Palembang No. 2/2004 tentang Pemberantasan Pelacuran.Palembang District Regulation No 2/2004 about the banning of prostitution.
30. Peraturan Daerah Tasikmalaya No. 3/2001 tentang Pemulihan Kemanan dan Ketertiban yang Berdasarkan kepada Ajaran Moral, Agama, Etika dan nilai-nilai budaya daerah
31. Peraturan Daerah Kabupaten Garut No. 6/2000 tentang Kesusilaan.Garut District Regulation No 6/2000 about the morality.
32. Peraturan Daerah Batam No. 6/2002 tentang Ketertiban Sosial di Kota Batam.Batam District Regulation No 6/2002 about the Social Conduct in Batam City.
33. Peraturan Daerah Indramayu No. 7/1999 tentang Prostitusi.Indramayu District Regulation No 7/1999 about the banning of prostitution.
34. Peraturan Daerah Kabupaten Jember No. 14/2001 tentang Penanganan Pelacuran.Jember District Regulation (East Java) about the banning of prostitution and social illness.
35. Peraturan Daerah Sulawesi Selatan tentang Amar Ma'ruf Nahi Munkar, Perda ini meliputi: Perda tentang Zakat, baca tulis Al Quran dan busana muslim, perjudian, miras, narkoba dan prostitusi.South Sulawesi Provincial Law about the Amar Ma'ruf Nahi Munkar conduct, which covers the following regulations: Zakat regulation, Quranic literacy regulation, Muslim/mah dressing regulation, regulation to ban gambling, alcohol drink, drugs and prostitution.
36. Peraturan Daerah Bulukumba (Sulawesi Selatan) No. 6/2005 tentang Pandai Baca-Tulis Al Quran Bagi Siswa dan Calon Pengantin.Bulukumba District Regulation (South Sulawesi) No 6/2005 about Quranic literacy for pupils and students as well as bride-to-be.

37. Peraturan Daerah Bulukumba No. 2/2003 tentang Pengelolaan Zakat, Infak dan Sedekah.Bulukumba District Regulation (South Sulawesi) No 2/2003 about the management of Zakat, Infaq, and Alm-giving.
38. Peraturan Daerah Bulukumba No. 3/2002 tentang Larangan Penertiban dan Penjualan Minuman Keras.Bulukumba District Regulation (South Sulawesi) No 3/2002 about the banning of alcohol drink sale.
39. Peraturan Daerah Solok (Sumatra Barat) No. 10/2001 tentang Wajib Baca Al Quran untuk Siswa dan Pengantin.Solok District Regulation (West Sumatera) No 10/2001 about Quranic literacy for pupils and students as well as bride.
40. Peraturan Daerah Tangerang (Banten) No. 7/2005 tentang Menjual, Mengecer dan Menyimpan Minuman Keras Mabuk-mabukan.Tangerang District Regulation (Banten) No 7/2005 about the banning of the sale of alcohol drink.
41. Peraturan Daerah Kabupaten Pasuruan No. 10 Tahun 2001 tentang Pemberantasan Pelacuran.Pasuruan District Regulation (East Java) No 10/2001 about the banning of prostitution.
42. Rancangan Perda Kota Mataran Tahun 2003 tentang Pencegahan Maksiat.The Plan of Mataram District Regulation Year 2003 about the banning of social illness.
43. Rancangan Peraturan Daerah Kabupaten Cianjur tentang Pelaksanaan Syariat Islam di Kabupaten Cianjur.Cianjur District Regulation about the implementation of Sharia Islam in Cianjur District.
44. Rencana Strategis Kabupaten Tasikmalaya Tahun 2001-2005.Strategic Plan of Tasikmalaya District Year 2001-2005.
45. Peraturan Daerah Kabupaten Cianjur No. 08 tahun 2002 tentang Rencana Strategis Kabupaten Cianjur Tahun 2001-2005.Cianjur District Regulation (West Java) No 08/2002 about strategic plan for Cianjur District Year 2001 – 2005.
46. Pedoman tentang Lembaga Pengkajian dan Pengembangan Islam (LPP) Kabupaten Cianjur.Guidance about Board of Islamic Research and Development for District Cianjur.
47. Pedoman Pelaksanaan Gerakan Aparatur Pemerintah Berahlaqul Karimah di Kabupaten Cianjur.Guidance for the implementation of good moral conduct of the civil servants in District Cianjur.
48. Sosialisasi Gerbang Marhamah Melalui Pendidikan (Kabupaten Cianjur).Socialization of good moral conduct through education in District Cianjur.

Sources: *Divisi Reformasi Hukum, Komnas Perempuan* (National Commission on Violence Against Women) and *Medias Reviews*.

In the main these regulations seek to regulate how women shall (1) dress in public and (2) behave in the public sphere, including the curfew on women's freedom of movement after 10 pm. For example, Regulation Kabupaten Bulukumba (South Sulawesi) No 04/2003 concerns Muslimah attire, noting that Muslim women should cover what they call *aurat*, or those parts of the body which it is forbidden to show in public. That is all parts of the body with the exception of the face and the palm of the hand). The state obligates female civil servants to wear only one kind of uniform, which KOMNAS Perempuan views as limiting women's freedom of expression and civil liberty. Women who do not obey this regulation are at risk of losing their job. This regulation has been copied and inserted into another eight regulations, such as (1) Regulation Kabupaten Enrekang (South Sulawesi) No 6/2005 about Muslimah uniform; (2) Policy Letters from Bupati Cianjur No 025/3643/Org and No 061.2/2896/ Org about the obligation for all civil servants to wear Muslim/ah uniform during weekdays; (3) Regulation District Solok (West Sumatera) No 6/2002 about the obligation to wear Muslimah dress; (4) Walikota Padang Instruction (West Sumatera) No 0451.442/Binsos-III/2005 about the obligation to wear Muslimah dress; (5) Regulation Kabupaten Maros (South Sulawesi) No. 15, 16, 17/2005 about Quranic illiteracy, Muslim/mah dress and zakat management; (6) Policy Letters Bupati Garut about Muslimah uniform for all women civil servants; (7) Kabupaten Gowa regulation which obliges all civil servants to wear *jilbab* and study Islamic teaching; and (8) District Regulation Takalar (South Sulawesi) about Muslimah dress; Policy Letters Bupati Indramayu about the obligation of Muslimah dress and Quranic literacy. The previous nine laws obligate all Muslim women to cover all parts of the body with the exception of their face and the palm of their hands, and are directly inspired by a literalist interpretation of the Quran-Hadith on the so-called "aurat" of women. Muslim women, within these regulations, are responsible for the morality of the nation.

Besides placing absolute responsibility for morality onto women, the local government has sucked the sweat of migrant women workers as well. KOMNAS Perempuan has reported the following three regulations: (1) District Regulation East Jawa No 2/2004 regulating the income of migrant women working about so to ensure they meet their taxation obligations to the local government. Instead of protecting women's rights, this laws only regulates how to make a profit from the labour of migrant female workers aboard; (2) Regulation Kabupaten Cianjur No 15/2002 about migrant female workers, which does not focus on protecting their rights but instead focuses on allocating and managing female workers' income; and (3) Regulation Kabupaten Kerawang No 22/2001 about retribution to the service given to migrant women's workers. Women are only seen as commodity before this regulation.

After the concern with women's dress and the regulation of migrant female workers' income, comes the banning of women from public areas from 10 pm.

The restriction this imposes on women's access to economic activities after 10 pm in several district regulations has been criticized as violating women rights as workers. The impetus behind the introduction of this ban was the eradication of social ills, and most particularly prostitution. (1) District Regulation Sumatera Barat No 11 Tahun 2001 introduced this curfew in order to reduce and eventually eradicate social ills; while (2) Regulation Kota Gresik No 7 Tahun 2002; and (3) Regulation District Tangerang No 8 Tahun 2005 introduced this in the context of banning prostitution (*Jurnal Perempuan*, 2006). Jombang district in East Java will soon follow in implementing this ban. The point of departure for this ban is not only a desire to eradicate prostitution but also the socio-cultural construction that men are the breadwinners of the family. This belief denies women their economic rights as well as the fact that female vendors dominate most of the traditional markets in Indonesia and frequently start their work at 3 a.m. Instead of taking into account the social fact that women play significant productive roles in the public sphere, the propagators of these ordinances seek to confine women to the home. Indonesian women and men have worked together to make a living since time immemorial. Earlier legislature had established equal rights for women and men, and to some extent the dream of gender equality had actually been coming true with the expansion of women's education and employment. In this context, the banning of women from public places after 10 pm is evidence of a recent turn in the search for gender equality, and evidence of deterioration in the quality of women's life and freedom in Indonesia.

On the ordinances governing dress, women now have to wear the jilbab (Muslim headscarf). It is true that after the fall of Suharto, wearing the jilbab represented a form of expression or freedom against the restrictions imposed by Suharto. At that time, women celebrated their right "to wear or not to wear the veil". Today, however, Muslim women in the 40 regencies and municipalities concerned have no choice but to wear Muslim dress. The state has robbed women of their rights to decide whether to wear the jilbab or not and distorted the history of Sharia at the same time. Sharia has been interpreted in differing ways by Muslims at different times and in different contexts. The meaning of the veil has also changed from civilization to civilization and across time. Women themselves have interpreted the wearing of the veil differently. Some interpret Muslimah dress codes in a strict literalist sense (meaning that women can only show their palms and faces when in public), while other women insist that they are required only to dress modestly, and that a head scarf is not necessary. The veil controversy is a battle of identities now played out on a global stage. The future homogenization of the form and meaning of the veil may be an inevitable outcome that Muslim women will have to live with. Nevertheless, currently women's veils take various forms, from long black veils to short colorful ones.

The way women wear the veil also varies, with some having all of their hair covered, while others allow some of their hair to be revealed.

The question for the state now is "on whose interpretation are all of these Sharia ordinances that oblige women to wear Islamic dress and the veil based?" Whose rights are being ignored and denied by this interpretation? Certainly, it is women's rights. The current interpretation has circumscribed the rights of women in these 40 regencies and municipalities. Failure to provide these rights means that the state is denying the rights of women, who are also citizens. It will be true empowerment, therefore, if women can reclaim their rights to dress as they like in the public space. The denial of women's basic rights (such as to have access to the public space after 10 pm and to dress as they please) reveals the weaknesses of public policy makers in understanding the spirit behind the founding of the Republic of Indonesia. Supporters of Sharia are being guided by a patriarchal textual understanding of Sharia that views women as half-human beings who need to be controlled more than men. They are also inspired by the teaching of the Sharia as a text, per se. They have forgotten how Sharia is formulated, and the need for it to be accompanied by the philosophy of interpretation known as *ushul fiqih*, and for it to be adjusted to local social and cultural contexts, such as in the multiethnic Indonesia. To date, policy makers have focused solely on the interpretation they have acquired from clerics. The complexity of Muslims' interpretations of Sharia has been totally ignored. The imposition of a fixed interpretation on women has also meant that women have lost their right to interpret for themselves, on the basis of their spiritual and rational experiences. This only serves to prevent women from expressing their apprehension of present socio-cultural conditions. It is time to return to women in Indonesia the right to wear or not to wear the veil, and for the state to finally defend and and guarantee this right.

Many Indonesian women's NGO also object to the way that the substance of these district regulations, namely *Perda Sharia*, violate higher, national-level laws and conventions. These include violations of: (1) CEDAW (Convention on the Elimination of the Discrimination Against Women's Right) which was ratified by the Constitution of Indonesia in 1984 (Undang-Undang No 7 Tahun 1984); (2) the International Convention on Civil and Politic Rights which was ratified 2005 (Undang-Undang No 12 Tahun 2005); (3) the 1999 Human Rights Law (Undang-Undang Hak Asasi Manusia No 39 Tahun 1999); and (4) the International Convention on Economic, Social, Cultural Rights which was ratified in 2005 (Undang-Undang No 11 Tahun 2005), and which states that the Republic of Indonesia should protect workers' rights, family rights, the right to health and an adequate standard of living, educational rights and cultural rights.

A judicial review of the recent *Perda Sharia* has been proposed by the Law Reformation Division of KOMNAS Perempuan, which is coordinated by

R. Husna Mulya. She has noted that several *Perda Sharia* are weakly drafted due to their drafters' legal illiteracy. This lack of legal literacy and weakly drafted regulations has also made many of these *Perda Sharia* open to multi-interpretations. This has endangered the execution of the regulations particular in terms of law enforcement. As Komnas Perempuan has noted, in some cases regulations were not intended to discriminate against women, but due to the lack of legal literacy during their drafting, the expression of the regulations contradict higher laws of the land—such as the four noted above—which are meant to provide a structure and umbrella for lower laws and regulations. Based on the previous concern on legal illiteracy and legal drafting, as well as the lack of legal advisers in many district throughout Indonesia, Komnas Perempuan has proposed the following steps to regulate and administer new laws and regulations:

1. Republic of Indonesia's National Parliament (DPR RI). As the highest legislative body, the DPR should ask (a.) the Interior Ministry to check the consistency between the higher laws and the lower laws in the districts. (b.) Support the Ministry of Law and Human Rights to raise the capacity and quality of district legal adviser so that the products of legal draftings are concomitant with the higher laws of Indonesia. (c.) Take special steps to form ad hoc teams which could evaluate the work and the implementation of District Regulations that should be in conformity with UUD 1945 Amendment IV, and other laws.
2. Supreme Court should review the content of district regulations, which are opposed by civilian groups.
3. Indonesian Police Corps should protect the higher national laws, which are violated by the lower district regulations.
4. Constitutional Court should review law products which are insensitive and unjust with respect to gender issues.
5. The Regional Representative Councils or DPD (Dewan Perwakilan Daerah/District Representative Board) should monitor the application of District Regulations which violate higher national laws, particular the Consitution (UUD 1945 Amendment IV).

(Source: *Komnas Perempuan*. "Pernyataan Pers: Penertiban Perda-Perda diskriminatif adalah tanggung jawab negara yang tak bisa diabaikan". Jakarta, 20 June 2006).

4. Theological Pretext

Diverse forms of veils have traveled, proliferated, and resided in the Diasporas of Muslim countries. Along the history of Muslim community, *jilbab* have been identified, formed, reformed, and continually represented in the identity politics being affirmed Muslim worldwide in multiple ways. In Turki it is called *charshaf*, in Libya *milayat*, and in Iraq it is known as *abaya* (Walther, 1993:208). In Iran it is known as *Chador*, from the Persian language meaning tent, an all-enveloping piece of cloth covers woman's body from head to toe (Milani, 1992:20). In the Indian continent including Pakistan and Bangladesh it is known as Purdah. Purdah is from Indo-Pakistan, *pardeh*, meaning curtain (Mumtaz & Shaheed, 1987:77-81). In the Southeast Asia such as Indonesia, South Thailand, Malaysia, and Brunei it is known as *kerudung* or *kudung* in a traditional sense. In Indonesia after the fall of Soeharto in 1998, the veil got novel term and is popularly called *jilbab*.

Jilbab is not originated from Islamic tradition alone. It has been widely known, practiced, and embraced long before the onset of Islamic tradition. In the Jew tradition, the similar expression for *jilbab* is *tif'eret* stated in the Torah, Isaiah: 3:19-20 (Epstein, 1967:37). While in the Christian tradition it is called *redid*, *zammah*, *re'alah*, *zaif*, or *mitpahat* stated in the Bible (Epstein, 1967:37). Long before it is existed in the Semitic tradition, it had been known in the Assyrian tradition. The veil was wore when women entering into the public sphere. In the Arabic tradition, there are several type of women veiling, such as *khimar*, a veil donning the head; *dir'*, a veil donning the body; *niqab* and *burqa*, a veil donning the face except two of the eyes; *idzar*, a cloth covering the whole body until toes; *rida'* is donning outside of *idzar*; *jilbab* is head veil, covering head including *dir'* and *khimar* (Stowasser, 1994). The root of *jilbab* from the Arabic term is *jalaba*, meaning "to carry" or "to take". It is an outer garment which could cover the whole woman body. In the Islamic tradition, many jurists instruct the obligation to wear the veil for woman by relying on Quran Surah 24 An Nur verse 31 (hereafter Surah 24:31) as well as Surah 33 Al Ahzab verse 53 and 59 (hereafter Surah 33:53 and Surah 33:59). The following English translation of the Quran is taken from *Interpretation of the Meanings of the Noble Quran in the English Language*, by Muhammad Muhsin Khan and Muhammad Taqi-ud-Din Al-Hilali, Al Haramain Foundation, Riyadh, Saudi Arabia:

> And tell the believing women to lower their gaze (from looking at forbidden things), and protect their private parts (from illegal sexual acts) and not to show off their adornment except that which is apparent (like both eyes for necessity to see the way, or outer palms of hands or one eye or dress like veil, gloves, headcover, apron), and to draw their veils all over ***Juyubihinna*** **(i.e. their bodies, faces, necks and bosoms)** and not to reveal their adornment except to their husbands, or their fathers, or their husband's fathers, or their sons, or their husband's sons, or their brothers or their brother's sons, or their sister's sons, or their (Muslim) women (i.e. their sisters in Islam), or the (female) slaves whom their right hands possess, or old male servants who lack vigour, or small children who have no sense of feminine sex. And let them not stamp their feet so as to reveal what they hide of their adornment. And all of you beg Allah to forgive you all, O believers, that you may be successful (Surah 24:31).

> O you who believe! Enter not the Prophet's houses, unless permission is given to you for a meal, (and then) not (so early as) to wait for its preparation. But when you are invited, enter, and when you have taken your meal, disperse without sitting for a

> talk. Verily, such (behaviour) annoys the Prophet, and he is shy of (asking) you (to go); but Allah is not shy of (telling you) the truth. And when you ask (his wives) for anything you want, **ask them from behind a screen**, that is purer for your hearts and for their hearts. And it is not (right) for you that you should annoy Allah's Messenger, nor that you should ever marry his wives after him (his death). Verily, with Allah that shall be an enormity (Surah 33:53).
>
> O Prophet! Tell your wives and your daughters and the women in the believers to draw their cloaks (veils) all over their bodies **(i.e. screen themselves completely except the eyes or one eye to see the way)**. That will be better that they should be known (as free respectable women) so as not to be annoyed. And Allah is Ever Oft-Forgiving, Most Merciful (Surah 33:59).

The following analysis discusses the theological pretext of derivative meaning of Arabic in Quran related to the translation coming from previous Saudian jurists. The analysis aims to unveil the historical context behind the revelations of each verses as well as the political subtext that underline the production of Islamic legal formulations of religious obligation on the act of women's veiling. Particular political, social, economic, cultural subtext climates the birth of particular theological pretext.

5. Political Subtext of Androcentric Reading

In the Arabic peninsula, the veil for woman body is popularly known as *hijab*, meaning "to separate" using curtain. According to Fatema Mernissi, in the beginning of Islamic civilization, the meaning of *hijab* is "curtain", after the process of politicization of women in Islam, the meaning of *hijab* was shifted into *jilbab*, meaning "to cover" (Mernissi, 1991:184-185). Lila Abu-Lughod further explains that veiling is that which covers sexual shame and that it communicates deference, but its vocabulary is that of sexuality and chastity (1986:159). In Surah 33:53, the phrase *min wara' al-hijab* (from behind a screen) emphasizes the element of separation or partition. The notion of *hijab* in Islam refers to a sacred divide or separation between two worlds or two spaces: deity and mortals, good and evil, light and dark, believers and nonbelievers, or aristocracy and commoners (El Guindi, 1999:157). Neither women's seclusion from the public sphere nor gender segregation do previous three verses denotes and signifies. *Hijab* represents purity and sacred spaces.

The meaning of *hijab* then transferred into full covering of the whole woman body including the face except two of the eyes as well as women's seclusion and gender segregation with the arrival of political subtext into the ramifications of theological interpretation. Political coercion on women's veiling was famous during Caliphs of Ummayah (661-750), Abbasid (750-1258), Mamluk (1250-1517), and the last Ottoman Caliphate as well. Practice of polygamy was exercised by the previous dynasties. Khalifah al-Mutawakkil (847-61) owned 4000 concubines, besides legal wives; as well as Khalifah Harun al-Rashid (786-809) owned hundred concubines (Hitti, 1940:342 & Abbot,

1946:138). Those among who protested the practice of androcentricism were Sufi order, Khariji and Qarmatian. Rabiah Al-Adawiyah (d.801) and Hasan al-Bashri (d.728) lived during the Abbasid Caliphate. Both advocated gender equity in reading the Quran and Hadith (Prophetic Tradition). The most important and famous intellectual during the Abbasid Caliphate was Ibn al-Arabi (1165-1240) who was against misogynistic approach in reading and interpreting the holy texts. His poetry compilation, *Tarjuman al-Ashwaq*, unearthed an approach of feminine Allah. During Ottoman dynasty, progressive readings were proposed by Rifa'ah Rafi' al-Tahtawi (1801-73), Jamal al-Din al-Afghani (1839-97), as well as Muhammad Abduh (1849-1905) who advocated reciprocal and equal relationship between men and women. Their progressive and sensitive gender approach toward Quran and Hadith, however, were neither the mainstream nor the formal legal formulation most caliphates employed in Islamic jurisprudence.

The previous Islamic dynasties exploited androcentric reading in approaching the Quran and prophetic tradition, Hadith. Androcentricism is dominated by or emphasizing masculine interests and a masculine point of view, placing masculine point of view at the center of one's view of the world and its culture and history; while feminine perspective and worldview are seen as deviance and complimentary. One of the prominent androcentric reading approaches is the religious obligation for women to wear face veil. Quran translation (*tarjamat al-quran)* that is used to argue that Prophet's wives used to wear *niqab* (face veil) is found in Surah 33:53.

The time of the revelation was during which Muhammad spent his time in Madina in which the growing number of early Muslim converts flooded the mosque and the Prophet and his wives compartments surround the mosques to paid a visit. With the growing number of visitors, Aisha bin Abu Bakr and Umm Salamah, Prophet's wives, put and built some type of screen to their hut to separate their privacy from the public. Prophet's other wives such as Sawda, Hafsa bin Umar bin Khattab, Zainab bin Jahsh, Maimuna, Safia (Jewish), and Miriam (Egyptian concubine) presumably might do similar action. *Asbab al-nuzul*, the reason and context behind the revelation, Surah 33:53 is to instruct male visitors wishing to speak and talk to Prophet Muhammad's wives from behind the curtain (Stern, 1939:116). This event reveals that after the wedding feast some of the guest lingered on in Zainab's hut and several tactless guests remained lost in conversation during the wedding supper of the Prophet and his new wife, Zainab bin Jahsh. The Prophet was unable to rid himself of them and grew impatient and visited his other wives, waiting for their departure. Only after he went to Zainab's hut for the second time did they finally leave the newly wedded pair alone.

The witness of the revelation was the third person of the wedded pair, called Anas ibn Malik, one of Prophet's Companions. The *Asbab al-wurud*, the reason and context of the prophetic sayings, Hadith, suggested the synonym of the word *hijab*, that is to separate between the Prophet himself (and his wife) and Anas. The previous two evidences, *asbab al-nuzul* and *asbab al-wurud*, suggest that the revelations disclose privacy and sanctity of the home and private life of the Prophet from the public. Quran and Hadith advocate neither gender segregation nor women's seclusion from the public space.

Surah 33:53, however, has been exercised to obligate women to cover their faces, especially translation that is exercised and coming from Arabic Peninsula. Another important androcentric reading has substantiated the plight of Saudian women, especially regarding the marriage and family law which put rights of polygamy, divorce and child custody solely to "men". Turkey, Iraq, Syria, Tunisia and Kuwait has undergone law reform toward new modern law which asided ulama of Sharia Law (Ahmed, 1992:146 & 241). They introduced measure critically to redefine and amend the law on polygamy and divorce in ways that fundamentally curtailed male license and privilege.

If Saudian English translation of Quran advocates women's face covering with *niqab* and *burqa*, Indonesian's Quran translation (Surah 24:31, 33:53, and 33:59) by Ministry of Religious Affair did not mention that women shall cover their whole bodies including their faces except two of the eyes. Obligating women to cover their faces using *niqab* or *burqa* contradicts with the literal meaning of the verses. First, the verses do not employs the word *niqab* rather *hijab* which in this context means a curtain. Second, in Surah 33:53 the reason and context behind the revelation recommends putting a barrier between two men (the Prophet and Anas ibn Malik), not a man and a woman. Different from Indonesia, in the Middle East these three Surahs have been understood to require women wearing face veil, *niqab*. It contradicts the complexity and plurivocality of juristic debates and divergent voices that have been generated by previous communities of interpretation in relation to these verses. Furthermore, the operative word of *juyubihinna* in Surah 24:31 which is interpreted as a complete covering not only of woman's hair but also of the body, face, neck and bosom is unauthentic.

One of important modern contemporary Islamic Jurists, Khalid Abou El-Fadl, has unearthed the intellectual dishonesty in the Quran translation from Saudi Arabia or those which were funded by petrodollars such as the previous cited English translation co-translated by professors from Islamic University al-Madinah Al-Munawwarah (El-Fadl, 2001). Many English speaking countries are unaware of the dishonest Quran translation in their Islamic centers and bookstores. At present Muslim worldwide rely mainly and exclusively on the meaning of translation from Arabic in Quran due to illiteracy to Arabic and little knowledge on the history of Islam. El-Fadl exposes the interfering additional dishonest explanation of the meaning of particular verse in the Quran by adding parenthetical utterances "(…)". The additional parenthetical explanation signifies the political subtext that might have been exercised by Orthodox Wahabi Mazhab to exploit particular agenda different from the authentic and factual meaning of verses in question.

In verses of veil Surah 24:31 & Surah 33:59, both translators invented novel parenthetical intervention to assert that God's command is that women should cloak themselves in a large veil, and cover everything except two of the eyes. The cited parenthetical intervention is as follows: first, An Nur 31: additional phrase "*juyubihinna* (i.e. their bodies, faces, necks and bosoms)"; second, Al Ahzab 59: additional unauthentic obligation is "(i.e. screen themselves completely except the eyes or one eye to see the way)". Both wrote that God explicitly mandates that the cloaks or veil be drawn over a woman's entire body. The literal meaning of the verses would read: "O Prophet! Tell your wives and your daughters and the women of the believers to lower (or possible, draw upon themselves) their garments. That is better so that they will not be known or molested. And God is forgiving and merciful" (*Ibid*).

El Fadl adds neither a parenthetical intervention on the operative word of *juyubihinna* nor incorrect literal meaning of the English translation of Arabic. He explores further that the operative words of Surah 33:59 are *yudnina 'alayhinna min jalabibihinna*. It could mean as either "lower their garments" or "draw their garments closer to their bodies". *Jalabibihinna* literally means "their garments" and not a veil. A *jilbab* (a singular for *jalabib*) is a garment like a dress or Arab robe which has stitches and threads. *Yudnina* means, literary, "to bring closer" or "to lower something" in this case a garb. This verse can be interpreted to require the covering of the legs, or a more vigilant covering of the torso, or simply, modesty, but it does not support the previous Medinian translation as requiring the covering of everything except one or two eyes and hands. The Medinian translation purports a clear Wahabian agenda in dictating ideal Islamic formula for women of Islam.

A number of divergent and conflicting views on the meaning of the verses of veil are found ubiquitously in the opinions of early Muslim jurists. Some claimed that it mandates covering of the legs or bosom. Majority maintained that it requires the covering of the full body except the face, hands and feet. A minority view asserted that the verse requires women to cover their faces. A minority other maintains decency and modesty. The claim on the religious suggestion and not obligation to veil for women of Islam is found everywhere in Islamic jurisprudence. Religious obligation on veil has undergone constant debate and dispute. Almost all of the Islamic jurists, however, agreed that the verse was revealed to protect women from verbal and physical abuse during Prophet Era. During Muhammad Prophethood, several group of fraudulent men in Medina used to harass and molest women at night. The targeted women were apparently not women of Islam, but slave women. *Jilbab* was put on to signify a free woman, and thus was not going to be molested; while non-*jilbab* wearing slave women were considered to be legitimate targets. Even slave women who wore *jilbab* were considered unruly, disobedient and thereby should be punished. The seventh century Arabia was a slave owning community. It is conspicuous that the reason behind this revelation was to distinguish between free and slave women. It implies neither religious connotation nor religious obligation.

In Surah 24:31 parenthesis interjection is added on the phrase *juyubihinna*. *Jayb* means the beginning of cleavage from women's chest or bosom where neck and chest meet. *Khimar* (head veil) was usually worn by women of Pre-Islamic era on the head. It was the habit of women in Mecca and Medina to expose most of their chests in the public, although their hairs were covered with *turban*. *Turban* is *khimar* being worn on the head. *Khimar* was put on usually to cover women's neck and left the head and bosom unveiled and exposed. The verse suggests drawing the khimar, a piece of cloth, to veil and covering women's bosom. It importantly asks women to cover their chest. The word *khimar* signifies and refers neither to the covering of face nor hands.

The previous discussion discloses that it is important to note several considerations in reading, interpreting and translating the Quran. Tracing the historical accounts as well as contextualization of particular revelation unearthed the interpretational considerations particular jurists take. It thus uncovers the political agenda behind particular translation and legal decision on particular religious obligation. Notably by unveiling the derivative meaning of particular word or phrase or sentence in Quran might play significant role in determining the lot of Muslim women worldwide. Otherwise, unjust and fraudulent reading and interpretation might create plight for women in Islam. Muslim feminists' propagation in introducing different perspective approaching Quran and Hadith might overcome the previous gender injustice practice in Islam examined from manifold dimensions.

6. Under the Rite of Morality

In modern time, the meaning of *jilbab* shifted along with the development of women movements around Muslim countries. In Indonesia during authoritarian New Order Era, the wearing of *jilbab* was forbidden in the state-owned schools and universities. Short before Suharto's fall, a number of *Tarbiyah* activists (New-Islamists movement) from state-owned universities insisted and protested the government that they are to be granted permission to wear *jilbab* in the school and universities. *Tarbiyah* movements were flourishing short before the fall of Suharto and enjoyed the right to wear head veil during post-authoritarian Indonesia, popularly called as Reformation Era. They translated *jilbab* into a heroic form of speaking against the authoritarian Suharto. On the one hand, New-Islamist women have affirmed the meaning of *jilbab* as a means of covering, thus giving up their own right of their own bodies under traditional orthodox interpretations. On the other hand, contemporary Islamist women have acclaimed the rights to *jilbab* as a means of resistance toward the corrupt regime whom apparently hindering them, which thus such action of self-donning grants them with civil liberty. From 1998 until recently, more and more Muslim women wear *jilbab*.

The expression of wearing *jilbab* takes various forms of meaning. For a large amount of women, the wearing of the veil is one and foremost the fulfillment of Islamic code of conduct for womanhood. Yet this expression is denying the historical facts that during Muhammad era, many Muslim women were free to show their hair. The propagation of *jilbab* in Indonesia is partly highly influenced by the Iranian Revolution in 1979 in which Iranian women standing tall wearing *jilbab* to speak against the despotic monarchy. It is a politics of identity in affirming self as a Muslim which is different from the other. Inaugurating self as a Muslim is becoming important with the arrival of globalization. Globalization is seen as agent of "homogenization", especially the "West". Being modern, being a good woman of Islam, and being non-Western are amongst the *raison d'etre* of self veiling. Globalization is then seen, perceived and paralyzed with homogenization. Homogenization then entails possibility to the extent to which voluntary-induced veiling flourishes in heterogeneous community. Globalization circulates homogenized economical and political subtext from various different rich compartments. It furthermore fosters homogenization of various religious-culturally based compartments such as Islam. Modern technology thus assists in disseminating the incorporeal Islamic image and message to Muslim worldwide across the globe. Affirming self veiling defines inauguration of tangible and intangible manifestation in politics of identity. Self donning bears plurality of meanings in particular contexts.

For particulars women *jilbab* is celebrated as an expression of particular ideology of particular Islamic movements. *Jilbab* is regarded as a political means in speaking against the other. *Jilbab* is then being embedded into novel political subtext of particular Islamist Parties such as PKS, PBB, PPP and PBR. Besides being used as a political card, *jilbab* is self-affirmed by many women in the self renunciation before Allah. The bodies are seen as sources of temptations to reach the bliss of heaven, *Saada*. To reach *Saada*, every Muslim is obliged to tame the desire of the body. Women's bodies are seen, within this *Weltanschauung* (worldview), as source of temptation. It is suggested, therefore, to cover the whole of women's bodies as well as women's hair so to reach the bliss of heaven. Furthermore, in the patriarchy cosmology, the world is being seen from the masculine eyes. And women bodies are an exposed "to-be-lookedness" spectacle. The patriarchy is the spectators, those who undergo the process of seeing and beholding. Yet women are shouldered with the role of "to be seen", "to be looked at", or "to be beholden". Consequently women take the responsibility of the cosmology of human morality. This kind of morality is defined by the way woman could cover herself and hide the bodies from the spectators. Politics of morality thus defines the way the community could and are able to control woman's body. It is thus under the rite of morality that woman's body is being placed to be in service.

7. Captives of the State

1966-1998 Suharto's political pretext had been defined, constructed, and proliferated in manifold representations among its dissenting movements close to his downfall. Among them which brought constant grass root fame is Islamist representation whether in sociopolitical or sociocultural template. One of its defining factors are designed by ideology *Al-Ziyy Al-Islami* (Islamic dress) calling for decency and conformity to the ultimate Islamic mores. The ideology hereafter exercises novel modern Islamic conduct of womanhood in the 21st century Indonesian unisexual society. It precedes norms of a more conservative construction of women's bodies from a theological perspective inspired by the imagination of the founding discourses in the seventh century Arabic peninsula, a community in which gender hierarchy prevailed from the onset of pre-Muhammadan Islam.

After the Iranian revolution in 1979 and other prominent Islamist resurgences in other Arab Middle Eastern Asian countries such as Egypt and Pakistan, the discourse of veil has traveled and is being gradually affirmed into the psychosocial of Indo-Malay Muslim. Those among the influential replications are Egyptian Hasan al-Banna's Ikhwanul Muslimin that inspired Indonesian Tarbiyah movements following other subsequent political and cultural embodiment such as the famous Justice and Prosperous Party (PKS). The increasing and amassing of self-donning attest crucial emblem of women's quest for "authentic" and "original" Islam amid ceaselessly global "Western" cultural stream. Self-donning "autonomy" as well as "authority" is structured to speak against the failed modern state. Unfortunately, states regimes took charge of power in respected countries embellished its political administration with corruption and moral bankruptcy. Islamic moral "purification" recharges aforementioned limpid crisis. *Jilbab* seen as dissenting manifestation struggles to free itself from the government formal banning in formal schools.

Soon after Suharto's fall discourses of self donning gained victorious standing among Muslim activists and community. Furthermore, *jilbab* is exercised as political and cultural resistances toward so-called pathetic scene of adulation on material and secular visualization. It inspires many hearts to turn into God for unending hope of a just and humane world. Self donning thus demonstrates women's autonomy and subjectivity rather than subordination on the basis of sociopolitical precepts. Women of veil enjoys public sphere as much as bare-head women, including mingling with other sexes across diverse public spheres. It is rather a pretext of ethics—spirit of Sharia as ideal Ethics—that colors the act of self veiling in Indonesia, and certainly not doctrinal segregation mounted on the founding discourses during the Abbasid Caliphate (750-1258) where marriage inflicted conspicuous gender hierarchy that put vast access of divorce and polygamy as well as child custody to "men".

Self donning imbued Tarbiyah movement is partly evidence of lower and middle classes upward mobilization into upper sociopolitical and sociocultural ruling class. Its ethics impregnate self-discipline, autonomy and morality against corrupting setting. They permeate ethical and spiritual quest for a just Indonesia. Economic crisis is being viewed brought about by unjust greedy capitalism, while social and cultural crisis is being foreseen caused by immoral conduct of Godless behavior. Reconstruction as well as re-symbolization of past practice of the 9th century Arabic Peninsula found its crux spectacle in the piece of cloth. Modern fashion code embeds discreetly into the Islamic dress. A novel style of Islamic dress and headscarf fashion different from those being worn by women of Muhammad era are being invented, produced, and consumed under the aegis of modern capitalism. Modern technologies escort the way this novel invention to be circulated across different Muslim countries worldwide.

Indonesian headscarf and Islamic dress textile industries have loomed the economic situation for the emergency native pockets. Indonesian trade marks are well-known among hajj pilgrimage in Mecca. Muslim women enjoy and indulge themselves in variety of colorful and array style of Islamic dress and *jilbab* in the market. Capitalism thus situates this novelty into conspicuous prism of consumerism among Muslim women. Self donning thereafter despite provides its users a way of liberating self from the trap of capitalism as well as creates vibrant Muslim economic vehicles, *jilbab* could redirect its users as well into lavish consumerism. Preceding terrain demonstrates interpenetration and cohabitation among conflicting factors surrounding the practices of self veiling, particularly under the auspices of modern secular capitalism vis-à-vis Islamic purification. Love and hatred configuration frequently embody Muslim women personification and cultural production deliberately as well as unconsciously. It is not merely theological pretext but yet capitalist subtext exemplifying the practice of self veiling.

The rigorous festival enjoyed by Muslim women in the act of self donning in the realm of ethical shift in sociocultural as well as sociopolitical life, however, is discreetly being battered by recent political subtext that produces Sharia Bylaws in several districts in Indonesia. If previously women enjoyed greater freedom whether to adopt the veil or not, at present they are then being compelled to put the *jilbab* on. If previously the authority of *jilbab* belonged to women, now they lost such freedom as well as autonomy toward the veil. The state coerces the veil upon the plurivocality of women's Islamic dress interpretations. It is not a mystery that *Al-Ziyy Al-Islami* has been interpreted in diverging ways in different schools of Islam. Multivocality of meaning production is reflected vividly in the very heart of Islamic tradition. There is no single truth regarding this code.

Several minor alternative schools such as Sufi order, Khariji, and Qarmatian provide no coercion, while the dominant established Mazhab (school of interpretation) enforces coercion. Such dialectic and constantly celebrated-rich-perspectives entrenches into the cemented-culture throughout the course of Muslim history. With the arrival of the state along with political parties as its apparatus, one dominant interpretation is then being appropriated in householding unjust agendas as well as concealing its failure to bring prosperity and just society. In conjunction with *jilbab* coercion upon women, the state curtails women not to entering the public space after 10 pm in suspicion of their carrying out prostitution. The State hurdled women back from economic sectors as captives of their own houses by not considering that industrial women workers usually have their 12 pm night-shift, while women vendors starting their works at 3 am in the urban traditional markets. It is thus an impulsive and an impetuous political standpoint the state discriminates against women's economic, social and civil rights.

Indonesia non-segregate and unisex community has replicated as well as launched civil liberty for different gender—men, women, and sexual minority—across centuries. The adoption of one version of the interpretation of Sharia, namely *fiqih* (the law governing relations between God and Human), by neglecting among other multivocal interpretations, has impeded the way Indonesian defines the plural melting pot of Indonesianness. *Jilbab* compulsion and public segregation exercised upon women are thus further enshrining women as captives of their own houses as well as prisoners of the state.

8. Jilbab as State's Control against Women's Bodies

With the arrival of Sharia Bylaws, the practice of women veiling has shifted the meaning of the veil. From 1998 onward the rights wearing *jilbab* belongs to women. Yet in the last two years, in which around 27 out of 88 districts (Indonesia owns 423 districts in 33 provinces) laws seen as violating women's rights, the rights to wear *jilbab* or not is being politicized and becoming the political subtexts of particular Islamist parties as well as state's control. State is now has license and sole right to compel women wearing *jilbab*. Even in Aceh and Bulukumba (South Sulawesi), those who wear no *jilbab* will be put onto the truck and face several lashes as well as punishments and humiliations before the public gaze. While in Padang (West Sumatera), minorities and non-Muslim students are required to wear Islamic dress and *jilbab* in state-owned schools. *Jilbab* revolution in 1998 in speaking against authoritarian regime has now being inserted to impede Indonesian women's civil liberty. The state exercises this piece of cloth, *jilbab*, in controlling women's bodies manifested in the politics of piety.

Along with Sharia Bylaws, in 2005 the state proposed as well a bill draft on law against pornography. Yet the content of the bill shoulders morality into women's bodies alone. Women bodies are seen as sources of temptation and should be regulated. The law, anyhow, forgets to regulate the spectators. The bill is unable to unread the process of complex ramification of woman body's commodification under the umbrella of capitalism. When the laws are practiced in the field, it is glaringly obvious, that Sharia Bylaws and Anti-Pornography bill draft are primarily concerned with regulating woman's body. The government then enjoys the benefit to increase the level of corruption unwatched. Religious leaders are busied and politicized to guard the morality of the masses, while the morality of the top leaders is left unobserved. When Islam is reduced into a sole interpretation, the manifold history of reciprocal hybridization of Islamic ethics and Indonesian values is then partly ignored, forgotten and finally rejected. Many Ulemas and Muslim scholars and their communities strongly support the introduction of Sharia Bylaws; however just as many Ulemas and Muslim scholars and their community strongly oppose them. Two of the best known Ulemas and scholars opposed to Sharia Bylaws are former President Gus Dur, who is head of Indonesia's largest Muslim organisation Nadlatul Ulama (NU), and Syafii Maarif from Muhammadiyah, the second largest (Maarif in *Republika* 11 Juli 2006).

The dilemma of Sharia Bylaws results from different interpretations of Sharia within Islamic community. The transformation and rejuvenation of Sharia in the Indonesian context has been driven by two important actors, those who play from the theological level and those who engage from civil and socio-cultural level. From theological perspective, two notable poles—that of the conservative and of the progressive position—have contributed to a highly dynamic debate on the role of Sharia in Indonesia. The conservative circles are satisfied with expressing a literal interpretation and application of the Quran and Hadith, whereas the progressive circles criticize such literal applications, arguing the need for greater historical inquiry in order to find a more contextualized, germane, and progressive interpretation of Sharia.

Two influential and theologically-informed feminist groups within progressive circles are Rahima and LKAJ. These organizations are mostly led and dominated by daughters of NU (Nadlatul Ulama). Rahima stands for the Centre for Education and Information on Islam and Women's Rights Issues, and is led by Farha Ciciek. Rahima is a rural-based Islamic women's NGO, which focuses on the empowerment of women from Islamic perspective. Rahima originally developed in response to the need for information regarding women's rights issues within Islam. In the beginning Rahima's focus was on the training and dissemination of information (concerning women's rights within Islam) to local community, Muslim groups, and Pesantrens (Islamic boarding schools). However, with the increasing interest in gender issues in Indonesia in recent times, Rahima has now extended its network to a wider range of women's NGOs, Islamic women's organisations and university groups. Its vision is achievement of democratic society, which Rahima believes can only be achieved when women's rights are fulfilled, as necessary component of the execution of human rights. Rahima's mission is to empower women through various awareness raising activities concerning women rights within Islam, focusing on women, men and institutions, where gender discourses are raised, resonated, and proliferated. Its goal is to motivate and encourage Islamic discourses, in order to strengthen the position of women within Islamic society. Through strengthening the position of women (based on equality and justice) and raising gender awareness, Rahima hopes to engender a public democracy within Indonesian society.

The second prominent progressive organization is, LKAJ (Lembaga Kajian Agama dan Jender or Organization for Gender and Religious Studies), which was founded by Siti Musdah Mulia. Mulia saw that the ratification and formalization of Sharia Bylaws solely hindering women's rights as its interpretation was apparently gender insensitive (Mulia in *ICRP*, 2006). She criticizes that while the Sharia is universal in its teaching as given by God to the Prophet Muhammad, nevertheless the interpretation of this teaching has always varied on the basis of different formulations of Islamic schools of thought. In this way, *fiqih* is always relative and open to rejuvenation and re-interpretation depending on the context. Mulia has proposed a more context-based and gender-conscious interpretation of Sharia (Mulia, *Swara Rahima*, 2006). At present a more gendered interpretation of Sharia has been proposed by a number of Muslim feminists who consequently have risked the accusation of being infidels and faced severe *fatwas*. For example, Siti Musdah Mulia and team's proposed re-construction of the Muslim Marriage and Family Law, known as the CLD (Counter Legal Draft), has been seen as violating the Islamic law (Kompilasi Hukum Islam 1974), resulting in the rejection of the proposal by MUI (the Council of Indonesian Ulema). Mulia further suggests that better propagation and circulation of "education on Sharia Law" is urgently needed, so that people have the opportunity to reflect upon it critically, contextually, and progressively, and not merely accepting the interpretation from conservative Ulemas (Mulia in *Swara Rahima*, 2006)..

Two Muhammadiyah sister wings organizations have played an important progressive role at the civil and social cultural level. Aisyiyah and Nasyiatul Aisyiyah have played significant role in transforming the meaning of womanhood since the fall of Sukarno's presidency in 1965 (Syamsiyatun, 2007). Through their activities they have enabled women to extend the role from the domestic sphere into the public sphere. In practice, many women in Muhammadiyah organizations have been self empowered to transform and negotiate the Islamic ideology they profess and the values they receive outside of Islamic teaching.

Transformations are apparent in the rejuvenation of *jilbab* in a form different from that usually being worn by women of Arab, and the rare practice of polygamy within Muhammadiyah circles. Muhammadiyah's daughters are well-empowered at the practical, socio-cultural level, while NU's daughters are well-informed at the theological level. What is lack from both of these two movements is women's active participation at the political level. Gendered political movements in Indonesia's Islamic organizations have been very low.

Male domination over the interpretation of Sharia has engendered severe shortage of women in leadership positions compared to the number of men. Women's further representation in the political arena is severely limited with women's representation in Parliament which is based more on "charity" than on "political will" (Hasyim in *Swara Rahima*, 2006). The positions are mostly related to their husband's position either in the parliament or governmental bodies. Lack of women representation was addressed in the establishment of KOMNAS Perempuan (National Commission on Violence against Women), which was established in 1998 in response to the mass rape of Indonesian-Chinese women in Jakarta during the "May 1998 Tragedy".

9. Mainstreaming Gender

The apparent lack of gender equity in leadership positions within the political arena does not mean that women's resistance at the civil society level has not continued to voice and develop. Women activists have been vocal in their criticism of Sharia Bylaws. Many urban-based women have rejected them along with other district regulations, such as *Perda Anti Maksiat dan Anti Pelacuran*, which apparently violates the rights of female workers to access economic activities after 10 pm. They criticize as well the forced wearing of *jilbab* for female civil servants, arguing that such a decision should be based on civil liberty and not on state's coercion. State's coercion reverberates violence against women's right. Women have not been granted rights to choose uniform or way of dress up in line with their choice of identity. New district regulations are expected to enhance women's rights and not merely deteriorate women's rights.

Detailed inquiries into the many districts regulations and Sharia Bylaws have been conducted thoroughly by R. Husna Mulya, coordinator of Law Reform, and her team from KOMNAS Perempuan (Mulya, 2006). The team found that many Sharia Bylaws had not been intended to be discriminatory in their formal legal content. Lack of legal knowledge and legal illiteracy rather resulted in weak and multi-interpretational legal drafting. The formulations of district regulations therefore need to be accompanied by experienced legal advisers who are expected to be well-informed and well-versed with respect to the higher national and international laws. Legal experts who are going to help formulating future regulations are expected to be familiar with the policy issued by State Ministry for Women Empowerment, known as gender-mainstreaming strategy as policy realization from CEDAW (Convention on the Elimination of all Forms of Discrimination against Women).

By considering various factors behind the formulation of Sharia Bylaws, thorough and meticulous assistances on gender-sensitive law formulations might change the lot of Indonesian women. At the social civil level Indonesian women are highly empowered, whereas at the political and policy level women's voices are unfortunately left behind and poorly represented. The need for gender-based interpretation of the prevalent grand *fiqih* needs to be revisited and rejuvenated to meet the ideals of Indonesian Islam. The state thus has enormous task to ascertain that the plural and multivocal interpretations celebrated within Islamic tradition will do no harm against women's rights and minorities' rights.

Chapter VI
Muhammadiyah at the Crossroad: between Sacred Text and Pragmatism

1. Introduction: Interviews Charted

Chapter VI is written to provide the current picture of Muhammadiyah's English Departments, where I conducted field research for two months, from mid July until mid September 2007. I delineated three distinct interview groups representing three distinct organisational groups and sets of opinions within Muhammadiyah. The first group was composed of members of the Board of Muhammadiyah Education Yogyakarta (Diktilitbang Yogyakarta, hereafter DIKTI). I argue that these board members can be seen as 'ideology initiators' due to the power and influence they exercise over the curriculum from the highest level. Questions posed to this group dealt with Muhammadiyah's policy relating to the position of English departments. In recent decades there has been a massive growth in the establishment of English departments within Muhammadiyah universities. I wanted to investigate whether this trend was triggered by Muhammadiyah's commitment—inspired by an Islamic educational ideology—to expand its horizon by gaining greater knowledge of other cultural values, in this case Western ones. Or whether the establishment of English departments was a more pragmatic decision related to the increasing market demand for English. In Muhammadiyah's Education faculties, English departments, usually, have the largest enrolment of student compared to other departments.

The second group of interviews was with the people who execute the curriculum (or 'curriculum executors'), namely the lecturing staff who teach in the English departments in Muhammadiyah universities. I chose two Muhammadiyah universities that are Universitas Muhammadiyah Surakarta (UMS) and Universitas Muhammadiyah Ahmad Dahlan (UAD), both are located in Central Java. In the first instance, I wanted to configure their general perception of the current English literature canon. I was specifically interested to know how they defined this canon, and what they believed should be taught to students. Is the canon only comprised of western works of literature that become a "must" recipe or could it draw from other resources, such as postcolonial writers. I asked their opinion of Muslim literature, specifically literature written by women writers from Muslim countries. I was curious to know how they tackled problems dealing with the clash of values experienced by students in their classes. Many of the questions were inspired by my own experience of teaching English literature at UMS. I found that much of the time, I had to bridge students' Islamic cosmology and the western literature that they were asked to read. This was not an easy job.

The third type of interview was with students from USM or 'curriculum acceptors'. I selected students in terms of four categories, that is, those who were in second year, third year and fourth year, as well as those doing their final paper on literature. I asked all students in my sample the same set of questsions. My focus was to investigate the level of horizon the students have connecting with the current western canon contained in the curriculum. Besides investigating their perception of the western values contained in the current canon, I examined as well their perception of the different gender constructions found within the framework of Islamic cosmology and those in the works of literature they read. I wanted to know how their Islamic and Muhammadiyah education consolidated with the so-called secular education they received in these English departments.

2. Between Ideology and Pragmatism: The Establishment of English Departments

Among its 168 institutions of higher education, Muhammadiyah owns around 32 universities, in which 16 English departments were been established during Suharto's presidency (1966-1998). Muhammadiyah is known widely in Indonesia and this in part is due to its extensive educational network, as well as its other health and other social services. The contribution of Muhammadiyah to the education sector in Indonesia amounts to around 10 percent of the total sector and 6 percent of the higher education sector. It has established around 18.000 senior and elementary schools as well as 168 higher education institutions. This number is not static as from year to year, more and more Muhammadiyah education institutions are established. At the same time, many Muhammadiyah schools have closed down due to demographic falls in certain regions in Indonesia. Nevertheless, the rate of establishment of Muhammadiyah schools and universities is, higher than the rate of closure. Muhammadiyah educational institutions are considered as an additional source for the education of Indonesians and helps meet the shortfall in the state-owned educational institutions in many regions.

The large number of Muhammadiyah schools and universities, however, is not accompanied by a qualified and solid management. Even the number of educational institutions will vary according to each leader. This is caused by the unprofessional management of data within the Muhammadiyah Education Board (DIKTI), which is mainly due to a lack of human resources at the leadership level. The growth of Muhammadiyah's educational sector is, most of the time, happening at the grassroots level, which causes problems at the leadership level where there is no human resources to manage this mushrooming growth.

Apart from ineffective management at the highest level, Muhammadiyah faces two additional major problems. The first relates to the quality of education within Muhammadiyah educational institutions. In Indonesia there is a board of accreditation that measures the quality of educational institutions, called as BAN-PT (Badan Akreditasi Nasional Perguruan Tinggi Perguruan Tinggi). BAN produces certificates of accreditation to each university. Only around one quarter of Muhammadiyah universities have received accreditation from BAN. Muhammadiyah has spent its energy in increasing the quality of its educational institution by fostering a more advanced high education management system. Secondly, the demands from the Muslim community for high quality Islamic education have challenged Muhammadiyah to design more progressive and modern approaches to teaching Islam as one of its products, in addition to secular subjects.

The lack of effective management within Muhammadiyah has led to the creation of several umbrella organisations within Muhammadiyah designed to tackle aspects of this broader problem. DIKTI was established to function as an umbrella organisation for all Muhammadiyah universities. Yet DIKTI has never been given the human resources required to fulfil this function. Effective communication between Muhammadiyah universities and DIKTI is hindered by the lack of human resources in DIKTI. In fact, Muhammadiyah universities are better off than DIKTI in terms of their human resources as DIKTI was established only recently when most of Muhammadiyah universities were already well-established.

Lack of effective management is also a problem faced by Indonesia's education sector at present. Poor quality education management is caused mainly by the ineffectiveness of management and a lack of qualified human resources. The other problem facing Indonesia's education sector is the uneven and unequal distribution of educational resources across Indonesia. In an archipelago comprising of more than 13.000 islands and no guaranteed quality of transportation, geographical obstacles are significant stumbling blocks to achieving equity of access.

During interviews with DIKTI members in Yogyakarta, I found that the main problems with management were not only caused by a lack of human resources but also the lack of systematized data coming from Muhammadiyah universities around the archipelago. Prof Edi Suandi Hamid (Head of DIKTI) said that updated data play an important role in their decision support system which in many cases functions as a support system to future planning. Most of the time new schools and universities did not report their current data. Besides a lack of awareness of the importance of this data, DIKTI itself is a relatively new sub division within the organization of Muhammadiyah. He commented shortly that the DIKTI was 'better late than never' into existence.

After posing questions on the internal management of the system of Muhammadiyah organization, I moved onto questions on ideology. I was interested to know whether the establishment of English departments was mainly derived from the philosophy of Islamic education itself, that is, that it is necessary to know other cultural values, such as those from the West; or whether their establishment was mainly due to pragmatic considerations and in particular to the growing market demand from prospective students that Muhammadiyah teach English. The discussion of pragmatism here also relates to debates during the last decade as to whether Muhammadiyah should establish English department at the university level, or simply English courses at the informal level. English courses are mushrooming and now widespread throughout Indonesia. Even, Muhammadiyah kindergartens have considered introducing English classes—a development that astonished my college in Muhammadiyah University. In many Muhammadiyah universities, the English department is the department which is most popular and has the biggest number of students compared to other departments. The increasing number of students, of course, means the increasing amount of financial revenue.

In considering this fact, I had intense discussions during my interviews, with members of DIKTI, university leaders and university lecturers. The answers given to the previous question were variable. At the leaders' level, it was revealed that the establishment of English departments was derived from the philosophy of Islamic education to know and learn other cultural values. They mentioned three popular hadith (prophetic teachings): "*Uthlubul ilma wa lau bi tsin*", seek knowledge though you have to go to as far as China. The second hadith: *Tholabul ilmi faridhatun a la kuli muslimin wal muslimatin*, to get knowledge or to study is mandatory obligation for Muslim male and female. Third hadith, *Tholabul Ilmi minal mahdi ila lahdi*, the obligation to seek knowledge from the cradle until laying in the grave. From these three hadith Muhammadiyah leaders saw that the establishment of English departments was necessary and even obligatory from the perspective of Islamic education philosophy.

The answer from the university level was paradoxically different from the leaders of Muhammadiyah. During my interview with Prof Bambang Setiaji, the Rector of UMS, I found an interesting answer that, basically the establishment of the English department was derived from the need of society to learn English. Besides meeting a growing market demand, the English department was established in Muhammadiyah as a complimentary program to the state-owned universities. According to the Indonesian Government, state-owned universities alone can not meet all the market demand for English instruction throughout Indonesia. This is in accordance with the government's decision to open its economic sector to the global arena. For the government, English has become inseparable to the need to keep pace with other countries.

At the faculty level, the answer varied as well. The faculty saw that the existence of the English department was a necessity as it has become the only feasible form of financial revenue in the past decade. In UMS as well as

UAD, English departments in the faculty of Teacher Training and Letters, were becoming the sole and largest source of financial revenue. As a "rich department", as they usually called it, the English department has six times more students than other departments. In the past decade, the English department in UMS received around 600 prospective students per semester. And the financial revenue drawn from students' fee was around one million Rupiah per semester per student. Basically the English department now supports the financial revenue at the university-level as well. This is where the pragmatism of Muhammadiyah lies, with other Islamic universities, relatively new and small, copying this strategy to keep the university financially viable.

Muhammadiyah's basic educational philosophy as expressed by leaders within the universities and DIKTI shows a positive appraisal of the importance of knowing other cultural values. This contrasts with the vision and mission stated in each of the department's curriculum, where it is clearly shown that the establishment of the English departments was mainly done in a spirit of *dakwah Islamiyah*, that is, in a deeply ingrained spirit of the propagation of Islam. During my visits to the two Muhammadiyah universities, UMS & UAD, I found that this spirit blanketed the process of teaching-learning. Since 2000 both universities have imposed an obligation on female students to wear the head veil. This informal law, was, uniquely, not mentioned at any formal laws. Before 2000 female students with no headscarf were still allowed to join classes. There were even a good many female teachers and lecturers who wore no headscarf. The gender lens has been unfortunately ommitted with respect to making this informal headveil obligatory law. Female students who happen not to wear a headscarf are banned from entering into classes. They are told that they can only join the class when they dress appropriately, meaning wear the headscarf. And female lecturers are advised to wear the headscarf. The process is practiced peacefully and there is almost no physical threat to those who wear no headscarf. The public regime, however, imposes an unforgettable experience, stigmatizing those wearing no head veil as morally un-Islamic and unacceptable to the community. It has become more demoralizing for those who feel forced to wear a headscarf, even though they do not wish to, who then pull the headscarf off soon after they leave the campus.

The movement of dakwah Islamiyah is mostly propagated through informal situations, such as through Islamic Youth Mentoring, which is propagated and organized by groups of students inspired by Salafi and Ikhawanul Muslimin movements. This student-led movement has crept into the higher levels of Muhammadiyah of time, as these students graduate and taken on teaching and administrative positions within the university. It is almost impossible now for female students and lecturers who did not wish to wear the head veil entering the uni without a head veil. According to one of my interviews with a UMS lecturer, I found that organizations which exert a strong influence over students stem from PKS (Partai Keadilan Sejahtera—one of Indonesia's influential Islamist Parties). This Islamist party has established a formidable cadre recruitment processe through its youth-based organisations in most universities and senior high school in Indonesia. The conservatism in Muhammadiyah of late is mainly influenced by its own students who have been highly motivated by dakwah Islamiyah. Though the attitudes of Muhammadiyah leaders are mainly pragmatist, logical and progressive, the spirit of ultra conservatism is on the rise amongst Muhammadiyah students. Details of students' Islamic cosmology were discussed in the previous Chapter, along with a detailed landscape of a heightened consciousness of the need of Muslims to unite in the spirit of Brotherhood and to practice 'kaffah'/total Islam.

Drawing upon these differences, it is clear that there is a generation gap within Muhammadiyah. The perception of Islam of the older generation is different from the younger generation. Quite recently, Muhammadiyah leaders have swept away any activities on campus done in the name of PKS. For example, in 2007 Muhammadiyah issued a decree to protect its assets from being used for Islamist political practice and agendas. The tension between Muhammadiyah and the PKS is a tension of ideology as well as a tension of generation. From an ideological point of view, Muhammadiyah believes that Dakwah Islamiyah is best achieved on the basis of social and educational services to the *Ummah*, while PKS seeks Dakwah Islamiyah through the political arena, and in pursuing this has used Muhammadiyah assets a good many times. Though Muhammadiyah leaders have sought to limit such activities and the use of Muhammadiyah campus as a site for PKS political ambitions, the mentality of most of the students who I interviewed was still in the spirit of propagating Islam through political means, a position which Muhammadiyah has openly rejected. Genealogically Muhammadiyah is older than PKS and was established as a non-political organization in 1912 under Dutch colonization. At that time the Dutch only allowed Islamic social and educational organizations. In contrast, PKS was born in the euphoria of the burgeoning of Indonesian democracy in 1998. Most PKS leaders come from within the Muhammadiyah circle. From the organizational level, PKS is very pragmatic. Though its ideology is static and conservative, its members and leaders exercise, most of the time, a pragmatic approach. Both Muhammadiyah and PKS are similar in their ideological construction, which is conservative, yet very pragmatic at the practical level.

There is an apparent split personality within Muhammadiyah, as one half seeks to hold on to its ideology on the one hand, while the other half faces the burgeoning globalization, on the other. Its approach to Islamic cosmology, emphasises the puritan and textual, yet on a daily basis in line with practical reality, it adheres to pragmatism. While Islamic teaching is still taught in a traditional way, the secular subjects flood with an unstoppable force the universities. This has resulted in a cultural clash for many students in their classroom interactions. In the morning they receive a rigid textual interpretation of Quran-Hadith, where there is no space given to the use of creative and critical skills. Then in the afternoon they receive secular-humanist texts, like a piece of Western literature, where they are expected to show criticality and creativity. Lecturers of UMS & UAD reported this cultural clash without being able to understanding the root of the problem or identify why this could occur.

3. Studies on Islam and Muhammadiyah: Transforming the Cognitive to the Affective

The cultural clash was caused first and foremostly by the introduction of a program of Study of Islam and Muhammadiyah (hereafter, SIM) to be taken by Muhammadiyah students in the first three years of study. In the UMS Curriculum for the 2005/2006 academic year, there were a series of Islamic-related subjects introduced across five semesters, namely, *Islamic Studies I* in the first semester; *Islamic Studies II* in the second semester (accompanied by *Indonesian State Ideology*); *Kemuhammadiyahan* in the third Semester; *Islamic Studies III* in the fourth semester, followed by *Indonesian Civics* in the fifth semester. One of the lecturers of SIM whom I interviewed stated that these subjects were introduced to because the curriculum had so far failed to transform students' understanding of the values of Islam, especially the content taught in the class. It was triggered by students' failure to apply Islamic values in daily life, as could be seen by the absence of Islam in most social processes and the deterioration of social interaction. For young people, throwing trash everywhere—to mention one of the many problems identified—is not considered sinful, although in terms of their ritual behaviour many of these people were basically religious. The current curriculum, I was told, was largely based on the former curriculum made in the Suharto era (1965-1998), where religious subjects were politicised in the sense that they were taught in order to maintain the stability of the state. Religious subjects were thus treated in a more rational manner rather than seen from an affective approach. This resulted in a massive amount of incorrect social behaviour and led to a situation where people may be personally religious but socially irreligious.

Since educational reforms in 2003, religious subjects, such as Islam, have been subject to open criticism. Much of the severest criticism has chartered how Islamic teaching has been unable in tackle social ills such as corruption. The most corrupted department is even the Ministry of Religious Affairs. This information shocked the public who demanded reforms to the curriculum for religious subjects in state-owned universities and schools as well as in Muhammadiyah. Indonesians felt that the crisis of morality was caused partly by the failure of religious education. The 2006 National Curriculum, Permendiknas No. 22, 23, and 24/2006, stated that the standard of religious education shall aim at creating Indonesians with high moral standards, that is, who are smart, honest, just, disciplined, show *tasamuh*—tolerance, and keep harmony between the personal and the social.

The present Minister of Religious Affairs, Maftuh Basuni, has said that religious education has no social function as it only develops cognitive aspect than affective. He said that it is better to implement religious values than learn those doctrines by heart. Religious teachings should focus on how religious values are ingrained into students' way of thinking and behaving personally as well as socially. Intellectual verbalism has no correlation with social morality. Students need not only *hikmah*/conscience and *mau'idhatul hasanah*, but also good role models, a good methodology, and a better teaching-learning atmosphere. He argued that religious education shouldl be transformed to cohere with the present social-cultural-political problems Indonesia faces. Values of togetherness, multiculturalism, and plurality could enhance dialogues among students from different religious background. Religious teaching is still an important subject in Indonesia, as the Indonesian state insists that all citizens have one of six official religions. Given the plural reality of Indonesia, the teaching of religious doctrines should be enhanced to promote the values of social integrity rather than differences. Unfortunately, the teaching of religious doctrines prescribed in the various religious subjects within schools has merely sharpened the sense of difference between religions in Indonesia. This resulted in the massive social fractures in the post-1998 era up to the present. The focus of religious instruction should be directed at improving *tasamuh*/tolerance. Indonesia's multicultural background forces religious education to not only performs formalistic-ritual education at the personal level, but also to implement the essence of religion at the social level.

Despite this lack of religiosity at the social level—exacerbated by the doctrinal teaching in the formal education system, there is also a lack of internalisation of religiosity at the academic level. Students view that cheating during the test is not sinful, while they may be, at the same time, ritually disciplined. Islamic teaching has not been rejuvenated in the modern context to meet problems, which specifically occur in the present era. Throwing garbage is not sinful, say for example, while they may be, once again, ritually disciplined. They may feel sinful and guilty when they miss one of the five daily prayers, for example, while consider that cheating in a test and throwing garbage on the street are not sinful. The problems with this then became acute when students consider bad behaviour that is not connected to Islamic ritual to be unimportant. The failure of Islamic religious teaching is that it only focussed on the theological level and forgot to teach and implement an ethical orientation to daily life and social engagement.

The doctrinal approach on Islamic teaching has also in turn influenced the way students perceive other subjects, which are categorized as "secular subjects" by the Muhammadiyah Board, such as English. Students perceive secular subjects to be irreligious; it is only for the world of the living. They endure a split personality, meaning that they are ritualistically disciplined—that is, personally religious—while at the same time socially irreligious. The epistemological construction of learning in Islam is that learning and studying subjects outside of the religious teaching is important and Islamic as well. Religious affection is rich at the personal level yet short at the social level. It is no wonder that the level of corruption in the government is so extensive in Indonesia, a problem that may be caused by the failure of religious teaching within formal education. The cognitive approach to teaching Islam as part of formal education met with the spirit of pragmatism in Muhammadiyah universities, where some subjects were separated as "Islamic teachings" while others were commodified as: "secular subjects". Sacred texts are not approached contextually and hermeneutically, but in a textual way where meaning is cut off from the context in which Islam was born. On the other hand, anything Arabic is considered Islamic, regardless of both its cultural difference from Indonesian and its social fabrication. Muhammadiyah's recent swing to the Right and ultra conservatism has deteriorated the way students perceive Islam in relation to secular subjects, such as English.

The trend amongst students is now to discuss the establishment of Khilafah Islamiyah, an Islamist state, where secular values are replaced by pure Islam. Students tend to forget their own heritage as Asians, as Indonesians. They change their names to that of an Arabic warrior because they feel ashamed of their Indonesian name. Change to everyday conversation starts when they cluster in their cell-group-community. If, previously, they just said "hari ulang tahun" for birthday, now they use the Arabic term, "milad". In a similar vein they call other girls "Akhwat" and boys "Ikhwan". These trends influence their perceptions of their own histories and the histories of their families as Javanese, for example. They chose to connect directly to the history of Muhammad, and specifically focus on the epoch of Muhammad's life during wartime. The use of the names of Muslim warriors has become a trend in internet communication. Anti Western sentiment is also a characteristic of this. It is now much more difficult to teach students English literature, than five years ago. They are, however, pragmatists as well. They view English as "merely" a means of communication and seek to ignore the cultural values behind it. They like, for example, internet, or using Yahoo email, while curse the advancement of technology as an evil mechanism. This split personality acutely influences the way they think at the academic level. There is an apparent rise of ultra conservatism in Muhammadiyah students. Islamic teaching with Muhammadiyah has not helped the way students perceive academic achievement as Islamic. The current doctrinal approach has exacerbated the situation.

Two of the main foundations in the religious subjects in Muhammadiyah universities are the Quran and Hadith. These two texts are sacred to the Muslim community. The way the texts are formulated in the curriculum and taught in the class preserves this sense of sacredness. Texts are introduced to students immune from an historical approach. Students are encouraged to accept the texts as having descended from heaven and to have no connection whatsoever with the history of Muhammad in the Arabic peninsula. The teaching of the Quran, specifically through rote-learning, implies that students are expected only to learn it by heart which then forces them to approach it uncritically. There is no way students can critically evaluate these texts. These texts are immune from any critical analysis and should be treated as "text" per se.

In one of my interviews with students in their second year, I posed questions on several issues which have been interpreted differently by Imam in different Muslim countries around the world. One of these issues was polygamy. Students expressed quite innocently, without pausing to think, that polygamy is preferable as the Quran stated so clearly in the chapter entitled 'An Nisa', verse 03. In the verse, the Prophet Mohammad says that a man could marry up to four wives. What these students did not mention was that this statement is followed by other statements on the importance of "justice", which has been used by some scholars to argue that polygamy is not preferred because it would be impossible for most men to show true justice to all their wives. A hermeneutical approach however was rarely used. Moreover, hardly any historical approach to the text is exercised in their religious subjects. This is a great loss, in my perspective, as students perceive Muhammad's era to be similar to their own. If an historical approach were used then they could begin to appreciate why polygamy could be permissable in the eyes of the Prophet in the 7th century AD but not today. While students are introduced to the history and life of Muhammad, this is not used to enable them to capture the historical context of behind a particular verse in the Quran and Hadith. Historical approaches to Quran are only studied by students who specialising in Islamic studies, but not by those who are from secular departments, such as English. As noted above, the students then treat the Quran and Hadith as "text" per se.

By perceiving that the text in the verses as texts only, students fail to connect present-day phenomena with the context of the text in the 7th century AD. They treated the text as holy and beyond criticism. Similar cases happen as well to the history or the figure of Muhammad. Denmark cartoons or Salman Rushdie's Satanic Verses are considered an insult. Students fail to address these two phenomena from an academic level. In several interviews, students expressed their anger while unable to give a rational explanation for their fury. When I asked further why they decided to react in this way and who mostly influenced their decision, they said that it was mostly due to the Imam. The role of the Imam in the Mosque played a significant role in moulding the identity of Muhammadiyah students. When I posed the same questions to the DIKTI members and to lecturers, surprisingly, they said that they did not have a problem with these phenomena. For them, academic life in Muhammadiyah Universities should be enhanced by critical engagement. They saw that phenomena could occur within any religion and the role of university was to strengthen the rational response of the religious community in order to manage such issues.

From this we could conclude that there is an apparent gap between the understandings of the professor at Muhammadiyah universities and the Imams on the Muhammadiyah board itself. It shows that at a practical level, Muhammadiyah universities have an advanced code of conduct in managing issues related to Islam. Most important point is its criticality. While at the ideological level is still rigid and conservative in handling cases related to Islam. It needs to be understood that there is no Priesthood/Imamhood in Muhammadiyah as a modern Islamic organization. The power of the Imam is not as powerful as in Iran, for example. The Imam's opinion does not necessarily represent the organization of Muhammadiyah as a whole. Other faces of Muhammadiyah can be seen vividly through its educational and health sectors. A clear example here is the case of HIV/AIDS patients in Muhammadiyah hospitals. On on occasion, the Imam said that HIV patients should not be treated as HIV/AIDS is one of the most sinful types of illness. They interpreted this epidemic as satanic and sinful. However, the professors and the doctors in Muhammadiyah hospitals posed a counter argument. Although there was a high degree of contestation over the treatment of HIV/AIDS patients, in the end the professors and doctors won the day and patients with AIDS continue to be treated at Muhammadiyah hospitals (PKU). Muhammadiyah educational and health sectors have proven to be the most rational compared to the ideological holders within Muhammadiyah bodies. Still the Imams play a significant role in defining Muhammadiyah morality at the national level. In the current discussion it is important to note how they moulded the landscape of Studies of Islam and Muhammadiyah (SIM) in the educational sector.

4. "The Current Western Canon" is still sacred

The previous interview material, focussing on the implementation of the curriculum as well as class interactions in Islamic Studies in the English department, was meant to uncover problems experienced by Muslim students in encountering English literature. The following interviews dealing more directly on the practice and process of teaching and learning in English literature classes. The first questions posed were on the notion and definition of an English literary canon addressed to the teachers of literature in the English department of UMS and UAD. I was interested to know how lecturers perceive the English literary canon, including their ideas on which works should be considered as part of the canon.

The most frequent answer to this question related foremostly to the ethnicity of white western writers who write the works of literature. Despite an emphasis on ethnicity, geographical location played a key role as well, as writers coming from Britain or America were considered to belong to the canon. New writers from different ethnic backgrounds and geographical locations outside of British and America were still considered outside or foreign to their memory of the so-called "English literary canon". Their memory of the English literary canon was of writers firstly, who came from these two countries and secondly, were taught as "literary" in the western academy. New postcolonial writers, for example, were also catagorised as unfamiliar to them. If, for example, students proposed a work of literature coming from outside the present prescribed canon in the curriculum, he or she would be directed to turn back to the list of writers proposed by the English department.

"Literariness" was defined in very restricted terms as well. British and American literature from contemporary writers who originated from a non-white or minority ethnic group was once again found to be foreign to the present definition of Muhammadiyah curriculum. Works from writers such as Salman Rushdie, for example, were not being placed in the canon. Works coming from postcolonial areas such as the prolific Indian writers or Caribbean were still foreign to them. Literature coming from, areas of British settlement, such as Australia and Canada, were also not well-regarded. Muhammadiyah curriculum defined the canon as falling into one of three categories of literature only, that is, fiction, poetry and drama. Works such as memoires or travelogues by particular writers were not considered to be literary. At UMS, the concept of literariness over the past ten years has been largely defined by one textbook, written by Sylvan Barnet, Morton Bermen & William Burton. Their *Introduction to Literature: Fiction, Poetry, Drama* (1963) has been set as required reading for many years (Kurikulum UMS 2005/2006, 2005: 229).

The list of poetry writers in the subject *Poetry* required to be read by students and prescribed in the curriculum has not changed either in the last ten years. They are Robert Frost, A.E. Housman, John Donne, Shakespeare, Langston Hughes, John Boyle O'Rilley, Robert Browning, W.H. Auden, Emily Dickinson, John Keats, and Dylan Thomas (*Ibid*, 242-243). In this way works from earlier writers are regarded as part of a 'sacred canon' that is not so different from the way in which the present Muhammadiyah curriculum approaches Islamic teaching based on exlusively on the Quran and Hadith. Students must consult with lecturers before drawing on works in their final paper which are not on the prescribed list given to students. Hence, new works outside of the canon which may meet a concept of literariness are not recognised.

This approach also happens in the subject *Fiction*. Although students are introduced to a variety of fictional forms, such as the short story, novel and novella; as well as to non-fiction, such as satire, diary, autobiography, nature writing, the works exemplified in the curriculum are restricted to a limited number. The list of fiction writers in the curriculum are: Flannery O'Connor, Ernest Hemingway, D.H. Lawrence, and Richard Wright (*Ibid*, 244-245). It is clear that the prescribed texts come exclusively from British-American literature, while those outside of the Muhammadiyah defined canon are not considered. In the subject *Drama* the list of writers are as follows: George Bernard Shaw, Henrik Ibsen, Oscar Wilde, and William Shakespeare (Ibid, 245). The above subjects have as their aim to introduce students to a range of poetry/fiction/drama and to help them with their appreciation of these forms of literature. The subjects are designed to support students' major competence. The Muhammadiyah curriculum is designed to provide students with a valuable reading experience, one which not only supports their language (English) competence but permits them to develop greater appreciation of cultural diversity as well. Students are also expected to understand the variety of the different genre as well as understand the aesthetic elements of the genre. The previous background for the subjects and expected competence in the curriculum shows Muhammadiyah's openness and desire to learn other cultural values outside of Islam. However, the practical classroom interaction as revealed through the prescribed canon shows an inherent limitation in terms of this desire to understand western cultural values. Western cultural values are merely represented by a limited number of writers coming from limited social and cultural backgrounds.

Students within the English department at UMS also study two new subjects, designed to enhance their understanding of English literature, these are, *History and Background of Western Culture* and *History of English and American Literature*. These subjects have only been introduced in the last two years at the request of lecturers and in response to findings based on classroom interactions that showed that students were having great difficulty grasping the different cultural background of western literature. *History of Western Culture* aims to support students to better understand the English language and thus enhance their major competence. By taking this subject students are expected to increase their understanding of the background of Western culture in order to develop a deeper understanding of the values underlying western thought and the English language in particular. Topics introduced in the subjects are as follows: 1. Greek mythology: the greater gods, 2. Greek mythology: the lesser gods, 3. Greek schools of thoughts, 4. Roman mythology, 5. Christianity: doctrine and practice, 6. Christianity: history, 8. Renaissance and the Revival of Helenic thought, 9. Scientific revolution, 10. Linear thoughts and Mass production, 11. Materialism, 12. Democracy and individual freedom, 13. Marxism, 14. Pragmatism and Philanthropist perspective, 15. Women's liberation (*Ibid*, 252-253).

Another important subject introduced to students at the third year is *History of English and American Literature*. This subject aims to introduce students to the history of English and American literature. The subject is designed to support students' major competence and students are expected to understand the history of English and American literature, which contributes to the deeper understanding of English literature (*Ibid*, 254). The topics discussed are: 1. English literature: the old period (450-1066); 2. English literature: the Middle English period (1066-1485); 3. English literature: the Elizabethan Age (1485-1603); 4. English literature: the seventeenth century; 5. English literature: the eighteenth century; 6. English literature: the early nineteenth century; 7. English literature: the late nineteenth century; 8. English literature: the twentieth century; 9. American literature: the colonial period; 10. American literature: the rise of a national literature; 11. American literature: the American renaissance; 12. American literature: the civil war and the gilded era; 13. American literature: the era of realism and naturalism; 14. American literature: the twentieth century (*Ibid*, 254).

The English department of UMS is the only Muhammadiyah University to introduce these two important bridging subjects for students. This is unfortunate as these subjects' help students grasp a different cultural value from their own and provide an important and necessary bridge during classroom interaction. Although the history introduced to the students takes them well into the twentieth century, the works introduced are limited. There are for example no works by postcolonial writers from the twenty first century. After several interviews with lecturers at UMS, it became apparent that they were unfamiliar with this so-called English literature as well. When I asked them what level of flexibility they had to change or refresh the canon, they said that they had this flexibility but that the difficulty they faced in accessing new works of literature coming from English speaking countries made such reform difficult to realize. Lecturers at both UMS & UAD, said that changes to the canon were "possible"—meaning that they have every right to do so—but difficult due to scarcity of resources.

When I visited the libraries of UMS and UAD, the lack of a collection made the potential list of works of literature that could be read by students limited as well. Lack of information on the works coming from new writers was one of the major problems faced by these Muhammadiyah universities. Besides technical problems in accessing the new works, lack of epistemological definition over the terms literary and literariness played a major role in influencing lecturers' decision as to whether particular works could be included in the canon or not. Presently, lecturers' epistemological construction of the English canon was restricted to works of literature that come from Britain and the Unites States of American, and did not include any works after the mid twentieth century.

When I contacted the library management regarding this matter, they reported that the library provides every possible opportunity for staff to order new material but that this has not been responded actively. Lack of communication between the library and the English department in both Muhammadiyah universities exacerbated the scarcity of new resources for the students. Financial support in allocation of books and materials are abundant but those who make use of these services are rare, as reported by the Rector of UMS. He said that it is mostly due to the lack of a reading culture within Muhammadiyah universities. This influenced their performance in the field of research and academic achievement, both amongst lecturers and students. UMS, for example, has paid for the *opac* library system, a service that is regarded as expensive by local universities in Indonesia, but the academic usage has not been maximal, even rare. This lack of a culture of reading contribted to their limited perceptions of what counts as literariness and the acccepted canon. This is why they still regard the present canon as sacred, why new works were considered foreign by them, and why the concept of literariness remained highly influenced by an out-of-date academic atmosphere.

Fortunately, though the range of works being read and studied was limited, students were introduced to the following Subjects: *Literary Research Method* (LRM), *Literary Criticism* (LC), and *Seminar on Literature* (SL) (*Ibid*, 255-259). LRM aims at introducing students to the different concepts as well as approaches used in literary studies and at helping students with the necessary steps and procedures in conducting a literary study. Students are expected to be able to prepare a literary research proposal following their introduction to the following topics: 1. Introduction to a literary study, its difference from literature, and the relation between literature and other studies; 2. the characteristics of the study of literature; 3. background, problem statement, literature review; 4. data-collecting techniques, note-taking, data-analysing techniques; 5. structuralism and structural analysis; 6. heuristic and hermeneutic interpretation; 7. the sociological approach; 8. generic structuralist approach; 9. Marxist analysis; 10. Gender/feminist analysis; 11. Existentialist analysis; 12. semiotic analysis; 13. Psychoanalytic analysis (*Ibid*, 255). The last five approaches were only introduced in the last two years. When I interviewed one UMS lecturer, M. Thoyibi, MA, he said that it was a bit difficult for students to accept Marxist and Feminist approaches. He said that students find it difficult to accept a Marxist approach due to the trauma experienced by Indonesians during the Suharto era in which the Communist Party was banned in 1965, so much so that Marxist terminology is always connected to the Indonesian Communist Party. He sought to overcome this problem by introducing students to the history of Marxism in Europe, especially, in order to detach any connection with the Communist Party in Indonesia.

The approach most difficult for Muhammadiyah students to appreciate is that of feminist approaches to literature. Feminism has an extremely bad reputation among devout Muslim in Muhammadiyah, especially amongst its clergy. This then influences the way students in Muhammadiyah perceive feminism. Feminism is seen as antagonistic to Islamic ritual practice such as the wearing of the head veil and the practice of polygamy. Muhammadiyah's appreciation of women's roles in the public is quite progressive, when one looks at the number and achievements of Muhammadiyah women in public office, but its theological construct of womanhood is highly influenced by a textualist interpretation of the Quran and Hadith, one that is unable to separate the position of women from their socio-cultural position in the Arabic peninsula in the era of Prophet Muhammad. In Muhammadiyah universities, for example, female students can apply to study technical engineering, something that might be restricted for female students in Saudi Arabia. In the social and practical landscape, the everyday life of Muhammadiyah female students is nearly similar to female students in the West, say in Germany. Their theological construct, however, is still dominated by textualist and conservative interpretations of the Quran-Hadith.

In interviews with male and female students, I asked whether women can become a leader. Astonishingly the answers from both female and male students were similar, that is, that "women should not become a leader, as the holy text say so". When I posed the following question: "If the choice is between an incompetent male leader and a capable female leader, which one would you choose?"; their answers were also surprising: the would chose the second capable leader, even though she was a woman. From several interviews, it was clear that the *das sollen* is that woman should not become a leader, while the *das sein* is that women could become a leader. This led me to question one of UMS lecturer who supervised students' final paper on the proportion of students who used a feminist approach in their research projects. The answer was an astounding 15 percent of students used feminist approach, and all within the last two years after the theory had been introduced into the curriculum. When I asked this lecturer what was the biggest problem facing such students, I was told the lack of materials, such as novels written by women, in the libraries. The lack of material had become a major barrier for these students in researching and writing their final paper. Lack of materials then unconsciously influences the way lecturers perceived and defined literariness especially connecting with the reading practices that are implemented in classroom interaction. The present western canon in the curriculum is apparently still sacred, as sacred as their holy texts.

5. Clash of Values, the Bridge is needed

After observing the data from the perspective of curriculum materials, I then moved to conduct interviews from the perspective of classroom practice. I was interested to know whether students experienced a clash of values when they came to their literature class after their Studies of Islam and Muhammadiyah (SIM). I captured an interesting doubt experienced by students studying western literature when they try to connect this with their Islamic belief. Around five years ago, I taught the subject *Prose*, and I asked students to go to the local theatre to watch the film *The Scarlet Letter*. Amazingly, nearly a good quarter of the students commented that the film was immoral and pornographic. In this research I sought to unravel this response and to assess whether such a phenomenon still existed after five years. The interviews showed clearly that students in their first few years at university were much more conservative than those doing their final paper. The younger students were more closed-minded. The interviews charted students in their fifth semester and showed that they were much more resistant to values coming from the West that they perceived in the prescribed works of literature they read. There was an apparent clash of cultures for students in the earlier stages of university study, when they were not yet in close contact to the prescribed works of literature. When I investigated the reason behind this resistance, they said that their religious beliefs had been contrastive to the Western values contained in the works of literature.

They saw the works as corrupt and secular. But when I asked why they kept reading them, they answered that it was because of the expectations of their lecturers. It was apparent that their reading was not for enjoyment, out of curiosity and due to real engagement, rather it was only to complete a task assigned by their lecturers. Students at this earlier stage were prone to a rigid interpretation of the holy texts, and this then influenced the way they perceived literature. One female student I interviewed even said that woman should not become a leader because woman is emotional in contrast to men who are rational: that is why Allah created man to lead the world. I asked these students why they thought in such a way. They replied that their Ulema had taught them in this way. I ran after them with more questions, to the female students, as to whether they were emotional or rational. Their answers were a bit gauche and unclear. It seems that female students have no confidence at all that they are indeed rational. This then influenced the way they read the texts: the apparent clash they experience within their own cosmology hardly permits them the ability to learn the goodness of other cultural values, especially coming from the West. Moreover, they were not truly engaged in the process of reading. It was obvious that their prejudice towards the West took priority in their reading of literary texts.

This led me to question teachers as to whether such clashes frequently happened in classroom interaction. They confirmed that they were indeed frequent amongst students in the earlier stages of studying literature. One of the lecturers, Bapak Nurhadi, even said, that most of the time, he had to bridge the students by mentioning verses in the holy sayings that stressed the importance of learning about other cultural values, and the need to respect these values as Prophet Muhammad did in the 7th century. The dramatic transition from Islamic studies in the morning to literary classes in the afternoon presented students in the earlier years with a great disjuncture of cultural horizons. It was like entering two totally different rooms at the same time, having to move from one horizon to the other with no advice on how to understand and negotiate the differences. There was simply no proper or adequate bridge which could help students perceive the richness of differences. Differences for them were perceived as a great threat. Homogeneity and sameness and lack of critical thinking were much safer territory for them. Students reported that Islamic studies allow only one interpretation; other different interpretations are considered harmful and looked down upon. This influenced the way they perform at the academic level, where differences of perspective and angle are necessary and a must. This is the core area in which Muhammadiyah students under performs in academic tasks. Students' critical skills have been weakened by an approach to religion that emphasises absolute truth in the interpretation of their religion. Absolute truth impairs students' creativity as well. Consequently, creative thinking and writing in reaction toward works of literature are scarce and few.

The older the students and the longer their exposure to reading literary work, the more open-minded they become compared to their younger cohort. Students in their seventh semester, having encountered several Western literary works, were able to make an ambiguous yet firm decision on particular issues. They could accept, for example, woman as a leader, while still asserting that under ordinary conditions leaders should be men. They were able to see the movie, *The Scarlet Letter*, to use the above example, and appreciate it, while still standing firmly on their own footing and unable to grasp another perspective. Islam and its "high morality", they called it, was the central footing from which they viewed the world. This kind of worldview influenced the way they appreciated and criticized literary works. In many ways this centralized worldview, which clustered around their notion of a higher morality, made their logic weak and not particularly vibrant. Their horizons could not be renewed or refreshed from the reading of these literary pieces. They, however, were able to accept that there existed a world outside of their own, no matter how much it contradicted their own. This was an important step in building their sense of tolerance and respect.

Students from the tenth semester, especially those working on their final paper, were the most open-minded of all the students. In addition to being able to understand a different world outside of their own, they had the ability to think in terms of a different perspective, outside of their own central footing within an Islamic high morality. They were aware of the insights, of the conscience and of the good values that they had absorbed through reading these literary peices. Students could even consider outside values to be Islamic, if they demonstrated virtue and universal conscience/*hikmah*. At this level, they had an ability to self-critically review their own position on interpreting Islam. They were no longer dependent on the teachings of Ulema but had the self confidence to make their own interpretation of particular texts. Students in the tenth semester, who are not doing their final paper on literature, still reacted in the same way as those in the seventh semester. It seemed that students focusing their final paper on literature have a higher appreciation of the value of literary works than do students doing their final paper on English language teaching or phonology, for example.

The previous findings shows that there is an urgent need to equip students with the necessary bridge to enable them to negotiate the Western values contained in their English literature classes in relation to their own Islamic cosmology. This should be part of the process of buidling their logical thinking, both in the process of reception and expression. In their classroom interaction, lecturers attempt to bridge the situation where students approach the English literature they read from a high prejudiced perspective. Lecturers reported that it seemed like they were constructing a "hidden curriculum" by talking about religion and Islam in a different way in their literature classes. This fact should be communicated to lecturers in Studies of Islam and Muhammadiyah (SIM). Yet this had not taken place as lecturers felt that it would be difficult to break the conformity of vision students where exposed to in SIM on the interpretation of Islam, even though this closed and homogenized teaching of religion impacted negatively on students' approach to their other 'secular' subjects.

Lecturers at UMS said that almost half of the classroom practices were taken up with clarifying misunderstandings and overcoming students' prejudices. It was indeed an unproductive and non-conducive setting for teaching and learning. In the other Muhammadiyah University, the lecturers and students from UAD took this situation for granted, as if it never happened, resulting in a monotonous uncritical literary appreciation and criticism. With an apparent lack of material and lacklustre class dialectics, it is no wonder that only a small number of English departments within the Muhammadiyah system are accredited by the government. UMS is one of these universities which have received B accreditation from the government. The findings show as well that UMS's curriculum has introduced a much wider variety of literary theories compared to other Muhammadiyah universities.

More clashes happened in the inner cosmology of the younger students compared to the older ones. In the case of students still in the junior semesters, I found many had never been attached to or even read western literary works. So their encounter with western literary works at the university level was their first experience. No wonder that they had a more negative judgment of the values they found in these literary works. Those younger students who had come with a wide variety of reading experiences expressed a more positive appreciation toward the western values in these works. Most of these students expressed ambiguity towards values they perceived as outside of Islam. On the one hand, they were prejudiced against what they saw as western values, but on the other hand they very often practiced these values in everyday life. One vivid example was female students' attitude on women's public role. When asked they defined an Islamic women in terms of their ideal of women of the Arabic world. When I told them that, to take one example, women in Saudia Arab are forbidden to walk alone in the public, they were surprised. Most female students in Muhammadiyah universities would travel to the university alone and did not feel that it was necessary for them to be accompanied by a male guardian, like women in the Arabian Peninsula. It was quite clear that Muhammadiyah students' own dream of living an Islamic life like that in Saudi Arabia was ambiguous. They had never experienced the reality of what it is like to be a woman in the Arab world.

Basically they defined their Islam-ness by affirming what they already had, that is, a set of strongly held Javanese values and lifesyles that they had inherited through their long upbringing, but which they themselves rejected on the surface. So for example, they rejected calling friends by their Javanese name preferring to use an Arabic name. Yet they were unaware that they lived in an unsegregated society, where female students in Muhammadiyah universities could sit next to male students. They had no idea of the partition of class found in the Arabian Peninsula. It was obvious that their theological constructs were is basically conservative but that their everyday practice was basically progressive, just like students in Germany, for example. The way they perceived Studies of Islam and Muhammadiyah (SIM) influenced the way they thought about the world outside them. Unfortunately, the exploration of the contextual situation of Indonesian life has not been incorporated into the materials and teaching sources in the teaching of religion. The split within students' inner cosmology, made it difficult for them to connect the disjuncture between their received beliefs (based on the religious teachings of SIM) and their own everyday life, let alone their academic life.

This clash of values was basically caused by one doctrine being absorbed by students textually, in which there was an unquestioned acceptance of the concepts of a "good deed" and of heaven. They were taught that good deeds outside of a belief in Islam had no value useless. So people, who performed good deeds, including Westerners, would not enter heaven unless they had the faith of Islam. This view influenced the way they perceived Western people, in this case, western writers whose works they read in class. A fascist mode of interpretation occured when they felt that the works were not Islamic. When I asked them if I could introduce them to the work of Salman Rushdie, they said that they would not read it as it was a dangerous book, they said. When I asked them, who said that? They answered the Ustads/Ulema told us. Are you going to burn the book? I asked them again. They answered this time with a little less certainty. I asked them again: are you angry with him? Yes, they answered. Why? I persisted. They answered that Salman Rushdie defamed our Prophet. So have you read it? *The Satanic Verses*? I pushed. No, they said. From this interview, it was clear that the role of Ulema was still strong amongst Muslim students and this, in my perspective, could hinder their creative and critical skills.

When I reported these facts to the leaders of DIKTI and the Rectors of the two Muhammadiyah universities in my sample, their answer contradicted the students' responses. They said that it was permissible for lecturers to introduce Salman Rushdie's works in the class, students could react rationally. It did not run counter to the principles of education within Muhammadiyah. Those two findings, one from the leadership level and one from the student level shows gap between the policy makers and the recipients of this policy, the students. There needs to be a bridge to overcome this problem, and part of the bridge could be in the form of curriculum reform. Leaders are unaware that there is a process of silent radicalization amongst students. When I asked students why they think in such a way, they answered that they felt that the West dominated the world. They felt that they were ashamed that they are no good Muslim novelists like those in the West. I continued with the question that if there were Muslim novelists would they read their works. They reaction was astonishing; they said that they didn't believe it. When I showed them the novels of Fatema Mernissi, the memoir of Leila Ahmed, and the novels of Nawal el Shadawi and Carmen Bin Laden—all of whom are postcolonial Muslim women writers—they expressed great joy. They said, I want to read them!

Their reactions exemplify the need for Muslim students to read Muslim writers who take Islam as their main theme in order to bridge the gap between the Islamic values they embraced and the world outside them. I consciously chose the writers who have already crossed—and written about this crossing—two different worlds, i.e. the West and Islam. By presenting students with the life and experience of these writers who had experienced both values, students could grasp an important projection of their own role model. It helped them to be critical and creative as well. To be critical, in that they are able to criticize their own present position, and to be creative, in that they are be able to open up to a much wider horizon which forces them to must situate themselves in a new position and perspective. These literary works are the site of a dialogue across different cultures and values, specifically Islamic values and the Western values. These dialogues, through the intense interaction of the major characters in the Islamic and Western worlds, provide a fascinating as well as necessary experiences that could be shared by Muhammadiyah students.

Besides presenting a site of dialogue, postcolonial Muslim women writers' works could become a strategic bridge that could amend the negative prejudices cast by Muhammadiyah students upon Western values. Reflecting upon these field findings gained through interviews with leaders, rectors, deans, lecturers, students; and librarians and through research into the curriculum, it is obvious that such a bridge is needed, and that it might be in the form of curriculum reform through an introduction of the works of Muslim women writers who have experienced these two different worlds. The major characters in their writings provide exemplary role models for students who are forced to seek his/her own identity amid the rampant cultural flows of globalization. These novels could help them configure the landscape of western values through the eyes of the major characters and in this way help students to negotiate their own value system with Western values. By experiencing a moving from one horizon to another in this way, students could develop the ability to negotiate their values in such a way that can find common values which are universal and shared by different cultural and religious backgrounds. The success of this reform, however, is dependent on how religious education is executed within Muhammadiyah universities. Greater efforts to reform the curriculum in secular departments will only work if such efforts are followed as well in the religious departments.

6. Conclusion: Tension in Islamic Curriculum Reformation

Over the past ten years, more and more prospective students of Muhammadiyah universities have chosen to study within secular departments than the religious departments, such as those offered within the Faculty of Islamic Studies: Ushuluddin/Theology and Philosophy, Syariah/Islamic Law, and Tarbiyah/Islamic Education. The number of prospective students in the Institute for Ushuluddin at UMS has declined over the last ten years with only 10 students now studying per semester. Syariah students number around 80 students per semester and Tarbiyah has about 120 students per semester. Compared these numbers to those of the English department, where there are around 1000 applicants and 600 students accepted each semester. The declining number of students applying to the religious departments is caused foremostly by the shortage of employment opportunities in this area. As a result, the curriculum policy makers in Muhammadiyah have cut back on the amount of religious subjects in the curriculum. Some Muhammadiyah schools have even reshaped their schools by placing more emphasis on learning English than Arabic. Students of secular departments in Muhammadiyah universities are learning less Islam and more English nowadays. Many progressive Muslim leaders in Indonesia, especially in Muhammadiyah, campaign to have textbooks rewritten, time-honored teaching methods changed and a reduction on the amount of religion in the curriculum. It is still, however, a subject of agonizing dispute.

Much of the education debate has focused on how—or whether—the religious curriculum promotes intolerance and extremism. But Muhammadiyah has chosen a dramatic course, deciding not just to rewrite textbooks but also aiming to prepare its graduates for a more participatory and economically competitive future. The curriculum should incorporate elements of Muhammadiyah's identity, drawing on Muhammadiyah's own history and the religion of Islam. But broader reforms have not been carried out and many conservative Muhammadiyah leaders have blamed outsiders for unfairly tarring their religion-focused educational system. This proposed reformation is a chance to push through educational reforms that would not only promote religious tolerance but also seek to introduce notions of greater citizen participation, individual choice and entrepreneurship amongst students. Many progressive Muhammadiyah leaders endorse the idea of broader change and have issued a manifesto calling for more progressive Muhammadiyah education that results in better educated students better educated, better able to compete in the modern economy.

This research found three things that hinder development in Indonesia—rising unemployment in a region accustomed to working in the agricultural sector, ineffective and old-fashioned teaching methods, and failure to adapt to the Internet age in the schools and universities. There are shortcomings in Indonesia's developmental path and reformed system as it does not provide people with the basic skills demanded by the marketplace. This is why it is necessary that the Indonesia Government should declare war on "violence and fanaticism" and undertake a study of textbooks that might promote extremism as part of their religious curriculum. Religious textbooks describing jihad as mandatory war on non-Muslims and Israel as the religious enemy of all Muslim shall be replaced by textbooks that promote "brotherhood, equality, love, caring, mercifulness and coexistence". This process is still underway and not a word has been changed. Islam should not be interpreted in a fashion which leads to extremism, as progressive Muhammadiyah leaders have recently said (interviews to Prof Dr Syafii Maarif and Prof Dr Amin Abdullah).

Progressive leaders have stressed that Muhammadiyah students should know that Indonesians are not religious fundamentalist, or extremists and only a very few people although they are strong. The majority of the population is peace loving and moderate in a country of diverse cultures, geography, and natural beauty. The first challenge that Indonesian Muslims facing is religious extremism, sectarian tension and terrorism. The second challenge is poverty and illiteracy; both are major factors of social backwardness, a lack of true democracy, good governance and quality institutions. The education system that Muhammadiyah adopts is an entirely Western concept but the practice is far from being Western. Teachers and professors do not encourage students to speak out, express their ideas freely or disagree with teachers. Furthermore, the most modern technology and updated information are not provided and available to the students. This is entirely due to lack of financial resources. Teachers and professors are not trained in the modern techniques of teaching and do not have up-to-date information. Most of the time there is only a one-way lecture system, no proper class room discussions, and with questions from students discouraged as students who ask questions are considered to be students with poor knowledge. The content and curriculum do not match the requirements of the modern age. History books only give one perspective and are biased. There is also an outdated examination system in which students are supposed to read huge books before their final exam. Many students do not have access to these books and consequently cheating becomes common practice in the examinations. Education is used just to get a degree or certificate, not as a means to promote personal growth or development. On the other hand, there are very expensive private educational institutions that provide the most modern techniques, instruct course in English, and are based on the pattern of education in the West. However these institutions are only for the rich and poor people have no access to these institutions. Misery, poverty, sectarian tension, as well as corruption are part of daily life in Indonesia. Many people do not have basic amenities or the necessities of life, such as electricity, clean drinking water, proper health care, and access to education. Life is very stressful for many Indonesians.

These people usually attend the madrasah or religious schools, a tradition which can be traced back though nearly a thousand years of Islamic teaching. Over the last few decades, however, these schools have increasingly played a role contrary to their original intent. Founded as centres for the next generation of Islamic scholars and clerics, the schools now increasingly dominate the education sphere, largely because this type of education is not expensive and affordable for those who are poor. Several of the madrasah are affiliated with extremist religious/political groups, who have co-opted education for their own ends. These specific madrassah schools teach distorted view of Islam. Hatred is permissible, jihad gets misinterpreted to allow murders of innocent civilians, including other Muslim men, women, and children, and the new heroes in these specific schools are terrorists. Martyrdom through suicide attacks is also extolled. Many of the radical religious schools and universities also include weapons and physical training in their regimen, as well as weekly lesson on political speechmaking (where anti-American rhetoric is memorized). The students in these radicals' schools are uneducated, young, dependent on the schools, and cut off from contact with their parents for years at a time, and thus highly susceptible to being programmed towards violence.

Female students' role in these Madrasah is underdeveloped. The schools are a male dominated society. Men are considered the sole head and bread-winner of the family with women supposed to staying at home. The birth of a boy in a family is celebrated, while the birth of a girl is not a joyous occasion. Mothers are even stripped of their own names, for example a Javanese name of 'Canti Besari', changed to 'Ummu Ja'far' (Mother of Ja'far, a baby boy). The traditional roles of women include domestic works such as cooking, washing, cleaning, child rearing, and collecting fuel wood for cooking, farming, weeding, threshing, and harvesting. Men perform task outside home such as income earning jobs, working in business, or doing heavy manual labour. Women are not supposed to talk back or make any arguments with men. A husband or other male members of the family may consider it their right to beat a woman if she doesn't follow the expected guidelines of Islamic female behaviour. Men are not supposed to perform any works assigned to women, to do so is socially unacceptable and taboo. Such a role has defined the meaning of womanhood in the teaching of Islamic education. And is thus incorporated into their curriculum. This was seen as a salient threat for the development of future Indonesia. Muhammadiyah education lies in the middle of the crossroad, whether defining it in a more modern-progressive way or traditional-conservative way.

Muhammadiyah suffers from lack of a comprehensive approach to the curriculum of Islamic Studies. The current batch of Islamic curricula, both those published and those still in process, usually take one of two approaches. These approaches are set by Muslim writers who are experts in formulating Islamic policies in the education system and are (1) the separated-approach (SA) and (2) the integrated approach (IA). SA, for the time being, is more practical than the integrated curriculum approach. Advocates of this approach point out that Islamic education has to be separated from the secular subjects, and assume that secular subjects are also Islamic by affirming the ideology that Islamic education should widen the horizon of Muslims by reaching them about values that go beyond Islamic values themselves. According to this interpretation something Islamic is *rahmatin lil alamin*, or a blessing of the universe, and can thus affirm the existence of common values embraced by people from different religious, cultural, and social backgrounds. In the separated approach, however, the religious subjects stress the importance of the students knowing a certain amount of information by rote. Such as, for example, the basic facts of the life of Prophet Muhammad will be taught repeatedly. The advantage of this approach is that the students receive the same material many times, and, therefore, it is more likely that they will remember at least its salient points of past history. There are two major disadvantages to this approach however. If most material is taught through repetition and by rote method, then other material, such as Islamic ethics/*akhlak*, which may be equally important, may not get taught at all. This method may cause some extremely important aspects of Islam to be missed or minimized, as well as caused more boredom amongst students. Too many students dislike their Islamic studies classes because they are always the same thing repeatedly, and the material designed to be memorized instead of to engage the students. Rather than learn the material well, they simply turn off their hearing as soon as the repeatedly materials is introduced.

The second approach is the integrated approach (IA). Proponents of this approach argue that Islamic studies should be an integral part of every subject, and not related to just Islamic studies classes. Muslim teachers in the other secular subjects according to this approach are expected to do a reasonably good job of Islamizing secular subjects for their students. This approach seeks a comprehensive approach to education based on the idea of *Tauhid*—God-centeredness in all its aspects. Yet this approach does not encourage the development of critical and creative skills. The authority of the truth is an imposed, top-down process. Students are discouraged from undertaking their own investigation of recent phenomenon and provided with an already pre-made set of logics. Stimulation of new ideas and intellectual exchanges is rare and hardly promoted. This approach is also less practical than the first as advocates of this approach are still at the stage of developing the necessary textbooks and learning materials. The greatest obstacle they face is finding experts within each of the secular subjects who have the ability to Islamize the subjects.

The two approaches have also attracted different proponents. Strong proponents of the integrated approach are the Tarbiyah movements, part of the rising 'new Islamism' in Indonesia, represented by Forum Lingkar Pena (an Indonesian Islamist literary movement) and Partai Keadilan Sejahtera (Islamist Political Party) (see Chapter V). The proponents of the first approach are Muhammadiyah and Nahdlatul Ulama (Indonesia's two largest Islamic organizations). Muhammadiyah is the oldest Islamic organization—founded in 1912 during the reign of the Dutch—and is much more socially and civilly engaged than the newest Islamic organizations, such PKS, which are much more politically engaged.

Muhammadiyah is once again at the cross-road of choosing between those two approaches. The present applied approach is the separated one, but it has been challenged by new-Islamist movements within Muhammadiyah education who felt dissatisfied with the separated approach. A constant battle is still taking place within Islamic education institutions as to whether the studying of secular subjects should be considered Islamic as well as the study of the so-called religious subjects. Present experts in Muhammadiyah education favour this position of seeing the study of secular subjects to be Islamic but

Muhammadiyah's present educational policy may shift in the next decade as the new-Islamist movements continue to consolidate power and challenge this current position. Their epistemological approach, however, to the secular subjects is not as friendly as current expert opinion. From the Islamist perspective, secular subjects are not Islamic as they have not yet been Islamized. It is a hotly contested argument which has caused much worry among many progressive Ulemas and Kyais in Indonesia. The sacred is still sacred textually, while the context has been blamed as being unholy and not sacred. Pragmatism is seen as errant. Pragmatism, however, has prolonged the life of Muhammadiyah education so far. Several ultra-conservative Ulama in Muhammadiyah, however, felt that it is immoral and corrupt. It is a point that may endanger the education in Muhammadiyah institution in the future. The internal tension and dynamic in Muhammadiyah has resulted in many of its educational institutions being left far behind other educational institutions owned by the state and Christian-Catholic missions. It is no wonder that only a quarter of Muhammadiyah's educational institutions have been accredited by the government, while the rest of its other thousands of schools and universities lack proper accreditation.

Chapter VII
Mainstreaming Gender through Postcolonial Muslim Women Writers

1. Introduction

In this Chapter I explore possible ways to tackle the problems faced by students in the English department of Muhammadiyah universities. I focus specifically on the way a multicultural approach to reforming the present curriculum could enhance students' reception and appreciation of literary texts. Students' ability here is hindered by the way they apprehend Islamic texts, that is literally and textually, resulting in a strict and narrow perspective on literature representing other value systems, such as the current Western canon in the Muhammadiyah curriculum.

There is no apparent bridge in the present curriculum that could help students expand their horizons. By exposing them to western works only, they are not encouraged to develop a self-critical perspective on their present situation. The present monocultural (i.e. western) canon only increased students' skepticism towards other value systems and resulted in an overly outwardly critical stance toward western values, which was unnecessary. The work of postcolonial Muslim writers could be one way in which students read English language literature—and hence develop their core competence—but also are given the opportunity to exercise a level of self-reflexivity as they consider other cultural values which are nevertheless based on similar experiences as Muslims.

The bridge that this study proposes emphasises two components, firstly curriculum reform in order to include literary works in which there is serious engagement with the theme of gender and, secondly the introduction into classroom practice of different reading techniques derived from multicultural, poststructural and critical inquiry approaches. The first seeks to develop students' comparative outlook and their ability to negotiate competing values. This is based on the assumption that in their writing, postcolonial Muslim writers are themselves engaged a similar bridging exercise. Whether between Western and non-Western values or different interpretations of Islamic values, postcolonial Muslim writers can be said to bridge two different worlds within their work. The second component seeks to equip students with the practical knowledge and reading techniques required to enable them to successful read and engage with such work.

The rest of the Chapter is devoted to a discussion of my proposed curriculum reform. In particular, I consider how the introduction of a proposed new syllabus for the teaching of a unit on *Prose*, one focussing on specific postcolonial Muslim writers, could tackle the problems of Muhammadiyah students noted in the previous chapter. In terms of this proposed syllabus, students will be introduced to the work of postcolonial Muslim writers from Morocco, Egypt, Pakistan, India as well as Indonesia. Specific attention will be given to work written by women from those regions. The choice of women writers is a conscious one. I argue that many postcolonial women's writing exhibit a high degree of self-criticism toward their own tradition, particular in their speaking out against conservative traditions which they see as having suppressed women in the course of the modern era. I regard these works as exemplary in two ways for students who are themselves in the process of searching for their own Islamic identity. Firstly, such writers are located in a recognizably similar cultural horizon that is broadly speaking an Islamic one. This does not mean of course that the cultures of the students and writers are the same. In fact, the differences are important as much as the similarities, as it may be the recognition of cultural differences across the Islamic world that most successfully initiates more self-critically modes of enquiry amongst the students. Secondly, these writers are also engaged in a profound review of influences that come from outside Islam, and most particularly those that have been introduced in their homelands by western colonizers in the course of the modern era. These women have traveled widely either in Islamic regions or western countries and have expressed something of their experience here through the voices of their main characters, many of whom likewise cross boundaries whether geographical or cultural. The experience of reading the work of writers who are in some sense similar (as fellow Muslims) but nevertheless different (because they originate from culturally distinct parts of the Islamic world) is one way of broadening Muhammadiyah students' horizons, particularly their apprehension of different cultural values. The proposed syllabus is aimed at sharpening students' ability in the following skills: respect, understanding, and tolerance toward cultural values coming outside of the Islamic tradition. In addition, to giving them equal opportunity to access and read materials written by fellow Muslim writers, the cultural pluralism reflected in such work will hopefully encourage a more self-critically approach to reading in general.

2. The Islamic cosmology of Muhammadiyah Students: religious setting in connection with the choice of literary text

Muhammadiyah students come to a text laden with Islamic cultural, social, ideological baggage, all of which influence their response to the literary text. Concomitantly, their subjectivity is structured by the texts they read, and this is an ongoing, never-completed process. Their process of reading is not an innocent act. Recent findings made this study aware of how their conceptions of gender are shaped by what they read. This is why strategies for reading against an Imam-male-dominated text are proposed here. While greater representation of Muslim women writers is encouraged in the proposed reformed literary canon, the question of 'who's in' and 'who's out' of the canon remains an open question at this stage. While in this chapter I have made a selection of Muslim women writers, these are only suggestions, and any selection would need to consider the specific curriculum context as well as the particular context of each Muhammadiyah university. The choice of texts and the approaches proposed for the students are particularly important at the introductory level, for it is here that students should be receiving basic training in the critical skills they will need for reading and writing throughout their academic careers and beyond. It is here too that their awareness of a literary canon is sharpened as well, including the skills that they could learn from reader-response and feminist criticism, along with a balanced representation of men and women writers.

In terms of teaching techniques, the proposed syllabus should be designed to encourage students to share their personal experience of reading the pieces with other students. This is meant to create a learning atmosphere which will make the class meaningful to each unique, individual student. The postcolonial Muslim writers selected for this research are all actively engaged in the examination, redefinition and at times abondment of traditional Islamic views on the roles of men and women. To support their study here, certain goals need to be emphasized in the literature program, namely: a) the exploration of self, including the gendered self and b) the exploration of the relationships between self and other. These goals can be accomplished through the inclusion in the syllabus of postcolonial Muslim women writers, whose characters reflect upon various gender-specific traditions as well as the newly developing options for women and men in society. It is through reading good literature that the unique qualities of individuals can be explored, while at the same time, exploring similarities of human experience which cross gender boundaries. By discussing these women's work, which explicitly or implicitly deals with sex role stereotyping or the breaking of traditional stereotypes, students can be helped to reflect upon gender differences and the effect of gender stereotypes on a person's expectations, communication styles, response to life's major issues and traumas, and on their plans for the future.

Muhammadiyah students, both male and female, need works which validate their own experiences but also challenge that experience, perhaps showing them options of which they have been unaware. Through reading and vicariously experiencing life from a different yet similar Muslim context, students can not only begin to increase their appreciation for and tolerance of alternate perspectives within a similar context, but learn how to bring a more self-critical perspective to their understanding of their Islamic world. The main characters in the works of postcolonial Muslim women writers exemplify characters of both sexes that interact realistically, reflecting both the prejudice of Muslim society and the characters' ability to overcome these. Students can draw on this to, interact in a more positive way and learn from one another. Students need to be exposed to those characters who reflect current and historic Muslim realities, however uncomfortable those realities might be, and then they need to examine why those stereotypes exist and to confront their own stereotyping of others, thus sharpening their sense of empathy. Empathy and a concern for others grow out of a sense of connectedness, and the result of this sense of interconnection is not moral judgment or a hierarchy of absolute values and rules, as usually espoused by Muhammadiyah students when evaluating English language literary works from the perspective of their Islamic morality. Rather; the effect is to encourage dialogue and networks of care and support as well as an ability to move beyond traditional modes of thought.

3. Theoretical approach: Multicultural Education

An increasing awareness of the importance and value of diversity has led this research to seek strategies for change. This has entailed, in particular, the effort to incorporate multiculturalism into the curriculum. In contemporary education, the question of whether to include material on diversity is no longer an intellectual debate. Transforming the curriculum is not just a matter of adding courses or sections within courses. True curricular transformation involves the recognition of gender and multiculturalism as important aspects of everyday human functioning and interaction and the infusion of this recognition into the areas of literary study. Scholars are beginning to consider gender, race and ethnicity as social constructions rather than biological characteristics. Gender has been addressed in a more complex way, addressing the intersections of identities as well as the experience of those identities which defy single categorization (Burke, 1996). Along with this has come the responsibility to ensure a safe and comfortable climate for all people, irrespective of roles and individual differences related to gender.

Following Lyotard, this study asks "Who transmits learning?", "What is transmitted?", "To whom?", "Through what medium?", "In what form?", and "With what effect?" (Lyotard, 1986: 48). In the context of Indonesian Muhammadiyah universities, the existence of a homogeneous Islamic enclave has been highly influential with respect to these questions. Teachers' professed Islam has a major involvement in the transmission of learning to the Muslim students. Yet what is transmiited (the second question) varies according to the different faculties and department. In the context of the English Department, the previous Chapter has shown that works by Western writers have predominated in the content material of the curriculum. The debate initiated over the current literary cannon within English Departments has nothing to do with political correctness; rather it is motivated by a perceived and urgent need for Muhammadiyah students to read as well as to appreciate works written by Postcolonial Muslim writers. By giving them this chance, students will be able to have a more comprehensive picture of how Muslim writers have resisted religious prescriptions on their behaviour. A further benefit is that reforming the canon by incorporating postcolonial Muslim writers along with Western writers in this way will encourage an atmosphere of multiculturalism. Students will thus be better prepared to critically evaluate the two major religious systems that bid for their attention, as well as the global influences that are paraded before them. By having in-out-critical awareness, students are accompanied with reading strategies in which self-independency in literary appreciation will be assured in the classroom context through the employment of many different writers either from the Western or Postcolonial Muslim countries. By exposing students to a rainbow of writers, students are presented with reading materials that are rich in terms of cultural contexts although still correlated in general terms with their religious identity. This is meant to meet the multicultural objectives that this study aims to achieve.

Multicultural education contains divergence in terms of visions and approaches. Sleeter and Grant (2003), for instance, outline four foci and approaches to multicultural education that have evolved since the 1960s: 1. The exceptional and culturally different approach which is based on a cultural deficit theory aims to assimilate minority students; 2. A human relations approach, which focuses on respect, understanding, and tolerance; 3. Single-group studies approach, which focuses on cultural pluralism and equal opportunities; and 4. Education that is multicultural and social Reconstructionist, which seeks structural equality by addressing sociopolitical issues including racism, classism, sexism, and so forth. These approaches can be roughly divided politically into right, left liberal, and left radical positions as suggested by other educators in their discussion of multicultural education (Kincheloe & Steinberg, 1997; McLaren, 1995; Nieto, 1995). Nieto (2000) provides the following definition of multicultural education:

> Multicultural education is a process of comprehensive school reform and basic education for all students. It challenges and rejects racism and other forms of discrimination in schools and society and accepts and affirms the pluralism (ethnic, racial, linguistic, religious, economic, and gender, among others) that students, their communities, and teachers reflect. Multicultural education permeates the schools' curriculum and instructional strategies, as well as the interaction among teachers, students, and families, and the very way that schools conceptualize the nature of teaching and learning. Because it uses critical pedagogy as its underlying philosophy and focuses on knowledge, reflection, and action (praxis) as the basis for social change, multicultural education promotes democratic principles of social justice. (p. 305).

One of the potentially culturally responsive approaches to reading is the use of life-based multicultural literary texts (particularly those written in students' voices) as a means for students to make sense of the lived world, to create bridges to worlds other than their own, and to see themselves in the stories of others. Culturally responsive approaches to reading help students develop an empathetic understanding toward others, enable them to learn to acknowledge and respect the cultural heritages of different ethnic groups and their own, and improve their dispositions, attitudes, and approaches to reading in the multicultural classroom. By developing such an approach to reading enables Muhammadiyah Universities to promote culturally responsive teaching and learning, which are compatible with the values of students' own cultures and languages. This will help students reach their highest potential in a multicultural and multilingual world.

4. Post-Structuralist Critical Pedagogies: Untangling Gender Inequality

Following the continental 'linguistic turn', post-structuralism has focused on relationships between discourse, power and subjectivity and has highlighted how language constructs the experience of reality and shapes the process of knowledge acquisition. The role of language is not problematic because language conveys a range of meanings, never fixed or static. Thus, post-structuralism tends to 'stress the shifting, fragmented complexity of meaning (and relatedly of power), rather than a notion of its centralized order' (Beasley, 1999: 91). This has at least four implications.

First, there is always ambiguity in the meanings which are shared in the everyday life. Post-structuralism challenges the idea that there exists 'a single, literal reading of a textual object, the one intended by the author' (Barone, 1995: 65). Although some readings are certainly more privileged than others, interpretation cannot be controlled. Each one of us brings one's own knowledge, experience, values and meanings to the text. This calls into question the transfer of intended meaning between teacher and learner (and vice versa) so that authorial (teacher) authority is never guaranteed. It means that teachers have to acknowledge the ways in which students each produce their own meanings and their own knowledges.

Second, the fragmented and multiple model of power challenges assumptions that power is both a possession and can only be exercised by those with authority above us. Building on the work of Foucault, some post-structuralists take up a model of power in terms of a matrix or capillary. This is important because it allows us to recognize that we all have some level of power, and that because power is constituted through discourse, we can all be positioned as powerful and non-powerful. This means that wo/men can acknowledge the inter-relations of discourses of 'race', class and gender and come to understand how, for example, women can exercise power over other women or over men. In addition, this model of power assumes a degree of human agency because it challenges the idea that we are simply passive bodies waiting to be colonized by ideologies into a state of false consciousness. Rather where there is power there is also resistance.

Third, post-structuralism emphasizes the shifting, changing nature of identity construction. The self is positioned by, and importantly positions itself within, the socially and culturally constructed patterns of language we label discourse. Thus 'practices create subjectivities so that no real human subject exists prior to the social practices within which she is subjected' (Walkerdine, 1989: 206). The focus on the self as process is an important aspect of some forms of feminist post-structuralism because it highlights the potential for change. It is linked to Foucauldian analyses of power because here power is not simply repressive but also productive. Rather than assuming, as in some forms of feminism, that patriarchal power represses the person I *really* am, post-structuralism illustrates how the operations of power and discourse produce identities.

Fourth, feminist post-structuralism highlights how the binaried nature of language shapes gender identities and possibilities. Language is organized in terms of hierarchical binaries of which male-female is a classic example. 'The structure of language and the dominant storylines combine, with powerful effect, to operate on our conscious and unconscious minds and to shape our desire' (Davies, 1997:9). As a consequence, some post-structuralists argue for the development of critical literacy which will deconstruct binaries in order to illustrate how they construct regimes of truth and so demonstrate, as Davies puts it, how they create 'what we might call speaking as usual' (*ibid*).

The implications of the above offer students a kind of reflexive knowledge that would allow them to recognize and critique the various discourses that are made available to them. This reflexive knowledge includes the practice of deconstruction, upon which critical literacy rests. Deconstruction contains two strategies: those of overturning and metaphorisation (Garrick and Rhodes, 1998). Overturning seeks to change the embedded hierarchies in language so that the dominant and marginal terms are recognized as such. One of feminism's aims, for example, has been to expose the dominance/marginality of man/women discourses. However, it is insufficient to seek a reversal of the binaries in terms of dominance/marginality. This retains hierarchical ways of knowing and being. Through methaporisation one seeks to hold in play the relation of the two binaried terms so that students can illustrate how they are dependent on each other for their meaning and how one continuously threatens the hegemonic power of the other.

Arising from these features, there are three pedagogic tasks that could be undertaken. First, there is a need to generate a level of critical literacy that enables Muslim students to recognize multiple discourses. Second, there is a need to facilitate a critical awareness of the ways in which the self is contradictorily positioned as colonized and colonizer and as oppressed and oppressive within these discourses. Third, there is a need to embrace, as one's own, the multiplicity of positions with which one wishes to identify. Feminism may be a challenge to dominant systems of thought prescribed by the Imams but it also represents a threat to the investments that many women have made in their identities and in the life practices arising from this. To not respect these investments is to fail in the responsibility of teachers as critical educators. It is to forget that a liberatory pedagogy should never become a dogma.

5. Procedure in Critical Inquiry: Classroom Practice

Critical inquiry is a classroom teaching method that provides Muhammadiyah students with the tools they need to do close, teacher-guided reading of texts. It assists the student in weaving together analyses about the narrative structure. Critical inquiry is not simply a rhetorical contrivance, but a process to discover and analyze plausible interpretations of texts. As such, the process is dynamic and maybe be practiced in group settings in classrooms or become an integral part of students' study habits after its routine introduction in the classroom. In sum, critical inquiry is a tool for the exploration and examination of texts.

The ground rules operating in a setting where critical inquiry is a principal tool are clear enough: first, texts are to be read in class at least twice in order to acquire a sense of what they are about, what important ideas strike the reader, what natural divisions in storyline surface, who the main characters are, what peculiarities of language use appear that appeal to the reader's intuitive sense, and what the reader takes to be the authorial motive and intent. Procedurally, the second step in the critical inquiry reading method requires the reader to mark everything—words and their meanings—that are unfamiliar. Third, in the second reading, the task is done more slowly and carefully. Fourth, the reader begins the process of annotating questions and markings in the texts themselves. With multicultural materials, this is an arduous task for students but an important step that must be done with discipline and thoughtfulness. In the annotative stage, readers circle or underline important ideas, words, phrases, or entire passages that seem to them relevant to the texts' themes; underlining is also a practical convenience to highlight ideas that may seem unclear or confusing and to attend to particular words whose meaning need to be checked. Passages in the texts that seem inconsistent are noted, and those parts or fragments of texts that generate strong reactions in the reader are duly specified for inspection and analysis. Fifth, and finally, the reader then prepares questions pertaining to the texts for the teacher to consider, or for the class to discuss, for further use in writing assignments.

The exercise of critical inquiry is dependent on questions addressed to a text. At least three types of questions are central to the critical inquiry procedure. The format consists of factual questions where such questions can generally be answered by reference to the text or by drawing simple inference. The goal is to deal with a fact or vocabulary that is essential to the comprehension of the text. Students posing questions is encouraged, allowing them to focus on aspects of the text that they have selected in order to learn how to identify the crucial elements in the text that might impede their understanding. In short, Critical Inquiry promotes self-learning habits.

More complex questions can yield more than one reasonable response that may be supported with evidence from a text. Interpretive questions are of this kind and ask students to judge what occurs or has happened in a text or to discern an argument in an essay in comparison and contrast to what the reader believes about behavior or experience. For example, in some Muhammadiyah English Departments students are assigned to read Richard Wright, as part of a selection of important figures in the history of slavery, "to raise consciousness". Questions such as these can reasonably support different answers and how readers use evidence from a text to formulate a variety of responses.

The third form of text analysis involves evaluative questions that represent another key process in the critical inquiry perspective. An individual's knowledge, personal experience, and values help to form a constitutive grid or schema for judging and assessing the quality of an author's work. Evaluative questions oblige the reader to connect their personal or vicarious experiences with a text. To repeat, all three types of questioning are ways to penetrate the meanings of a text and to draw its implications and their subtle expressions to the surface. And it is also worth repeating that the questioning process empowers students to control their own learning.

The context of multicultural studies—especially in a culturally pluralistic setting such as Indonesia—teachers can raise many questions of all sorts to stimulate discussion and debate as the students use their rich backgrounds as the basic framework through which they see the world. It might be asked in class how the role of religious ideas works in a society and how effective they are. This example suggests another larger, more general question concerning how effective religious ideas tend to be in producing other kinds of radical political change in Muhammadiyah universities such as anti-Jewish and anti-American sentiments—all in terms of putative religious ideas. Critical inquiry is not designed as a memory aid but rather as a strategy to promote critical understanding of texts. There is a need for textual annotative work through the elaboration of questioning techniques learned in class. The critical inquiry method urges the reader to focus on important ideas in a selection by underlining them for review and comparison; by noting confusing words or passages for clarification; and by highlighting passages the reader agrees or disagrees with; that a reader's group should examine together, and that may be cross-referenced with other materials that have already been read and studied, particularly through the questioning method.

6. Why Postcolonial Muslim Women Writers?

The choice of postcolonial Muslim women writers is designed to provide students the opportunity to thoroughly engage with literary works that not only intersects with linguistic games and literary allusions but also religio-legal intertextual references that contest Muhammadiyah students' own Islamic cosmology. This helps students in two ways. Firstly, it helps them to render into their own system of beliefs new perspectives and ideas that will hopefully flourish, and thereby nourish a self-critical outlook. Secondly, it helps them their more measured encounter with non-Islamic influences, by accelerating the development of tolerance and empathy. Students' interpretive schemes of their culture, including the system of social norms, values, and roles, impinge directly on perception and judgment, defining within the framework of a given society what is the right way to see and to feel and to think. For students at Muhammadiyah, this takes the form of the "Islamic student think". Overcoming this requires self-reflexivity and self-consciousness.

The development of self-reflexivity is important in achieving these outcomes. Self-reflexivity enters into the students' process of understanding the processes of self-mirroring. It is part of the process of becoming aware that what is seen in a text mirrors parts of our own self understanding/identity. For many Muhammadiyah students, this self-mirroring process could take the following form: "Since I am so unsure of myself and of how I look, and since I am so self-conscious about this, when I look at the world, I see myself reflected and, of course, the world is always then looking at me".

The next step required by students during the reading procedure is an attitude of self-consciousness, that is, a sometimes painful awareness of themselves and how they look or act, or how they fear others see them as looking or acting. Self consciousness is needed so that they become aware, or conscious, of the influences on them, including traditional values which are embedded in Islam. The proposed alternative literary canon drawing on postcolonial Muslim women writers is designed to encourage students to become self consciously aware of what their experiences in the world have been and how these experiences relate to the politics of gender in the Islamic world. It is meant to signal their ability to think critically about thinking but also their potential to become self-centered, which is manifested in the role modelling of the main characters in the literary works.

Literary works are written to enhance students' sensitivity in apprehending the world inside as well as outside them as replicated in the literary works. As a place of the negotiation of meaning, literary works provide innumerable insights through the roles of the main characters. The function of the principal characters is to provide role models, which students can then reject, embrace or direct their criticism, at. Many of the main characters in these works speak out against an overarching patriarchy, whose roots in social, religious, and political institutions is inscribed by the writers in relation to their characters' bodies and the gender constructions that shape their story. Role modelling functions as a mirror in which Muslim students cast their image upon the main characters. In this way, they can see themselves in the story, and begin to capture a story of themselves as told by these Muslim writers. By identifying with the roles of the characters they have the chance to explore the complex relationship between religious values and the social and cultural background manifested in the traditional values, as well as global values invading their own cultural-religious constructs. This helps students enhance and accelerate their tolerance, sympathy and sensitivity when encountering differences.

Besides sharpening students' tolerance to difference, students are also sensitized to the issue of individual agency through the methodology of critical inquiry. In this way is a notion of 'Islamic communal agency' transformed into a concept of 'individual agency', equipping students with their own voice. Being aware of their own individual voice is important in exercising critical awareness toward cultural repression, which is often their experience of studying a dogmatic Islam. This further gives them access to alternative and critical voices, that are quite rare in Islamic society. By transforming students' communal voice into students' own voices, students are faced with having to confront their own reasoning instead of relying on the reasoning of clerics. For female students in particular, this can mean a lot in terms of their self empowerment, which is no longer limited by the power of male domination in the Muslim community.

The works of the postcolonial women writers considered below are mainly in the form of memoirs, which retell their own life's journey from a communal traditional Islamic cosmology into a more progressive modern Islamic cosmology, whether geographically, culturally, or psychologically. The main characters are mostly women living in a postcolonial Muslim country. These women are described as posing a major threat to the position of the clerics and their hegemonic version of the interpretation of Islam. The protoganists typically find themselves cornered by radical clerics in their respective countries, and this provides a wonderful arena of encounter from which Muhammadiyah students can better apprehend their own Islam. Such texts demand that students interrogate their own version of Islam as tolerant or intolerant. Their reading and untangling of the complex relations of oppression and domination exercised by the radical clerics, demands that they question their own clerics, on the one hand, and consider Islam in much more contextualized and progressive ways, on the other. This further strengthens their self-critical evaluation of their own perception as well as interpretation of Islam. Through literary appreciation, students are encouraged to claim the authority of their own voice, rather than revere that of the clerics. These women characters liberate women from radical interpretations of Islam, interpretations which have robbed and eroded their creators' own rights. Students are empowered by the role model provided by the main characters to cross two boundaries that are the western world and the Muslim cosmology.

The melting of the two boundaries has provided postcolonial Muslim women writers with an ability to cross over from the western worldview to the Muslim worldview, an ability to project a particular phenomenon from both mirrors. The worldviews that they have traveled have given them an illuminating red thread of the commonality shared by the two different cultures which even could be perceived paradoxically by its inhibiters. History has proved that history of a particular civilization can never be separated from the history of other civilizations which are within themselves bound to each other, no matter how they resented to each other. History, of course, could only mean "whose story" with its core "story" in which a particular perspective is exercised. The history of colonization is perceived and written differently when seen through the colonizer's eyes rather than the colonized's eyes. Postcolonial Muslim women's stories offer a different story which is different from the previous two perspectives, i.e. those perceived by the western colonizer and those perceived by the colonized.

Herstory is the story told and written by these women writers in which woman's voice is enshrined in the public domain. To read a woman's story is to read woman's vision of the civilization in which her life is cast. This may be very different from the visions of men, which is commonly referred to as **history**. To read herstory brings the possibility of freeing oneself from the entrapment of both the colonizer's eyes and the colonized's eyes. In spite of coercive efforts to set up distinct categories and impose racial divisions, colonial territories always remained borderlines or 'intermediate' spaces (as Kipling and Trevelyan emphasize), contact zones criss-crossed by other cultural perceptions, multiple different histories and stories (Boehmer, Introduction to *Empire Writing*, xxiii). The history of colonization is indeed a history of complexity in which two civilizations met, negotiated and exercised their powers, for example western 'slavery' finds its synonym in the outcasted Dalith people in Hinduism's cosmology. They met and found their similarity to exercise the interests they had.

The above discussion has sketched the reasoning behind the proposal to introduce postcolonial Muslim women's writing into the English Departments within Muhammadiyah universities. There are some striking similarities across these women. Firstly, their home countries were previously colonized by European power, such as India in the case of Cornelia Sorabji (1870-1904), Egypt in the case of Nawal el Saadawi (1931-) and Leila Ahmed (1940-), Morocco in the case of Fatema Mernissi (1940-), and Indonesia in the case of Kartini (1879-1904). These countries represent contested territories, where Islamic values and western modern values meet and are *still* negotiated. Women writers were selected because they more than male authors illustrate women's struggle to speak against repressive religious and traditional rules as well as against the western imperialist. This is significant in assisting these countries further development. Besides challenging the oppression from those in power, their works provide a place of contestation where Islam can be defined and seen from their own perspective, a perspective which is apparently marginalized in Muslim countries today. This assists students to critically apprehend their own religion and, more importantly, to give them their own voices with which to appreciate and exercise Islam as a religion for their own selves. This voice is actualized during the crossing of boundaries, that is, from the traversal of an Islamic cosmology to a western one.

a. Why Cornelia Sorabji?

> "A Friend who has warmed her hands at two fires, without being scorched"
> Sir Mountstuart (*India Calling*, ix)

> Yes—it is true that I have been privileged to know two hearthstones, to be homed in two countries, England and India. But though it is difficult to say which "home" I love best, there has never, at any time, been the remotest doubt as to which called to me with most insistence.... Always, early or late, throughout the years, it has been "India Calling."...
> Cornelia Sorabji (*India Calling*, ix)

Cornelia Sorabji was the daughter of a Parsee (Zoroastrian Persian) and a converted Christian Gujaratee family. There is the dust of Zoroastrianism and Christianity in a name like Cornelia Sorabji, which gives witness to the crossing of two civilizations, that of the East—Persian-Indian—and the West—England.

Cornelia's interest is a woman's interest when she met a penniless widowed-Purdahnashin asking for her mother's help. "That is so", said her mother. "There are many Indian women in trouble in that way. Would you like to learn how to help them?" The small Cornelia answered, "Oh! I should!" (*India Calling*, 17). The small Cornelia then studied Law in India and England. Although she supported the British Raj and publicly denounced the Gandhian independence movement during in the rise of nationalism in India in the first half of twentieth century, her interests remained firmly on transforming a traditional-patriarchal Hindu cosmology into a more equal and progressive interpretation of the *Shastra* (Hindu's holy verdict). Her modern western education combined with her residence in India, shaped her views on the condition of women in India and her vision on how to improve this. Her cross-national contacts created an interstitial space between the cosmopolitan and the parochial (Boehmer, *Empire, the National, and the Postcolonial 1890-1920*, 21). Her view on the condition of women was born of a perspective of in-betweeness, where she perceived the negative and positive changes wrought by British colonialism. From such a perspective she reflected on the life of Indian women in her writing.

Her work is a collection of stories, stories of herself, her family and Indian women captured in her two memoirs (*India Calling* and *India Recalled*) and in her fictional work (*Love and Life Behind the Purdah* and *Sun Babies*). Herstories, narrated in English, are blended with Sanskrit and Urdu for particular terms which have no English cultural or linguistic equivalent. Cultural markers like *purdah*, *zenana*, *vakil* and *pundit* were left in their original to show the untranslatability of such Urdu words. Besides leaving such terms in their original words, Sorabji also retained colloquial forms of daily conversation and terms of address in their original form, in a way that leave us with the impression of the rich cultural codes she exercised in bridging the two cultural enclaves, that of the western colonizer and the colonized Indian. Her narrative is like entering into an Indian women's life, from with a distant perspective, which at the same time attaches us to the inner cosmology of Indian women's cultural construction of their bodies in relation to their Brahmo Hindu theology. Sorabji Cornelia clearly distinguished in her work between Indian women's perception of their own bodies in relation to their worldview and Sorabji's own vision and interest in transforming the quality of their apprehension toward women's bodies. Herstory reflects the struggle and resistance propagated by her and the other Indian women who were the characters in herstories.

Unlike traditional religions which center their cosmology on an impersonal god, like the belief of the *Geist* of their predecessor, big trees, mountains or rivers, post-traditional religions, like Hinduism, construct their cosmology based on a personal polydeity. In worshipping their god, worshippers theologically constructed like Brahma, the Creator; Vishnu, the Nurturer; and Shiva, the Destroyer. They constructed as well goddesses which resemble the power of the nature: like Devi Sri, goddess of Earth; Devi Durga, goddess of many-handed; Devi Kali, goddess of Birth, etc. The existence of feminine gods along with masculine gods reflected the clear segregation of male and female roles which were inherited from Old Babylonia (Persia). Old Babylonian was a pastoral community who segregated the public life of men from the domestic life of women. This segregation of roles was transformed into the system of women's seclusion. Female seclusion meant that women's roles were confined to the domestic sphere and that their domestic responsibilities were not to be brought into the public domain, the domain of men. Female seclusion incorporated two aspects, that of women's clothing and the covering of their bodies from public gaze; and the restriction of women to a constrained, domestic space. In the Indian subcontinent, these aspects were *Purdah* and *Zenana* respectively, whereas in the Middle East they were called *Hijab* and *Harem*. Their attitude toward the cosmos and cosmology was in turn highly influenced by this system of segregation, with the pastoral Babylonian history of segregation eventually affecting the construction of women's bodies and role with the Hindu cosmology.

The Hindu construction of women's bodies can be traced to the roles cast upon women. Child-marriage was prescribed by the Shastra to ensure that followers adhered over their life to the total Hindu cosmology. Child-marriage did not simply mean early sexual intercourse, it meant more than bodily perception as its significance expanded to that of religious deed connected to the reincarnation and afterlife experience of her parents:

> "The first three years of her life, a girl-child may not be married, because she belongs those three years to the Great God Brahma, to Vishnu the Preserver, to Siva the Destroyer—each in his turn. After three years of age she must be married; if married between the third and the fifth year her parents go to a first-class heaven (i.e. have the highest form of regeneration); if between five and eight to a second-class heaven; between eight and ten to a third-class heaven; thereafter to hells—only to hells." (*Shastras* quoted in "Giribala" in *India Recalled*, 21).

The legacy of child-marriage thus rested on such theological doctrine. After her early marriage, a girl would enter into the world of the Zenana and live with other girls. Their main duty was to worshop their husbands, which meant fulfilling their prescribed domestic roles within the so called "family". Sorabji wrote as follows:

> "She told me how she was often admonished of her duty to her husband. He was a god, and she must worship him; he could do no wrong; her head must be bent and covered, and no word must she speak in his presence, when any older than herself stood by—this, during the first year of marriage. But, throughout life, she must obey him and do his will, whatever that might be. And if for a sin committed in some past life her husband were taken away by the King of Death, she must spend her widowhood in fasting and prayer, and in bratas, sacrifices, for his re-birth in happier circumstances than his last appearing" ("Arnakali Devi" in *India Recalled*, 11).

The Hindu family cosmology, on the surface, might deny the rights of women, but if analyzed from its deep structure it basically constructs the unity of the family, in which husband and wife play roles prescribed by religious doctrine.

Besides assembling the foundation of family life, praying for baby boys is a must for Hindu women. A baby boy, within this tradition, is more precious than a baby girl. Sorabji wrote as follows: "Sashur-Ma (mother-in-law) said that the right meditation for girls at that age was for a husband and for many sons. As I had a husband, I prayed only for sons, which meant that I might be a good wife" ("Arnakali Devi" in *India Recalled*, 10). A good wife is a wife who could have a son. This related strongly to the metaphysical supremacy endowed by men in the Hindu cosmology. Before the arrival of Western medical science, which found that men were also responsible for infertility, traditional Hindu cosmology saw infertility and the sex of the child sorely as the responsibility of women. If a family had no children, or only had daughters, those held responsible were women, not men. The Hindu Shastra clearly stated that "There is no heavenly region for a Son-less Man"—*Hindu Shastra* ("Head-Shaving Ceremony" in *India Recalled*, 198). Given this, a wife would usually look for a new wife for her husband in order to maintain the stability of the family. In "Greater Love" (*Love and Life behind the Purdah*, 61-69), the story of Matha-Shri, a sonless woman, is recounted. Martha Shri sought to get her husband to marry her cousin named Sahai, in order to save their rights in heaven. Although her husband, Nano the Pundit, refused at first, she forced him to marry her cousin. Matha Shri then decided to retire to live in a cave in the mountains: "She went home, almost gaily. 'My Life!' she said, 'I have made a vow to feed the old faqir who live on the top of the mountain pass—thou knowest: and to-morrow my vow will crave redemption. Sahai will take care of thee: I will shoulder my gourd of oil and the offering of ground-nut cakes, which the god loveth above all things, as thou knowest; and ere cock-crow I shall be on the mountain-side'. ... 'What matter?' retorted Matha Shri—'gods cannot be defied, least of all by the barren. Farewell! Never was a childless woman so happy as hath been thy Matha Shri!'" (*Love and Life Behind the Purdah*, 61-69). The story relates her happiness in saving a place in heaven for her husband for the sake of their family's integrity in accordance with Hindu cosmology.

Sorabji wrote on last and final duty that an Indian woman was expected to endure, this time on the death of her husband. This is the practice of Suttee, when a woman follows her husband's dead body by following him in the cremation fire. Sorabji eloquently narrated the story of Indian women's misery here in *Suttee* in "A Living Sacrifice" in *Love and Life Behind the Purdah* (84-89). *Suttee* tells the story of Tani who had to swallow the ball of black opium which lay within the cake of grain-flour, which her indifferent appetite could not be tempted to eat, before the suttee stone burned her body. Tani had indeed accepted the sacrifice, her body which moisted in the heatened bambus next to her motionless husband. If a Hindu husband is dead, a Hindu wife is supposed to follow him as well, burning herself in the fire, *Suttee*. Devi Agni, goddess of Fire, will then unite their souls. The textual sources of this doctrine had, however, undergone many challenges from more progressive interpretations. Mathaji Maharani, one of the significant female Pundits mentioned by Sorabji in herstory, held an interesting theory about *Suttee*:

> "that the form of *Suttee* found in practice by the British upon their occupation of India had its origin, in her belief, in the wanton or careless transcription of an ancient *Shastra*. "When her husband dies let the widow *go within*", read the text. "When her husband dies let the widow *go into the fire*", copied the scribe. Sanskrit scholars will recognize the ease—the changing of a single word—with which the terrible custom was foisted upon religion". (Arnakali Devi in *India Recalled*, 13).

This careful interpretation was then adopted by the British Indian to ban the practice of Suttee in the Indian subcontinent.

Upon the death of her husband, the Hindu widow—who was not supposed to earn a living outside of their domestic domain—inherited the total amount of her husband's property. A Hindu widow's estate had peculiar characteristics. A sonless widow has a greater interest in her husband's estate than that known in English law as a tenancy-for-life. As Mulla, a well-known authority on Hindu Law has said: "She is in fact an absolute owner, subject to certain restrictions, except where by custom she is without restriction, and is entitled absolutely". She may spend the entire income of the property as she pleases, and dispose of it in whatever way she likes. She may even deal with accumulations of income, provided she has separated these from the *corpus* before she dies, or dealt with them in such a manner that separation may be presumed (Principles of the Hindu Law, pp. 163, 171. Calcutta, 1932, quoted in "The Position of Hindu Women" in *India Recalled*, 29). The income, in fact, becomes her *stridhan* or *peculium* of which she may dispose by deed or will, and to which certain female heirs alone may succeed—*stridhan* property being protected against males, including husbands ("The Position of Hindu Women" in *India Recalled* 29). Widows' lives were guaranteed fully by the system employed in the orthodox Hindu related to the ownership of property.

The Indian women's adherence to the cosmology exercised within orthodox Hinduism and Islam, which are similar in their segregation of women, shows their self-willed surrender to what they regard as religiosity. They diminished the word "I" by affirming the ego of the community, communal ego, the ego of god which basically characterized traditional structures. To be religious was to follow every prescribed dogma. They perform this self-willed surrender to achieve balance with their worldview. They viewed that their roles were domestic. They gave their individual rights to the rights of the community, the family and the whole Hindu and Muslim society. Their surrender may have meant that they did not feel oppressed, as we would understand the term today, because they embraced the norms of their community and vowed to leave their "ego", to diminish their "I". Their perception of their own bodies reflected their religious cosmology. The abhorration towards their bodies that they sensed in their deep pray was an abhorration constructed in the holy verdicts. Their cosmology of bodies and the roles they had to play were highly textual and heavily influenced by the doctrines that determined their worldview.

The previous brief sketch of the roles prescribed for women in the Hindu cosmology related to the influence of inherited pastoral and rural traditions in the formulation of Hinduism's doctrines, as exemplified in the Shastra verdict. With the arrival of the British East India Company and India's subsequent formal colonization by the British Empire, Hinduism's cosmology met with the modern western cosmology—including, the affirmation of the world of ego and the existence of "I". These civilizations had different perceptions of the roles of women. The meeting of the different value constructions between the British and India provided a space for dialogue and transition. Cornelia Sorabji was one of a small number of prominent Indian women who intensely re-toured both value systems, and as an outcome of this, cast herself as both the guardian of Indian women and culture, and a catalyst for their transformation. She was the product of western modern education as well as the product of her close inquiry into the progressive interpretation of the Hindu holy texts. Her cosmology was a melting pot, in which the world of the traditional (that which affirmed the world of "community") could coexist with the modern world's affirmation of the existence of "I". She witnessed the transition of public roles in nineteenth century Britain, and observed how they were not solely performed by men. With her modern gaze, she captured Indian women's resistances toward their traditional roles in the first half of 19th century.

In Sorabji's fictional work, *Love and Life behind the Purdah*, she let her characters tell their own stories. One notable introduction is "Love and Death" that introduces the rejection by two English-educated Indian youngsters of their arranged-marriages. Both were doctors who fortunately met and fell in love. The girl, an Indian lady with European qualifications was temporarily at the disposal of the chief medical officer. "I always thought it very nice of him to allow me an English education," she said; "and I have often built him up round that one kind fact. But I begged a year's freedom on coming to India—and now, however am I to face that inevitable introduction? "Where is he?" Ah! That I cannot tell; but I expect you would find him in his native village, a pampered only son, too orthodox to cross the waters himself, and managing the family property, in ignorant and comfortable self-satisfaction" (Love and Death in *Love and Life behind the Purdah*, 53). Her resistance was expressed in her resentment of her blind future husband that her parents had decided for her. The seed of rejection mediated the trace of two cultures that she inherited, the modern western education that gradually admitted women into public roles; and the traditional Indian brahmo-noble rank which conserved the traditional values of domestic roles for women. She became the site of the reduplication and production of those two civilizations into which she had to negotiate.

Other women's resistances are brought to the fore in Sorabji's story "Love and Life" which narrates the story of a Muslim of high noble rank, Raj, who owned four wives in his zenana. Four queens to a king is the scriptural limit: "'tis much wiser to run to your full allowance, or revolt with a single favorite" (Love and Life in *Love and Life behind the Purdah*, 41). The doctrinal Quran was indeed being interpreted textually with the support of traditional cosmological views on the roles of women in the domestic sphere. His little Rani (Queen), Piari, who was jealous of the new wife, depicted her jealousy and suffering in the following poem.

> There was the Door, to which I found no keys;
> There was the Veil, through which I could not see:
> Some little talk awhile of Me and Thee
> There was—and then no more of Thee and Me!"
> (Love and Life in *Love and Life Behind the Purdah*, 44)

The previous poem shows her desperate search of the new Piari and her only husband, who is apparently co-owned by the other three wives. She resisted the concept of sharing a husband in her cosmology. Piari's resistance is also shared by another queen in the story entitled "Urmi":

> "Urmi, the cleverest queen moaned and said: 'Tell my father how they hated me here. You remember, when I came, how they looked at me, and shook their heads, and said a 'God forbid!' because I read and wrote? And when the king, our lord, favored me above them all, and sought my presence, and listened to my words, I heard them whisper. 'Bold minx!' They said, 'child of the Evil One! She knows what it does not beseem women to know, for she talks to *him*, she lifts her eyes and looks upon his face. How know we that in her distant home she did not break her *purdah*? We hear that her father taught her many things which he learnt of the Feringhee'." (Urmi in *Love and Life Behind the Purdah*, 59).

She was one of the Raj's favorite wives that brought consequently the hatred and jealousy of other wives. The conflict among wives in the Zenana in Sorabji's writing vividly depicts the start of educated women's rejection of the practice of polygamy.

The resistance of Indian's women depicted and narrated by Sorabji throws light on the transitional roles Indian women were ready to share in the public domain. The former traditional cosmology that prescribed only domestic roles to women had been challenged by the modern cosmology that promoted women's more public role. Modern education played a significant role raising women's consciousness and resistance during this transitional time in India. Sorabji saw that western modern education had penetrated their deep conscience, and having grasped onto the idea of more equal gender roles, they were willing to share this equal role whether in the public or domestic arena.

Sorabji mediated stories of Indian women and situated their resistance in relation to the transitions within modern India under the British. Educating women was the cure for the ills of society (de Souza, "Recovering a Tradition", 644). Sorabji herself had cast careful thought in her stories about how to help transform the roles women were willing to share in public. "I saw that education could become significant mediation in bridging their emancipation. I hoped that the educated ones would make a bridge between the old and the new, turning the grandmothers from customs and practices dangerous to health, helping women to find the work for which God had fitted individuals" ("The Many-Headed, The Many-Handed" in *India Recalled*, 117). She did not propose a sudden-jolt revolution or immediate emancipation as she saw that this prescription would only bring unnecessary destruction to the un-ready transitional Indian community. She envisioned slow change within the framework of purdah as the pathway to free women from being entrapped in old traditions. She said "Let education come first within the purdah, keeping the god-rules about subjection—indeed, keeping all the rules of our race which it is possible to keep. Freedom can come to women that way alone" ("The Many-Headed, The Many-Handed" in *India Recalled*, 119).

She praised the basic characteristic of Indian women as living sacrifices for having saved India from further obstacles: "It has always seemed to me deep wisdom, the thought behind this harrowing ritual, making women, not men, the removers of obstacles" ("The Scapegoat" in *India Recalled*, 136). She knew that such a character endowed in women was a talent that could become a significant vehicle in fostering the new India. She herself was involved in the gradual raising of the age of marriage in the Sarda Act from 6 to 14 years old. Her gradual proposal set the age of marriage at 7, then 9 and 11, before finally setting it at 14. She believed that if she proposed 14 at the beginning, the brahm rank would reject outright the Act. That was why she gradually, over time, proposed raising the age of marriage.

In her traversal of Indian and British cultures, Sorabji found at times a profound commonality between them. She recounted the story of an Indian man and a British man who respected each other. The two men liked one another at first sight. The Indian Bawaji is recalled as saying:

> "'Bring that Sadhu Sahib of the English people to the Hindu Sadhus' discussion tomorrow night". Lord Radstock was delighted to go. He read them a chapter of the Book of Isaiah, which they discussed with him. (I acted as translator). It was a great experience for myself. The pure in heart would seem to find common ground, whatever their form of Faith. ("Bawaji" in *India Recalled*, 145).

Sorabji had found that universal goodness, i.e. a common conscience, united these two religions.

For Sorabji, the Empire was not merely a political entity but had a cultural and social content. She dreamt of India retaining a social and cultural bond with Britain even if the Raj ended. Her uncritical awareness toward the British Empire was reflected in her finding religious commonality between the two civilizations: One can see this in her story of a boy, named Chota Chaukidar, who fasted for the health of Queen Victoria: "When the highest [of the] High", our Queen Victoria, was ill, in the same faithful way did my little Chaukidar fast "to win her merit" ("The Chota Chaukidar" in *Sun Babies*, 38). She saw a similarity in their perception of the body. Her world of the "there and after" was perceived to be of a far higher status than the faculty of the body. At best, the body is only another shrine. Spiritually however the body, as Mathaji said, was a degradation of the soul. Any "house" is in measure degradation, and belongs to a state of travel. “Someday we shall be free of all ‘houses’, shall lose ourselves in the Great Soul. That is the final ‘twilight’, the hour of Union awaiting every individual soul.... Then alone, shall there be no more death” (“Mathaji” in *India Recalled*, 153).

For all their cultural differences, Sorabji believed that the commonality between the two religions of Hinduism and Christianity would enhance dialogue and foster the movement of women into future public roles. Sorabji narrated the dream of a little girl, named Fleetfoot, to be free and to be unveiled. “And indeed the change was noticeable. “In her country,” she continued,” the women are free and unveiled, and Fleetfoot would be such here also” (“Fleetfoot” in *Sun Babies*, 70). Sorabji, however, stressed the need for slow change. “But others there are, like Bishun Singh’s grandmother, who recognize the need for change; but feel that change should come slowly, with propitiation of the great forces which have held an ancient people captive for centuries; should come with conservation of all that can be conserved without damage to progress in essentials” (“Bishun Singh” in *India Recalled*, 246).

Cornelia’s stories tell the story of the *Purdahnashin*, the history of Hindu and Muslim Indian women, of high or noble rank. She was often criticized for her stance against the Gandhian independence movement (Gooptu, *India’s Woman Lawyer*, 183). For example, she criticized the movement’s overturning of the position of India’s outcast ‘untouchable’ castes, arguing that this issue was being used merely as political card by the movement. She felt that the critics of orthodox Hinduism had yet to demonstrate that they could better guarantee harmony and solidarity amongst Indians. While her views on India’s independence movement may be regarded as out of tune with the spirit of the times, she had, however, assisted Hindu women’s transition to becoming more modern and educated. Some compare her unfavourably to her contemporary, the Indian women writer Sarojini Naidu, who has received more praise and acclamation in Indian politics. In contrast to Cornelia Sorabji, Sarojini Naidu campaigned for the extension of voting rights to women (Mehrotra, *A History of Indian Literature in English*, 133). Cornelia Sorabji, however, provided pathways for women to access the law. The entire women’s movement in India cannot be separated from Sorabji’s mediation in helping widowed *Purdahnashin* defend their property rights in front of the law. She together with other Indian women writers established a remarkable group of women who contributed a great deal to the fabric of modern India, through the retelling of women’s stories, the mediation between the modern and the traditional, bearing witness to women’s resistances and transformations, all of which were indeed herstory, only.

b. Why Nawal el Saadawi?

No woman in the Middle East has been the subject of more polemic and inspires as much emotion as Nawal El Saadawi. No woman's pen has violated as many sacred enclosures as that of Nawal El Saadawi. Arguably no woman has her finger so firmly on the pulse of Arab culture and the contemporary Middle East. As Egyptian psychiatrist, novelist, essayist, short-story and novella writer, nonfiction writer, memoirist, and playwright, Nawal El Saadawi (1931-) is hailed as one of the most prominent voices in Middle Eastern feminist literature and women's rights activism. El Saadawi is an advocate of values that threaten the patriarchal Arab society, and her outspoken support of political and sexual rights for women has resulted in her arrest on more than one occasion. Her work exemplifies the subservient role that women are expected to play in a patriarchal society and details the torture, mutilations, and spirit-breaking rules and regulations that contribute to the oppression of women, especially in Egypt. She speaks against radical religious groups of all types as these groups are based on a distrust of women and blame women for the sins of mankind. One of her most damning critiques is directed at the strongly patriarchal relations in Arab society that, coupled with a hierarchical class structure, have subjected women to a great deal of discrimination and caused them to be victims to a very marked degree of physical, psychological as well as spiritual oppression.

Her writings advocate the recognition of women's rights to control their own bodies and destinies as a result of her childhood trauma when she was forced to undergo a traditional clitoridectomy, a memory recounted in *El wajh el ary lilma'ra el arabeya* (1977, *The Hidden Face of Eve*). The essays in this collection describe female genital mutilation, chronicle the rules and regulations governing the lives of women, and tell of the difficulties and shame associated with being a woman in a repressive patriarchal society. These themes are repeated throughout El Saadawi's writings. In *Emra'atan fi emra'ah* (1968; *Two Women in One*), Bahiah, the protagonist, goes to attend university and begins to make choices for herself concerning love and her future. Her father is unhappy with her stance that she is free to make these decisions, so he sells her into marriage. She flees and is eventually imprisoned.

Nawal El Saadawi's dream of being a physician had led to her reaching the top position as the Director of Health Education in 1958, a position which she had to renounce due to the negative response to her nonfiction book *El ma'ra wal ginse* (1971, *Women and Sex*). On September 6, 1981, she was arrested under Egypt's "Law for the Protection of Values from Shame" and imprisoned during the politically volatile administration of Egyptian President Anwar el-Sadat. El Saadawi's arrest attracted publicity as women throughout the Arab world, Europe, the United States, and Asia campaigned for her freedom, finally securing her release on November 25, 1981. Afterwards her subsequent works were subject to censorship under the Anwar Sadat regime. At present, although her books are no longer censored in her homeland, they have banned in Egypt and other Arab countries for a time, although many managed to find their way into most Arab nations.

Her imprisonment was the basis for her memoir, *Mozakerati fi signel nissa* (1983; *Memoirs from the Women's Prison*). Her contact with a prisoner at Qanatir served as inspiration for an earlier work, a novel titled *Emra'a enda noktat el sifr* (1975; *A Woman at Point Zero*). El Saadawi creates a story around Firdaus, who seeks to gain financial independence through prostitution and is ultimately sentenced to death for killing her pimp. After being labeled 'dishonored', Firdaus decides to turn to a more traditional career. Although she rises quickly to the top echelon of female workers in her field, the realization that she has not regained respectability and that she is still selling her body—albeit in a different way—prompts complete disillusionment with society and causes her to return to her former life as a prostitute. The story revealed that the main character has to play the game of submission or die.

Again El Saadawi implies that rebellion, sacrifice, and transcendence, as the only options to fight against oppression, are at the expense of life. Another of El Saadawi's political yet wide-reaching works is *Suqut al-Imam* (1987; *The Fall of the Imam*), which is set on a fictitious male-dominated island and exposes and satirizes the hypocrisy in politics—particularly theocracies—and the treatment of women in all societies. *The Fall of the Imam* is a study of the psychology of power that goes far beyond slogans of patriarchy under the name of Islam as a religion. The limitations of women's roles in a repressive society are further explored in this novel. The novel examines the dangers of religious fanaticism and asserts that women are often the most susceptible to abuse and suffering when religious laws become more stringent. *The Fall of the Imam* is an ambitious rewriting of patriarchy. Her works reflects that patriarchy is an all-inclusive system that informs social, political, and religious structures. The Imam by his name, of course, has become one of the religious sides of her character. She employs an infinitely more complex and important game, that of redefining male theology and constructing an alternate, feminist religious mythology. The religious intertext was exposed as well in her former works, which had already being exploited in some of her short stories. In *The Fall of the Imam*, however, this intertext becomes a dominant robust part of the narrative.

Many of El Saadawi's recurring themes are brought together in *The Fall of the Imam*: abuse of power by male officials, rape, exploitation, and the unjust punishment of women for crimes committed by men. The book provoked death threats from religious extremist groups, causing the government to protect El Saadawi by stationing a twenty-four-hour armed guard detail at her home. El Saadawi has also written two autobiographies. *A Daughter of Isis* (1999) covers El Saadawi's childhood and describes her activist role in Egyptian feminism; *Walking through Fire* (2002) continues to outline her political battles to change the role of women in Middle Eastern society that are considered revolutionary and politically subversive.

With her next to the last novel, *Jannât wa-Iblîs* (*The Innocence of the Devil*), Nawal El Saadawi boldly continued the project begun with *The Fall of the Imam*. Whereas in *The Fall of the Imam* the political dominated, redefining the social and religious structures with which it came into contact, in *The Innocence of the Devil* the religious intertext leads, redefining the political and social orders. The setting of the book is an insane asylum, where Satan (Iblîs) and God are confined together as patients. Who is the Deity? Who is the Devil? Her narrative redefines not only the relationship between God and Devil, but also that between Adam and Eve, between man and woman. She saw that Christianity and Islam are both guilty here, and the Devil, like woman, becomes but another victim of the patriarchal order. The body becomes the central player in the narrative, with the physical rape of the female merely one of its articulations. *The Fall of the Imam* uncovers a great deal of the dominance of a patriarchal ruler.

Her works and memoirs are not a mere chronicling of imprisonment and subsequent liberation. Rather, the first-person narrator of the texts weaves an intricate tale in which prostitutes and political prisoners sit side by side, in which fictional elements blend with nonfictional ones, and in which past and present merge as childhood memories redefine the incarceration. More important, the entire project that is the prison memoirs is one of metaphorical and literary violation. Investigation of these multiple violations makes it clear that the fall of the Imam, that is the death of Sadat, was a necessary act whose consequences go beyond the mere liberation of the narrator. The initial violation that set the metaphorical women's protest in motion is rectified gradually throughout the narrative, culminating logically with the death of the male ruler. The violations in El Saadawi's textual corpus are more than literary and metaphorical. They are also a social yet theological outcry. When Nawal El Saadawi, the world traveler, traverses borders, many intricate games of identity are played out as the narrator uses various locales to make savage social commentary and to dramatically and provocatively cross established gender boundaries in the postcolonial Muslim Middle East.

c. Why Leila Ahmed?

Unlike Nawal El Sadaawi, both Huda Shaarawi (1879-1947)—Egypt's first feminist who greatly influenced both Saadawi and Ahmed—and Leila Ahmed came from well-to-do Muslim families. They frequently traveled abroad and were educated in the West, mostly in Europe. These characteristic would most likely describe many of Egypt's upper-middle to upper-class families.

In *A Border Passage: from Cairo to America: A Woman's Journey*, Leila Ahmed describes her Muslim childhood in an upper middle-class and privileged family in Cairo. There was the private world created by her mother, her aunts, and her grandmother, all of whom embodied the pacifist, life-affirming qualities of an Islam that was steeped in a rich, living oral tradition. This was in sharp contrast to the more severe tenets of the official Islam—drawn by men from arcane written texts—that were beginning to be re-imposed with new emphasis throughout the Middle East. In writing this memoir, Ahmed found two of the most intractable issues to be Arab nationalism and the "cargo of negatives" attached to Islam by Western academia. In *A Border Passage*, Leila Ahmed lucidly addresses confounding processes by which her identity was constructed amid the intersection of several different values.

She saw that Islam (like other religions) already has all those internal differences and diversities, which is undergoing further tremendous permutations and transformations as a result, for one thing, of the process of "globalization". She lamented that Islamic "fundamentalism" is entrenched, and it would seem that the future of the oral tradition of Islam that she grew up with is simply hopeless. She foresaw that the future of the oral tradition in Islam could actually be enormously promising. She wrote in her memoir that the method of teaching Islam was thus totally different for men and for women, and that the understanding that women have of Islam was also not fundamentalist (in Chapter 5). Ahmed understands that women's aural/oral tradition of applying and regenerating the teachings of the Quran is different from men's visits to mosques, the preaching of ayatollahs, and the study of classical Arabic (a "dead" language like Latin) which is pursued and translated only by men.

Her memoir provides a wonderful way to study the history of a Muslim woman's trajectory from Muslim Egypt to the American liberal community. It offers a detailed glimpse into another way of life, another time, on a personal level which intersects the life of tradition with that of the modern. The language of her memoirs is lyrical. Her themes of geographical and gender-based alienation, moreover, both evoke empathy. She firmly believed that the silent majority of Muslims want to find a voice and not to leave the voice of Islam only to the conservative, so-called observant Muslims.

d. Why Fatema Mernissi?

Dreams of Trespass (1995) is her autobiography. She has penned an engaging memoir about her own childhood in a Moroccan harem into which she was born in the 1940s. "I was born in a harem in 1940 in Fez, Morocco..." So begins Fatima Mernissi in this metaphoric harem by which she meant women's seclusion rather than the building in which women are kept per se. The Mernissi harem is a large extended family in which female members, including divorced aunts and the several wives of some men in the household, are confined to their shared home and restricted in their behavior. While they accept their role in society, the women applaud changes in other Muslim nations and admire prominent women who promote these changes. It is a great portrayal of a girl who learns about her culture by discovering the issues of sex, gender roles, and family in the Fez harem. This book stated many of the inequalities women who lived in harems had to deal with, and explained them with certain flair of childhood innocence. For her a harem was about private space, and the rules regulating it and it did not need walls; once one knew what was forbidden, one carried the harem within; any space one entered had its own invisible rules; wherever there are human beings, there is an invisible rule; unfortunately, most of the time, the invisible rule is against women. The above insights reflect her strenuous opposition to women's discrimination, which is still prevalent in the Muslim community within which she took as its vivid example, the metaphoric harem.

Mernissi is very critical of the traditional Islam that frequently subordinated women through its narrow interpretation of Islam. Like Kartini (see below), she was taught strictly in school that she should memorize the Qur'an everyday. She was constantly berated, yelled at and beaten whenever she made a mistake. Thus she viewed religion as something to be afraid of. To her, how the Qur'an is read depends on one's perspective and perception. These holy verses could be the gate to escape from oppression, or instead be an obstacle to this. To her the Qur'an can lead towards the dream of women's liberation instead of women's subordination. Mernissi even makes a robust critique of several Hadiths (prophetic tradition) originating from the Kitab Bukhari, which state that the Prophet said: "Dog, donkey and woman would annul anyone's prayer whenever they pass ahead them, break off between the praying man and kiblah." She was shocked to hear that sort of Hadith and resolved never to repeat it in the hope that silence would wipe away it out of her mind. She asked, "How come the Prophet said that sort of Hadits which hurt me so much?... How could the beloved Muhammad hurt a little girl who in her growth, attempts to make him a pillars of her romantic dreams?" (*Woman in Islam*, p. 82).

Like Kartini and El Saadawi, Mernissi is very critical of polygamy. Yet despite the merits of the nationalists in the Middle East who allowed women to get an education, Mernissi admitted that many ideas of Arabic nationalism are still to be criticized. For example, polygamy is not yet forbidden, women cannot achieve equal status and democracy has yet to be established in the Arab world. As a well-known and prominent activist in the Islamic world, she protested against a Hadith opposed to female leadership. Her motivation to investigate such Hadiths was instigated by the Hadiths spoken by a trader in the market, who negated female leadership. Surprised by her questions, the trader quoted the Hadith that "there is no salvation within society led by females." To her, this indicated the extent to which the Hadiths are embedded within the Muslim community, despite the fact that the Qur'an discusses the leadership of Queen Bilqis.

In additon to her rejection of polygamy and the reputed prohibition on women leaders, Mernissi is critical as well of the Hijab, which she was taught is compulsory for every devout Muslim woman. In her view, however, she sees the Hijab as an instrument of limitation, segregation and isolation, which is used to keep women out of the public space. To her Hijab means segregation and is used as a medium of asserting hierarchy between the rulers and the people. She attempts to illustrate that religious teachings can be easily manipulated and for that reason she believes that the oppression of woman is not part of the real teaching of Islam. She believes that there are real and true teachings in Islam, and is careful not to oppose the sacred tradition.

e. Why Kartini?

Kartini (1879-1904), with the noble title Raden Ajeng later proceeded by Raden Ayu after her marriege, was an outstanding Javanese Muslim woman, born into a noble and well-to-do Javanese family during the time when Java, was still part of the Dutch East Indies colony. Despite being a devout Muslim, she was very critical of her religion. Kartini raised questions about the way religion was used to provide a justification for men to pursue polygamy. For Kartini, the depth of suffering of Javanese women had reached its nadir, when their world was reduced to the walls of their house and when they were prepared to accept a polygamous marriage. She questioned as well why the Qu'ran must be memorised and recited without an obligation to actually understand it. She also expressed the view that the world would be more peaceful if there was no religion to provide reasons for disagreements, discord and offence. She firmly believed that religion must guard against committing sins, but more often, she lamented, sins are committed in the name of religion. In addition to her criticisms of Islam, she was also critical of Javanese culture. The majority of her letters protest the tendency of Javanese Culture to impose obstacles on the development of women. She wanted women to have the freedom to learn and study.

Kartini was appointed posthumously Indonesia's national heroine, due to her pioneering work in the area of women's rights for native Indonesian women. Kartini's family allowed her to attend school until she was 12 years old. Here, among other subjects, she learnt to speak fluent Dutch, an unusual accomplishment for Javanese women at the time. After she turned 12 she was 'secluded' at home, a common practice among Javanese nobility, to prepare young girls for their marriage. During seclusion girls were not allowed to leave their parents' house until they were married, at which point authority over them was transferred to their husbands. During her seclusion, Kartini continued to educate herself on her own. Because Kartini could speak Dutch, she acquired several Dutch pen friends. One of them, a girl by the name of Rosa Abendanon became her very close friend. Books, newspapers and European magazines fed Kartini's interest and fostered the desire to improve the conditions of indigenous women, who at that time had a very low social status. Kartini's concerns were not just in the area of the emancipation of women, but also the problems of her society. Kartini saw that the struggle for women to obtain their freedom, autonomy and legal equality was just part of a wider movement.

After her death, Mr JH Abendanon, the Minister for Culture, Religion and Industry in the East Indies, collected and published the letters that Kartini had sent to her friends in Europe. The book was titled *Door Duisternis tot Licht (Out of Dark Comes Light)* and was published in 1911. It went through five editions, with some additional letters included in the final edition, and was translated into English by Agnes L. Symmers and published under the title *Letters of a Javanese Princess*.

7. Using Postcolonial Muslim Women Writers' Works in *Prose* Syllabus: discussion related to gender theme

The messages about gender roles, both explicit and implied in the settings of these postcolonial Muslim countries setting need to be discussed with and evaluated by Muslim students in the classroom context. Specifically, teachers and students could explore, both through their analyses of the main characters and through their own responses to this type of literature, the ways in which Muslim women and men are alike and different in their response to issues of gender relations in Muslim societies. Table 1 lists the names of several Muslim women writers which deals with key issues in gender relations in Muslim traditional communities which intersect with the approaching modern era, as well as several corresponding sources a teacher might consult, and several works which present progressive Muslim characters (female and/or male) responding to these issues.

Table 2, provides a sample of possible topics suitable for group discussion, which could be used to initiate a discussion on the role of women in modern Muslim communities. Through the example of Leila Ahmad, students could consider how modern Muslim women's identity construction intersects with the values coming from the West. Students could go on to explore how gender may influence their response to the world in general, by reading the memoirs and letters of postcolonial Muslim women, such as Kartini's correspondence with J.H. Abendanon in the Netherlands. Kartini's experience as a Javanesse princess may help Javanese Muslim students in Muhammadiyah universities to reflect upon their present identity in connection with the world outside themselves. The collection of Kartini's letters contains her indigenous speaking voice, including her agony, her triumph, her confusion and despair which echoed across the barriers of time and place. Her letters can therefore be read as the consciousness of the life-world of her society at that time, a consciousness that was neither wholly colonial nor what may be regarded as traditional Javanese, neither contemporary Western nor traditional. Her agonizing arises from this state of coming-into-being, this emerging freedom growing out of her journey of self-definition.

The works provide students with robust, admirable characters who manage to move toward the kind of integration of traditional mores and modern morality within the Muslim community. The main characters separate the self from the heavy burden of the misogynistic tradition in the name of "Islam" and judge their present situation based upon a progressive interpretation of the holy sayings in due respect to their religion. Each main character in the works is accorded the right to develop as an individual. The female moralities, which are mostly muted in the Muslim community, are grounded in the immediate. Empathy and concern for others grow out of a sense of rebellion, and the result of this sense of protest toward the rigid traditional Ulema/Imams/Ustadz is not moral judgment or hierarchy of absolute values and rules; the effect is to encourage dialogue and networks of care and support. There are main characters as well who reflect an ability to move out of traditional modes of thought and who learn to take a stand and to rely on her own judgment, even when they conflict with those of others, instead of relying upon the words from traditional Ulemas. Students are given chances to experience the life of different characters, such as a prostitute, a rebellious girl, a physician, a second-third wife, a first wife, a woman who became a killer, etc.

This alternative canon proposed for the *Prose* Syllabus will not be able to accomplish significant changes in attitude over night. This alternative canon, nonetheless, can change literature programs in English departments to indicate that students should value and respect diversity and that they appreciate women's interpretation in reading against the prevalent interpretation which maintains women's subordination in the Muslim community.

Table 1
Sample of *Prose* Syllabus for the English Department in Muhammadiyah Universities

Postcolonial Muslim Countries	Author and Title
Indonesia	Kartini (1879-1904)1920, *Letters of a Javanesse Princess*(1986-ed & 2005-ed, translated by Agnes Louise Symmers)1992, *Letters from Kartini: An Indonesian Feminist, 1900-1904*(Translated by Joost Cote)

India	Cornelia Sorabji (1870-1904)1902, 2003, *Loves and Life Behind the Purdah*Attia Hosain (1913-1998)1961, *Sunlight on a Broken Column*
Egypt	Nawal el Saadawi (1931-)1987, *The Fall of the Imam*(1988, transl. by Sheriff Hetata)Leila Ahmed (1940-)1999, *A Border Passage: from Cairo to America—A Women's Journey*(autobiography)
Morocco	Fatema Mernissi (1940-)1995, *Dreams of Trespass, Tales of a Harem Girlhood* (autobiography)

Table 2:
Sample of group discussion questions from Leila Ahmed's *A Border Passage*

Discussion Questions:

1. Were any of Ahmed's childhood memories similar to your own? If so, please describe them.

2. Did the cultural backgrounds of the women with whom Ahmed grew up in Egypt inform her childhood opinions of them? Consider especially how her perception of her traditional Arabic speaking mother was utterly transformed throughout the course of the book. Have you undergone similar evolutions in how you perceive your own parents? If so, what do you think caused this?

3. Ahmed said that she learned about religion through watching "hidden messages: attitudes, posture, a glance of approval." How did you learn about religion? Discuss what types of "hidden messages" influenced your spiritual development.

4. Before reading A Border Passage, what were your feelings about Islam? What were some of the misconceptions about Muslim women dismantled by Ahmed in the book?

5. One of the core issues addressed in *A Border Passage* is the process by which our identities are constructed. Discuss what you think were

your own "defining moments" or "formative years". What made them so crucial? Were they politically driven?

6. Do you think Ahmed succeeds in objectively disentangling the controversial political, religious, and cultural conflicts explored in her book? Can you pinpoint which narrative techniques were most helpful to you?

7. Although many cultures thrive on oral traditions, educational systems continue to emphasize the written literary tradition. In short, "if it isn't written down, it didn't happen." What are the implications of assigning more credence to the written word than to oral traditions? How did this affect Ahmed's experience in Abu Dhabi? How do you think it affected your own education?

8. "I think that we are always plural. Not either this or that, but this and that." What does Ahmed mean by this? What different traditions, cultures, and histories converge to make you who you are?

8. Conclusion

If the classroom in Muhammadiyah universities is a microcosm of Muslim society, then gender is a powerful factor in English classrooms and the study of gender issues must inform both the students and Muslim society. This research has sought to theorize the decisions taken within Muhammadiyah universitites that have contributed to the content and orientation of English departments. Specifically, it has sought to address the following questions: which story, taught to whom, by what methods, for what purposes, followed by what kind of assignments, evaluated how, by whom, and for what purposes. Of course, as the second largest Islamic social institution in Indonesia, Muhammadiyah contributes a great deal to the learning and socialization of students' literary appreciation within its English departments. While this study does not consider that teachers themselves are responsible for the specific gender roles that male and female students assume in life, teachers do need to consider carefully Muhammadiyah's contribution to stereotypical behavior of gender roles in the Muslim community. The more we recognize and address the prevalence of such stereotypical behaviour, the more students could be empowered through a tactful and careful transformation of the canon. This study cannot decide what pedagogy on gender can do without having decided at some level what Islamic educational values are and what it believes about teaching and learning gender issues. Muslim students' views about gender and the learning of English have been shaped by their individual experiences as part of a Muslim community as a whole. The postcolonial Muslim women writers I have proposed in a tentative new canon for the *Prose* syllabus are mostly Muslim women whose analyses of gender relations could play a significant role in transforming the Muslim community in general, as well as lead to inquiry and reflection on how students might change.

In the present literature canon and curriculum in Muhammadiyah universities, teachers, most of the time, ask students to ignore their gender role as they read, to immerse themselves in the literature, following the central point of view where it leads them, and reflecting on that experience, seeking the high artistic universals. What this study is proposing here is that it invites students to read with their full gender experience intact, to resist the central point of view when it contradicts that experience, and to seek artistry both in particulars and the universals. It is meant to raise students' critical awareness toward their own-given-values vis-à-vis values coming from the outside of their own community.

The current English curriculum requires a close look in the light of gender sensitivity if all students, male and female, are to fully develop the potential to hear the voices of others clearly, as well as equally, even those voices who are very critical of Muslim traditions. Exposure to the writings of postcolonial Muslim women through the proposed canon reform would enhance students' critical abilities to understand, shape, and share their worlds, as well as to imagine other worlds which are possibly completely different from their own, and have a full appreciation to these. This Chapter is an effort to begin such an inquiry.

Chapter VIII
Conclusion

1. Muslim students need a specific literary canon

The present twenty two Muhammadiyah English Departments in Indonesia have initiated a multicultural dialogue through the inclusion of the present Western literary canon in the curriculum. Muhammadiyah universities through its English Departments, however, have adopted merely Western literature in the formation of their curricula which is unable to cater to the spirit of multiculturalism, and is particularly unable to cater to students' own search for their own self identity as Muslim students. The lack of Muslim writers within this canon is a tangible problem, and one that this research has tried to respond to from the beginning. There are always pedagogical considerations when forming a literary canon. And the question "Who reads the canon?" is far less frequently addressed compared to the question "how to read the canon?" which has been much wrtitten about in literary theory. It is necessary, from my perspective, to build a specific canon for Muslim students to bridge the gulf of the cultural clash that happens during the reading process. They deserve to read a more multicultural literary canon where Western values and Islamic values meet and are negotiated in a contemporary dialogue.

The present context in Indonesia calls for an urgent response here in order to cater to the need for a multicultural literary canon, one which could enhance Islamic students' critical awareness of the rapid changes accompanying globalization. Expanding the literary canon to promote dialogue between the West and the East is itself an aspect of globalization. Instead of perceiving globalization as the agent of homogenization of particular values, that is Western values, students should be encouraged to perceive it as potentially extending the space where other different value systems can be appreciated and negotiated. One way to do this is through the range of literary texts incorporated as part of the literary canon in Muhammadiyah's English Departments. Many contemporary writers, be those from the UK, such as the contemporary novels of Hanif Kureishi, from the US, Australia, Canada, India or many other postcolonial Muslim regions such as Pakistan, Bangladesh, Malaysia, Tunisia, Morocco, Aljazair, Algeria, or even Indonesia deserve to be placed in the canon in order to enhance the dialogue between the West and the East, and specifically to enhance the skills of Muhammadiyah students in negotiating their Islamic values in relation to the values they read in such works of literature.

2. The limit of Islamic education and its consequences

Historically, support for the teaching of English in Indonesia was initiated by three major factors: (1) the government's positive attitude towards English language due to the adoption of a capitalistic economy; (2) private initiatives from (a) western-educated nationalist indigenous actors; (b) Christian as well as Catholics missionaries; and (c) modern Islamic institutions, e.g. the Persyarikatan Muhammadiyah, which played significant roles in propagating the education of the neglected Muslim majority; and (3) support from the US via the Ford Foundation which promulgated the soft core of the English department curriculum and in-service training for teachers of English. Although the Dutch colonial government's support of public education during the Ethical Policy is considered to have had only a limited reach, it did contribute to the creation of western-educated indigenous nationalists. This in combination with modernist Islamist elite—many of whom studied for many years in Egypt and Saudi Arabia—was influential in leading to the establishment of Islamic educational institutions, which then spread across Indonesia providing mass education at the grassroots level.

Islamic education has assumed a new definition and received wider application by traditional Muslims during the last two decades. In 1977 an important meeting—the World Conference for Muslim Education—was held in Mecca, where a group of predominantly fundamentalist Muslims emphasized the need for education relevant to Islam's sociocultural values, relevance being seen in moral and eschatological terms. They argued that education could redirect and reshape the attitudes of Muslim children by shifting their orientation from Western to Islamic values. The role of Islam, defined in terms of its worldview and dogma, was seen as determining the objectives of education and influencing educational process. This, they believed, could be achieved by rejecting current practices colored by Western cultures and ideologies. In short, these traditionalists viewed education as an important means of creating an Islamized society and an instrument for forging a new Islamic identity. With this in mind, they attempted to reformulate educational objectives, redesign curricula, and rewrite textbooks.

The total assimilation of all subjects into an Islamic moral and religious frameworks, especially when this is tied to the propagation of *dakwah* (as shown in the analysis of seven Muhammadiyah curricula), means that subjects are all to be judged on their moral outcome and to go through a process of scrutiny and censorship before being accepted within the so-called Islamic polity. As a result of this understanding, science at all levels is taught conservatively with critical and analytical methodology absent. Scientific knowledge develops critical thinking and avoids the uncritical acceptance of traditional answers to human inquiry. Science challenges the validity and relevance of all discourse of knowledge, because nothing is accepted as permanent and sacred. Unlike theology, science permits the critical comparison of competing theories and frameworks. While the mark of a scientific theory is that it is testable, religious knowledge is empirically untestable and demands unquestioning acceptance and practice.

The Islamization of knowledge is then followed by the Islamization of laws in Indonesia. The enactment of around *Sharia* laws in 63 regions in Indonesia has resulted in the oppression of vulnerable groups in Indonesian society, especially women and religious minority. The *ulama*, the military, and elites all benefited from Islamization in those regions. Emblematic of the legitimization of traditional elite show that Islamic ideology has failed to provide the promised equality and social justice. The *ulama* never reached a consensus as to what constituted an Islamic educational, economic, or political system, or how it could be implemented. Nevertheless, Islamic discourse gave tremendous power to the *ulama*. The emphasis on ideological education has intensified cultural and religious differences, resulting in cultural clash and resentment of other cultures.

The fall of the Suharto secular Indonesian government has led to the growing criticism among the new Islamist activists, including Muhammadiyah in the educational sectors. The New Islamist activists regard that the return to the 'total Islam' (*kaffah*) means that implementing *Shariah Islamiyah* on a state is a must. The propagation to perform the total Islam (kaffah) is to reach what they call "ideal *Ummah*" in the house of *Ummah* (*Darul Ummah*). The ideal norm of the Muslim community has been translated by the new Islamist movements in reaction against the more homogenized global world. It shows distinctive expressions and the use of Islamic symbolism which is unique to new Islamist literary genre which is significant in propagating the goal of New Islamist movements. This has represented the resistance echoed by the New Islamist literary authors in expressing their unique identity in what they call as the more secular and materialistic global world.

The way these new-Islamists movements resist globalization, especially secularization and western values is shared as well by many Muhammadiyah students. Such of a resistance hinders Muslim students' process of reading literary works coming from the Western canon. This finding is conspicuously evident amongst present Indonesian Muslim students. "An ideal *Ummah* is an ideal situation for Muslim life" said many Muhammadiyah students during the interviews. "And an ideal Ummah is an Ummah which implements Islam *kaffah*", they concluded. Their perspective further entailed acute anti western and anti secular values.

3. Muhammadiyah curriculum reformation

The education debate has focused on how—or whether—the religious curriculum promotes intolerance and extremism. But Muhammadiyah has chosen a dramatic course, deciding not just to rewrite textbooks but also aiming to prepare its graduates for a more participatory and economically competitive future. A curriculum should presents Muhammadiyah's own identity, own history, and the Islamic religion. But broader reforms have not been carried out and many conservative Muhammadiyah leaders have blamed outsiders for unfairly tarring their religion-focused educational system. This reformation is as a chance to push through education reform, changes that would not only promote religious tolerance but also seek to introduce notions of greater citizen participation, individual choice and entrepreneurship. Many progressive Muhammadiyah leaders endorse the idea of broader change and issuing a manifesto calling for a more progressive Muhammadiyah education with students better educated to compete in the modern economy.

This research listed three things that hinder development in Indonesia—rising unemployment in a region accustomed to agricultural revenue, ineffective and old-fashioned teaching methods, and a failure to adapt to the Internet age in schools and universities. Indonesia has shortcomings in its developmental path and reformed system as it does not provide people with the basic skills demanded by the marketplace. This is why it is necessary that Indonesia should declare war on violence and fanaticism, and order a study of and changes to textbooks that promote extremism as part of a religious curriculum. Religious textbooks describing *jihad* as mandatory war on non-Muslims and Israel as the religious enemy of all Muslim should be replaced by textbooks that promote "brotherhood, equality, love, caring, mercifulness and coexistence". This process is still underway and not a word has been changed. Islam should not be interpreted in a fashion which leads to extremism, as progressive Muhammadiyah leaders have said recently.

A constant battle is still taking place within Islamic educational institutions, whether to treat all subjects as Islamic—including secular subjects as well as so-called religious subjects. Presently experts within Muhammadiyah's educational institutions favour a more open approach, that is, one which appreciates that secular subjects as well as religious subjects are also Islamic. But Muhammadiyah's present policy here may shift in the next decade if the new-Islamist movements continue to consolidate power and challenge such a position. Their epistemological approach would not be as friendly towards secular subjects, and they have already stated that secular subjects are not Islamic. The sacred is defined as textually sacred, and the current context has been blamed as unholy and not sacred. Pragmatism is seen as errant. These are contentious points which have many progressive *Ulemas* and *Kyais* in Indonesia worried. Pragmatism, for example, has prolonged the life of Muhammadiyah education so far. Several ultra-conservative Ulama in Muhammadiyah, however, feel that such an approach is immoral and corrupt. It is a point that may endanger the quality and relevance of education in Muhammadiyah's institutions in the future. This internal tension and dynamic in Muhammadiyah has made many of its educational institutions lag far behind other educational institutions owned by the State and Christian-Catholic missions. It is no wonder that only a quarter of Muhammadiyah educational institutions have been accredited by the government, while the remaining over one thousand schools and universities lack of proper accreditation.

4. Mainstreaming gender through postcolonial Muslim women writers

Muhammadiyah's view towards the position of women is strongly influenced by the holy texts, the Qur'an and the Hadith. These texts are seen as sacred texts, and tend to be interpreted in a very literal and textual approach, in which the influence of a historical context is denied. The literalist readings of these texts then influence the inner Islamic cosmology that constructs perceptions on the roles of men and women, including women's public role. Their *das sollen* says that women should not become leaders, however, their *das sein*, suggests that if in any particular situation, the best available leader is a woman, then it is permitted for that woman to become the leader. This conception then brings forth the recent phenomenon of the Islamization of districts laws in Indonesia. Until the end of 2007, there are approximately 63 Sharia ordinances out of 423 districts in Indonesia, which apparently denied women's rights. Of course, Muhammadiyah is not the only organization responsible for this action. And within Muhammadiyah organization itself, there is an internal dynamic of perceiving women's roles in the public.

If the classroom in Muhammadiyah universities is a microcosm of Muslim society, then gender is a powerful factor in English classrooms and the study of gender issues must inform both the students and Muslim society. This research has sought to theorize the decisions taken within Muhammadiyah universitites that have contributed to the content and orientation of English departments. Specifically, it has sought to address the following questions: which story, taught to whom, by what methods, for what purposes, followed by what kind of assignments, evaluated how, by whom, and for what purposes. Of course, as the second largest Islamic social institution in Indonesia, Muhammadiyah contributes a great deal to the learning and socialization of students' literary appreciation within its English departments. While this study does not consider that teachers themselves are responsible for the specific gender roles that male and female students assume in life, teachers do need to consider carefully Muhammadiyah's contribution to stereotypical behavior of gender roles in the Muslim community. The more we recognize and address the prevalence of such stereotypical behaviour, the more students could be empowered through a tactful and careful transformation of the canon. This study cannot decide what pedagogy on gender can do without having decided at some level what Islamic educational values are and what it believe about teaching and learning gender issues. Muslim students' views about gender and the learning of English have been shaped by their individual experiences as part of a Muslim community as a whole. The postcolonial Muslim women writers I have proposed in a tentative new canon for the *Prose* syllabus are mostly Muslim women whose analyses of gender relations could play a significant role in transforming the Muslim community in general, as well as lead to inquiry and reflection on how students might change.

In the present literature canon and curriculum in Muhammadiyah universities, teachers, most of the time, ask students to ignore their gender role as they read, to immerse themselves in the literature, following the central point of view where it leads them, and reflecting on that experience, seeking the high artistic universals. What this study is proposing here is that it invites students to read with their full gender experience intact, to resist the central point of view when it contradicts that experience, and to seek artistry both in particulars and the universals. It is meant to raise students' critical awareness toward their own-given-values vis-à-vis values coming from the outside of their own community.

The current English curriculum requires a close look in the light of gender sensitivity if all students, male and female, are to fully develop the potential to hear the voices of others clearly, as well as equally, even those voices who are very critical of Muslim traditions. Exposure to the writings of postcolonial Muslim women through the proposed canon reform would enhance students' critical abilities to understand, shape, and share their worlds, as well as to imagine other worlds which are possibly completely different from their own, and have a full appreciation to these. This dissertation is an effort to begin such an inquiry.

Glossary

Allah	God.
al-Irsyad	Islamic modernist foundation belong to Indonesian-Arab community founded in Dutch colonial era.
Adabiyah School	HIS (Hollandsch Inlandsche School), Senior High School for the natives in Dutch era.
Aisyiyah	The women's wing organization of Muhammadiyah.
'aqli	Intellectual knowledge.
amar ma'ruf nahi munkar	Enjoining good and forbidding evil; call people to good, and prohibit them from bad.
aqidah	Faith, creed.
bid'ah	Innovation, novelty, accretion, deviation; some view, thing or mores of action the like of which has not formerly existed or been practised. The reformists in Indonesia combatted bid'ah in the field of din, pure religion.
din	religion.
dakwah	To invite or call one to the Islamic cause, or to respond to the invitation or call.
Darul Harb	Abode of War.
Darul Islam	Abode of Islam.
desa	Village.
Diniyah School	Literary Religious School. The name of a modernist religious institution in Padang Pandjang, founded in 1915.
direktori	Directory.
Djamiyat Chair School	Community of Goodness.
Djamiyat al-Islam	Community of Islam.
Dzikir	Remembrance of Allah.
jahiliyah	Pre-Islamic period; also age of ignorance.
jihad	War; fighting, not necessarily in the physical sense.
fatwa	Statement of legal issue; decision of religious character, given by a recognized religious scholar (ulama).
fiqh	Jurisprudence, law, covering all aspects of life.
Hadits	Tradition; statements and/or actions of Prophet Muhammad.
hajj	pilgrimage to Mecca.
haram	Forbidden, unlawful, sinful; refers to actions the perfomance of which is punished and ommission rewarded.

hijrah	Migration; the migration of Muhammad from Mecca to Medina in 622 A.D.; the Muslim calendar is dated from that event.
hisab	Calculation (for determining the days, months, years). In Indonesia, especially for determining the time for prayers, fasting and the two Id.
Hizbul Wathan	Party (army) of the fatherland; name of the scout organization of Muhammadiyah.
Hizbut Tahrir	Hizbut Tahrir means party of liberation. The group wants to unite all Muslims under a giant pan-Islamic state based on strict Sharia law. hukum Law.
Id	Celebration, feast, feast day.
ijma	Consensus.
ijtihad	The right of individual interpretation; exerting oneself to form an opinion in a case or as to the rule of law; independent reason in religious interpretation.
Ikhwanul Muslimin	Muslim Brotherhood.
iktisabi	Acquired knowledge.
Iman	Faith; to accept truthfully, to be convinced, to verify something, to rely upon or have confidence in something.
Insya Allah	God willing.
jahiliyah	Error, going astray, deviation from Allah's straight path, and negligence in His worship.
jilbab	headscarf for Muslim women.
kabupaten	District.
kaffah	Total adherence.
kafir	Unbeliever, non-Muslim.
kecamatan	Sub-district.
kerudung	headveil; see jilbab.
lillahi Ta'ala	also lillah or lillahi: For God the Almighty alone. For no one except God.
Madmum	Condemned or undesirable deed.
madrasa	Islamic school.
madzab	Schools of Islamic thought.
madaris	Plural form of madrasa.
Mahmud	Good or desirable deed.
maksiat	Vice deeds.
Muallimat	Islamic school for girls in Muhammadiyah.
Muallimin	Islamic school for boys in Muhammadiyah.

mubah	Refers to actions the perfomance or neglect of which reward nor punishment need be expected.
mudharat	Adverse.
muhdith	Initiator; originator.
mujtahid	Authoritative interpreter of the law; one who practices ijtihad.
mujtahidin	Plural form of mujtahid.
Muktamar	Convention.
Muhammadiyah	The name of social reigious organization founded in Yogyakarta in 1912.
muhrim	A person whom one is not allowed to marry because of blood relationship.
muslimah	Muslim women.
naqli	Transmitted knowledge.
Nasyiatul Aisyiyah	Juniors of the Aisyiyah which is the women section of the Muhammadiyah.
nikah sirri	Marriage which is not registered in the Office for Religious Affairs (Kantor Urusan Agama or KUA).
nusantara	The Indonesian archipelago which includes the entire island chain of the country.
Pengurus Pusat	Central Board
Pengurus Wilayah	Regional Board
Pengurus Daerah	District Board
Pengurus Cabang	Special Board
Pengurus Ranting	Village Board
pesantren	Campus where religious education is given.
Propinsi	Province.
purdah	Covering the entire body except for the eyes, wrist and feet.
Quran	The Holy Book of the Muslims.
Ramadhan	The ninth month of the Hijrah year; the Muslim fasting month.
rahmatan lil alamin	Bless to the universe.
sa'ada	Bliss of the hereafter.
Sharia	The law of Islam.
stridham	Women enjoyed full rights of property.
sunnah	Commendable; refers to actions the perfomance of which is rewarded, but its neglect is not punished.
Suttee	Sati; the Indian custom of a widow burning herself, either on the funeral pyre of her dead husband or in some other fashion, soon after his death.

syirik	Association of something with God, other than God Himself.
taqlid	Adopting the already established fatwa and practices as final and as having an authoritative character.
tanah air	land and water; Indonesian call their homeland.
Tarbiyah	Tarbiyah Movement; refers to to increase, to grow, to educate.
tasamuh	Tolerance.
taqwa	Protection and shield from what is harmful; a state of submission.
Tauhid	Declaring Allah to be the only God who deserves to be worshipped in truth and confirming all attributes with which He has qualified Himself or that are attributed to Him by His Messenger.
tawassul	Supplicating Allah by means of an intermediary, whether it be a living person, dead person, a good deed, or a name or Attribute of Allah Most High.
tausiyah	Recommendation.
ulama	Muslim scholars, especially in religion.
Ummah	Community.
uswatun hasanah	Muhammad as an excellent example.
wahyu	Divine revelation; vision from God.

Bibliography

1. Main Sources

a. Republic of Indonesia Laws, Government Regulations, Education Ministerial Edicts & Persyarikatan Muhammadiyah Edicts

Undang-Undang Republik Indonesia Nomor 2 Tahun 1989 tentang Sistem Pendidikan Nasional.

Undang-Undang Republik Indonesia Nomor 20 Tahun 2003 tentang Sistem Pendidikan Nasional.

Peraturan Pemerintah Republik Indonesia Nomor 55 Tahun 1998 tentang Perubahan atas Peraturan Pemerintah Nomor 28 Tahun 1990 Tentang Pendidikan Dasar.

Peraturan Pemerintah Republik Indonesia Nomor 55 Tahun 1998 tentang Perubahan atas Peraturan Pemerintah Nomor 28 Tahun 1990 Tentang Pendidikan Dasar.

Peraturan Pemerintah Republik Indonesia Nomor 56 Tahun 1998 tentang Perubahan atas Peraturan Pemerintah Nomor 29 Tahun 1990 Tentang Pendidikan Menengah.

Peraturan Pemerintah Republik Indonesia Nomor 57 Tahun 1998 tentang Perubahan atas Peraturan Pemerintah Nomor 30 Tahun 1990 Tentang Pendidikan Tinggi.

Peraturan Pemerintah Republik Indonesia Nomor 60 Tahun 1999 tentang Pendidikan Tinggi.

Keputusan Menteri Pendidikan Nasional Republik Indonesia Nomor 045/U/2002 tentang Kurikulum Inti Pendidikan Tinggi.

Salinan Keputusan Menteri Pendidikan Nasional Republik Indonesia Nomor 232/U/2000 tentang Pedoman Penyusunan Kurikulum Pendidikan Tinggi dan Penilaian Hasil Belajar Mahasiswa.

Keputusan Presiden Republik Indonesia Nomor 93 Tahun 1999 tentang Perubahan Institut Keguruan dan Ilmu Pendidikan (IKIP) menjadi Universitas.

Rancangan Keputusan Pimpinan Pusat Muhammadiyah tentang Qaidah Perguruan Tinggi Muhammadiyah.

Direktorat Jenderal Pendidikan Tinggi, 2005, Rekapitulasi Perguruan Tinggi dan Program Studi, Jakarta: Dirjen Dikti.

Majelis Pendidikan Tinggi Penelitian dan Pengembangan Pinpinan Pusat Muhammadiyah, 2006, Direktori Perguruan Tinggi Muhammadiyah (PTM): Profil Universitas, Sekolah Tinggi, Politeknik, dan Akademi Muhammadiyah se-Indonesia, Yogyakarta: Diktilitbang Muhammadiyah.

Muktamar Muhammadiyah the 45th, Malang, East Java in 2005.

Kurikulum Bahasa Inggris Universitas Muhammadiyah Prof Dr Hamka 2006-2007, Jakarta.

Kurikulum Bahasa Inggris Universitas Muhammadiyah Sukabumi 2003-2004 & 2006-2007, West Java.

Kurikulum Bahasa Inggris Universitas Muhammadiyah Surakarta 2004-2005, Central Java.

Kurikulum Bahasa Inggris Universitas Ahmad Dahlan 2000, Yogyakarta.

Kurikulum Bahasa Inggris Universitas Muhammadiyah Malang, East Java.

Kurikulum Bahasa Inggris Universitas Muhammadiyah Mataram 2005, West Nusa Tenggara.

Kurikulum Bahasa Inggris Universitas Muhammadiyah Makasar 2004, South Sulawesi.

Buku Pedoman Kurikulum 2005/2006 Universitas Muhammadiyah Surakarta, Fakultas Keguruan dan Ilmu Pendidikan, Jurusan Pendidikan Bahasa Inggris. Surakarta: Muhammadiyah University Press.

Pedoman Akademik 2006/2007 Universitas Ahmad Dahlan Fakultas Keguruan dan Ilmu Pendidikan, Jurusan Pendidikan Bahasa Inggris. Yogyakarta: Universitas Ahmad Dahlan.

b. Interviews

All the interviews were conducted within two months in Indonesia (Surakarta, Yogyakarta, and Jakarta), from mid of July until mid of September 2007 in Universitas Muhammadiyah Surakarta (UMS), Universitas Muhammadiyah Ahmad Dahlan Yogyakarta (UAD), Universitas Islam Indonesia Yogyakarta (UII), DIKTI Muhammadiyah Yogyakarta (DIKTI) and PP Muhammadiyah Jakarta (PP) in Yogyakarta and Jakarta, and Maarif Institute Jakarta (MI) Jakarta.

Interviews with Muhammadiyah Leaders (PP Muhammadiyah):
Prof Dr Syafii Maarif (Yogyakarta State-Owned University and Maarif Institute Jakarta)
Prof Dr Amin Abdullah (Rector of UIN-Islamic University in Yogyakarta and PP Muhammadiyah Yogyakarta)

Interviews with Dikti Muhammadiyah:
Prof. Dr. Edy Suandi Hamid, M.Ec. (Secretary to DIKTI and Rector of Universitas Islam Indonesia, Yogyakarta)
Prof Dr. Bambang Setiaji, M.Ec. (Rector of Universitas Muhammadiyah Surakarta-UMS)
Drs. Muhammad Musiyam, MPt. (Vice Rector I of UMS)
Drs. Maryadi, MA. (Vice Dean of Education Faculty, UMS)
Muhammad Sayuti, SPd. (Secretary to DIKTI Muhammadiyah, Yogyakarta)

Interviews with Lecturers of Literature in the English Departments of UMS & UAD:
Drs. Muhammad Thoyibi, M. Hum. (English Dept of UMS)
Nur Hidayat, S.Pd. (English Dept of UMS)
Ulaya Ahdiani, M. Hum. (English Dept of UAD)
Lia Nur Octavia, M. Hum. (English Dept of UAD)

Interviews with Students of English Departments of UMS:
The 5th Semester/the second year
Dina Zaina (female)
Fuad Fauzan (male)
The 7th Semester/the third year
Sapta Rini (female)
Hajar Sumantri (male)
The 10th Semester/the fifth year
Anissa Rakhmawati (female)
Heni Sumarah (female)
Henri Arina (male)

c. The History of Private Indonesian Universities on the respective universities websites [accessed per October 15th , 2006]

Sejarah Universitas Nasional, Jakarta, http://www.unas.ac.id/
Sejarah Universitas Indonesia, Jakarta, http://www.ui.edu/
Sejarah Universitas Muhammadiyah Dr Hamka, Jakarta, http://www.uhamka.ac.id/
Sejarah Universitas Katolik Atmajaya, Jakarta, http://www.atmajaya.ac.id/
Sejarah Universitas Katolik Sanata Dharma, Yogyakarta, http://www.usd.ac.id/
Sejarah Universitas Kristen Satya Wacana, Salatiga, http://www.uksw.edu/
Sejarah Universitas Kristen Petra, Surabaya, http://www.petra.ac.id/
Sejarah Universitas Kristen Tomohon, North Sulawaesi, http://www.geocities.com/CollegePark/Hall/1981/ukit.htm or http://www.reformiert-online.net/adressen/detail.php?id=11218&lg=eng
Sejarah Universitas Kristen Klabat, North Sulawesi, http://www.tagnet.org/unklab/

2. Secondary Sources

Abbot, Nabia. 1946. Reprint 1974. Two Queens of Baghdad: Mother and Wife of Harun al-Rashid. Chicago: University of Chicago Press & Midway.

Abdel Fatah, Moataz Bellah Mohammed. 2004. "Islam and Democracy: An Empirical Examination of Muslim's Political Culture," unpublished PhD dissertation, Western Michigan University.

Abdulhamied, Fuad. 1982. Competency-based Teacher Education and Teaching English as a Foreign Language: Perceptions of Faculty and Administrators of the English Department at Teachers College in Indonesia. Southern Illinois University at Carbondale (unpublished Dissertation).

Abdullah, A.R.S. n.d. Educational Theory: A Quranic Outlook. Makkah: Umm ul-Qura University. p. 83.

Abdullah, Taufik. "Historical Reflection on Civil Society in Indonesia". Manuscript.1999. Pp. 4-6.

Abu-Lughod, Lila. 1986. Veiled Sentiments: Honor and Poetry in Bedouin Society. Berkeley, CA: University of California Press.

Abuza, Zachary. 2003. Militant Islam in Southeast Asia. Bouden: Reyna.

Achebe, Chinua. 1959, rpt.1994. Things Fall Apart. New York: Anchor Books.

Ahmed, Leila. 1992. Women and in Islam. New Haven & London: Yale UP.

__________. 1999. A Border Passage: from Cairo to America—A Women's Journey (autobiography)

Alfian, Muhammadiyah: The Political Behaviour of a Muslim Modernist Organization Under Dutch Colonialism, Yogyakarta: Gadjah Mada UP, p. 310.

Alip, Francis Borgias. 1993. Social Norms and Variation in Language Choice: The Case of English-speaking Students in Java. State University of New York at Stony Brook (unpublished Dissertation).

Altieri, Charles. 1990. Canons and Consequences: Reflections on the Ethical Force of Imaginative Ideals. Illinois: Northwestern University Press.

Ali Said Damanik. 2002. Fenomena PKS: Transformasi 20 Tahun Gerakan Tarbiyah di Indonesia (The Justice Party Phenomenon: Transformation over 20 years of the Tarbiyah Movement in Indonesia). Jakarta: Teraju. pp. 231-2.

Almond, G., R. S. Appleby, and I. Sivan. 2003. Strong Religion: The Rise of Fundamentalisms around the World. Chicago: The University of Chicago Press. pp. 14-15.

Anita, Lie. 1994. Paired Storytelling: An Integrated Approach for English as a Foreign Language Students in Indonesia. Baylor University (unpublished Dissertation).

Antor, Heinz & Klaus Stierstorfer (eds.). 2000. English Literatures in International Contexts. Heidelberg: Universitaetsverlag C. Winter.

Arber, Ruth. "Defining Positioning within Politics of Difference: negotiating spaces 'in between'" in journal of Race Ethnicity and Education, Vol. 3, No. 1, 2000. pp: 45-63.

Ashcroft, Bill. 2001. Post-colonial Transformation. London and New York: Routledge.

__________. 2000. "Resistance and Transformation" in Antor, Heinz & Klaus Stierstorfer (eds.). English Literatures in International Contexts. Heidelberg: Universitaetsverlag C. Winter.

Ashcroft, Bill, Gareth Griffiths, and Helen Tiffin. 1989. The Empire Writes Back. London and New York: Routledge.

Auerbach, E. 1995. The Politics of the ESL Classroom: Issues of Power in Pedagogical Choices, in J. Tollefson (Ed.) Power and Inequality in Language Education. NY: Cambridge UP.

Badan Akreditasi Nasional (BAN), 2000.

Barone, T. 1995. 'Persuasive Writings, Vigilant Readings and Reconstructed Characters: the Paradox of trust in educational story sharing' in J. Hatch and R. Wisniewski (eds.). Lie, History and Narrative. London: Falmer Press.

Baugh, Albert C and Thomas Cable. 1993. A History of the English Language. 4th ed. London: Routledge.

Beasley, C. 1999. What is Feminism? London: Sage.

Bhabha, Homi. 1994, rpt.2003. The Location of Culture. London and New York: Routledge.

Bidang Kewanitaan DPP PK Sejahtera. 2004. Perempuan-Perempuan Pilihan: Profil Singkat 150 Caleg dan Politisi Perempuan PK Sejahtera. Jakarta: Misykat Publication, p. 38.

Blake, NF. 1996. A History of the English Language. Hampshire & London: Macmillan Press Ltd.

Bloom, Harold, 1975, Kabbalah and Criticism. New York: Seabury.

Boehmer, Elleke. 2002. Empire, the National, and the Postcolonial 1890-1920. NY: Oxford UP.

______________. 1998. Empire Writing: An Anthology of Colonial Literature 1870-1918. Oxford: Oxford UP.

Bosnia Handout. "Ethnic Cleansing" and Atrocities in Bosnia. p. 1. http://www.fas.org/irp/cia/product/bosnia_handout.html. Assessed at 23.06.2005.

Bourdie, P. 1991. Language and Symbolic Power. Oxford: Polity Press.

Brook, GL. 1958. A History of the English Language. London: Andre Deutsch.

Bruenessen, Martin van. 2003. "Post Soeharto Muslim Engagement with Civil Society and Democratization" in paper presented in workshop on "Indonesia in Transition", Jakarta August 24-28, 2003.

Bruinessen, Martin van. n.d. "Genealogies of Islamic Radicalism in post-Soeharto Indonesia," pp. 19-21. See also, International Crisis Groups, "Al-Qaeda in Southeast Asia: The Case of "Ngruki Network" in Indonesia," http://www.crisisgroup.org/home/index.cfm?id=1765&l=1

Brydon, Diana. 2000. Postcolonialism: Critical Concepts. NY & London: Routledge.

Bukhori, Mochtar. "The Hopefuls among the Distrusted" in Laksamana.Net (August 10, 2002).

Burke, P. 1996. Gender Shock: Exploding the myths of male and female. NY: Anchor Books/Doubleday.

Burlbaw, Lynn M. & Sherry L. Field. 2005. Explorations in Curriculum History. Connecticut: Information Age Publishing.

Burton, Antoinette (ed.). 2003. After the Imperial Turn: Thinking With and Through the Nation. Durham & London: Duke UP.

_______________(ed.). 2001. Politics & Empire in Victorian Britain: A Reader. NY & Hampshire: Palgrave.

_______________. 2001. "India, Inc.? Nostalgia, Memory, and the Empire of Things" in Stuart Ward (ed.) British Culture and the End of Empire. Manchester and NY: Manchester UP.

_______________(ed.). 1999. Gender, Sexuality & Colonial Modernities. London & NY: Routledge Research in Gender & History.

_______________. 1998. At the Heart of the Empire: Indians and the Colonial Encounter in Late-Victorian Britain. Berkeley/Los Angeles/London: University of California Press.

_______________. 1994. Burdens of History: British Feminists, Indian Women, & Imperial Culture, 1865-1915. Chaper Hill & London: The University of North Carolina Press.

Bush, Robin. 2002. Islam and Civil Society in Indonesia: The Case of Nahdlatul Ulama. PhD Dissertation, University of Washington.

Carter, Jimmy. 2004. "Indonesian Voting: Surprise: Muslim Majority, Fair Election," in International Herald Tribune, July 6, 2004.

Carre, Oliver Carre, 1995. "Banna, Hassan" in The Oxford Encyclopaedia of the Modern Islamic World, vol. 1. pp. 194-199.

Chambers Educational Course. 1888. History of the English Language and Literature. London & Edinburgh: William and Robert Chambers.

Chatterjee, Partha & Pradeep Jeganathan (eds.). 2000. Subaltern Studies XI: Community, Gender and Violence. London: Hurst & Co.

Collins, Elisabeth Fuller. "Islam is the Solution: Dakwah and Democracy in Indonesia," in paper presented at Syarif Hidayatullah State Islamic University, Jakarta, 20.06.2004. pp. 8-9.

Corson, D. 1997. Critical realism: an emancipatory philosophy for applied linguistics? Applied Linguistics, 18 (2), pp. 166-188.

Crombie, Winifred. 1985. Discourse and Language Learning: A Relational Approach to Syllabus Design. Oxford: Oxford University Press.

Crystal, D. 1997. English as a Global Language. Cambridge: Cambridge University Press.

Darby, Phillip. 1998. The Fiction of Imperialism: Reading between International Relations and Postcolonialism. Wellington: Cassel.

Davidson, Lawrence. 1998. Islamic Fundamentalism. Connecticut: Greenwood Press. p. 50.

Djaja, Tamar, Pusaka Indonesia: Orang-orang Besar Tanah Air 2 vols. Bandung: G Kolff, 1951, p. 296.

Davies, B. 1997. 'Constructing and Deconstructing Masculinities through Critical Literacy', Gender and Education, 9 (1).

DeCamp, David & Ian F. Hancock (eds.). 1974. Pidgins and Creoles: Current Trends and Prospects. Washington: Georgetown UP.

DeCamp, David. 1958. "The Genesis of the Old English Dialects: A New Hypothesis", Language, Vol. 34., pp.: 232-244.

DeCamp, David & Ian F. Hancock (eds.). 1974. Pidgins and Creoles: Current Trends and Prospects. Washington: Georgetown UP.

De Souza, Eunice. "Recovering a Tradition: Forgotten Women's Voices" in Economic and Political Weekly, April 29, 2006, pp: 1642-1645.

Dirlik, Arif. 1997. The Postcolonial Aura: Third World Criticism in the Age of Global Capitalism. Oxford: Westview Press.

Dheram, Premakumari. 2005. "English Language Teaching in India: Colonial Past vis-à-vis Curriculum Reform in Braine, George (ed.), Teaching English to the World: History, Curriculum & Practice. New Jersey: Lawrence Erlbaum.

Djojosoekarto. 1973. A Study of Several Delopment Factors in the Revision and Updating of the National English Language Program in Indonesia with Specific Reference to In-Service Teacher Training and the Preparation of Teaching Materials. Unpublished doctoral thesis. Austin, Texas: University of Texas.

Eagleton, Terry. 1996, rpt.2002. Literary Theory: An Introduction. 2nd ed. Oxford: Blackwell Publishers.

Edwards, Richard & Robin Usher (eds.). 2003. Space, Curriculum, and Learning. Connecticut: Information Age Publishing.

Eickelman, Dale F. & James Piscatori. 1996. Muslim Politics. New Jersey: Princetown UP. pp. 139.

Eisenstadt, S.N. 1973. Tradition, Change and Modernity. New York: Wiley. P. 25.
El-Fadl, Khalid Abou. 2001. The Conference of the Books: The Search for Beauty in Islam. Univ Press of America: Lanham, Md.
El-Guindi, Fadwa. 1999. Veil: Modesty, Privacy and Resistance. Oxford & New York: Berg.
El Saadawi, Nawal. 1987. The Fall of the Imam (1988, transl. by Sheriff Hetata).
Engineer, A.A. 1978. "Islam and Reformation", Islam and the Modern Age 9, no. 1, pp: 86-95
Epstein, Louis M. 1967. Sex, Laws and Customs in Judaism. New York: Ktav Publishing House.
Esposito, John L. 1984. Islam & Politics. New York: Syracuse UP. pp. 60-64.
Esposito, John L. and Azzam Tamimi. 2000. Islam and Secularism in the Middle East. London Hurst and Company.
Fanon, Franz. 1967. Black Skin, White Masks. New York: Grove Press.
Freedom House. 2006. http://www.freedomhouse.org
Freire, Paulo. 1970.1993. Pedagogy of the Oppressed (trans. Myra Bergman Ramos). NY: Continuum.
__________. 1992. Pedagogy of Hope: Reliving Pedagogy of the Oppressed. (trans. Robert R. Barr). NY: Continuum.
Foucault, Michel. 1977, rpt.1991. Discipline and Punish: The Birth of the Prison. Translated by A. Sheridan. London: Penguin Books.
____________. 1980. "Two Lectures" in Power/Knowledge, edited by C. Gordon. Brighton: Harvester.
____________. 1982. "Afterward: The Subject and Power'" in Michel Foucault: Beyond Structuralism and Hermeneutics, H. L. Dreyfus and P. Rabinow (ed.). Brighton: Harvester.
Gellner, Ernst. 1994. Conditions of Liberty: Civil Society and Its Rivals. London: Hamish Hamilton. Pp: 23-29.
George, TJS. 1980. Revolt in Mindanao: The Rise of Islam in Philippines Politics, Kuala Lumpur: Oxford University Press. pp. 19-20.
Gooptu, Suparna. 2006. Cornelia Sorabji: India's Pioneer Woman Lawyer. India: Oxford UP.
Gorak, Jan. 1991. The Making of the Modern Canon: Genesis and Crisis of a Literary Idea. London & NJ: Athlone
Graddol, David; Dick Leith & Joan Swan. 1996. English: History, Diversity, and Change. London & NY: the Open University & Routledge.
Groeneboer, Kees. 1998. Gateway to the West. The Dutch Language in Colonial Indonesia 1600-1950: A History of Language Policy (translated by Myra Scholz). Amsterdam: Amsterdam University Press.
Guha, Rajanit. 2002. History at the Limit of World-History. New York: Columbia UP.

__________ (ed.). 1997. A Subaltern Studies Reader 1986-1995. Minnesota: Regents of the University of Minnesota.

Guillory, John. 1995. "Canon" in Critical Terms for Literary Study, F. Lentricchia and T. McLaughlin (ed). Chicago and London: University of Chicago Press.

Gullick, John M. 1995. Adventures and Encounters: Europeans in South-East Asia. Kuala Lumpur: Oxford University Press.

Hall, Stuart. 1993. 'Cultural Identity and Diaspora'. In Colonial Discourse and Post-Colonial Theory: A Reader, edited by P. Williams and L. Chrisman. New York: Harvester Wheatsheaf.

———. 1997. Representation: Cultural Representations and Signifying Practices. London: Open University.

Haneline, Douglas, "Reading 'Whiteness' in English Studies", May 2001, Vol. 63, Issue: 5, pp. 669-672, Urbana: College English.
http://proquest.umi.com/pqdweb?TS
Assessed at 26/7/2002; 2.30 p.m.

Hardin, Joe Marshall. 1999. Teaching Resistance in Composition: Culture, Ideology, and Rhetoric. University of South Florida (unpublished Dissertation).

Hardjasoemantri, Koesnadi. 1981. Study-Service as a subsystem in Indonesian Higher Education (unpublished Dissertation). Rijkuniversiteit te Leiden, Netherlands.

Hasyim, Syafiq. "Mengkritisi Perda Syariat Islam di Aceh; Perspektif Perempuan" in Swara Rahima, Edisi 2: Kontroversi Posisi Perempuan dalam Syariat Islam.
http://www.rahima.or.id/SR/02-01/Fikrah.htm
[retrieved at 28 October 2006].

Heffner, Robert. 2000. Civil Islam, Muslim and Democratization in Indonesia. Princeton: Princeton University Press.

Hefner, Robert and Patricia Horvatich (ed). 1997. Islam in an Era of Nation-States: Politics and Religious Renewal in Muslim Southeast Asia. New York: Amazon.

Hitti, Phillip K. 1940. History of the Arabs, 2nd ed., rev. London: Macmillan.

hooks, bell. 1981. Ain't I a Woman. London: Pluto Press.

_________. 1989. Talking Back. Boston: South End Press.

_________. 1994. Teaching to Transgress. London and New York: Routledge.

_________. 2003. Teaching Community: A Pedagogy of Hope. NY & London: Routledge.

Hourani, Albert. 1983. Arabic Thought in the Liberal Age, 1798-1939. Cambridge: Cambridge UP. p. 83.

Howatt, A.P.R. & H.G. Widdowson. 2004. A History of English Language Teaching. 2-nd ed. Oxford: Oxford UP.

Huntington, Samuel. 1997. The Clash of Civilizations and the Making of World Order. New York: Simon & Schuster. p: 112.

Hurst, Paul. 1983. "Africa and Middle East", International Handbook of Education Systems, African and Middle East, vol. 2, ed. J. Careron and P. Hurst. London: Wiley. Pp.: 1539-40.

Hussain, S.S. and A.A. Ashraf. 1979. Crisis in Muslim Educatio. Jeddah: King Abdul Azis University/Hodder & Stoughton.

Jameelah, Maryam. 1983. Modern Technology and the Dehumanization of Man. Lahore: El-Matbaat ul-Arabia. p.8.

Johnston, Ingrid. 1996. Re-Mapping Literary Worlds: Postcolonial Pedagogy in Practice. University of Alberta Canada (unpublished dissertation).

Jones, Sidney. 2002. "Al-Qaeda in Southeast Asia: The case of the "Ngruki Network" in Indonesia," in ICG Indonesia Briefing, 8 August 2002.

Joshi, Svati (ed.). 1994. Rethinking English: Essays in Literature, Language, History. Delhi, Bombay, Calcutta, Madras: Oxford University Press.

Jurnal Perempuan Online, "Sejumlah Perda Sebabkan Hak Ekosob Buruh Tidak Terpenuhi". Depok, Jakarta, 9 August 2006.

Kachru, Braj B. 1986. The Alchemy of English: The Spread, Functions and Models of Non-native Englishes. Oxford, NY, Toronto, Sydney & Frankfurt: Pergamon Institute of English.

___________. 1983. The Indianization of English: The English Language in India. Delhi: Oxford UP.

___________. "The Sacred Cows of English", English Today, 16 (1998).

___________ (ed.). 1982. rpt. 1983. The Other Tongue: English across Culture. Oxford, NY, Toronto, Paris, Frankfurt: Pergamon Press.

Kahin, George McT. 1952. Nationalism and Revolution in Indonesia. Ithaca, NY: Cornell UP.

Kartini. 1920. Letters of a Javanesse Princess (1986-ed & 2005-ed, translated by Agnes Louise Symmers).

Kartini, 1992. Letters from Kartini: An Indonesian Feminist 1900-1904 (translated and introduced by Joost Cote). Melbourne: Monash Asia Institute in assoc with Hyland House.

Kasbollah, Kasihani. 1988. A Syllabus for the Course in Teaching/Learning Strategies for Students of English Education in Indonesia. University of Kansas (unpublished dissertation).

Kastovsky, Dieter & Arthur Mettinger (eds.). 2001. 2003 (revised Ed.). Language Contact in the History of English. Frankfurt, Berlin, Bern, Bruxelles, NY, Oxford, Wien: Peter Lang.

Kearney, R. 1988. The Wake of Imagination. Minneapolis: University of Minnesota Press.

Khadduri, Majid. 1995. War and Peace in the Law of Islam. Baltimore: The John Hopkins Press. pp. 51-54.

Khan, MM and M. T. Hilali. 2001. Interpretations of the Meanings of the Noble Qur'an, Riyadh: Alharamain Foundation.

Kincheloe, J.l. & Steinberg, S.R. 1997. Changing Multiculturalism. Buckingham, UK: Open UP.

Knowles, Gerry. 1997. A Cultural History of the English Language. NY: Arnold.

Komnas Perempuan. "Pernyataan Pers: Penertiban Perda-Perda diskriminatif adalah tanggung jawab negara yang tak bisa diabaikan". Jakarta, 20 June 2006.

Kramer, Martin. 1996. Arab Awakening and Islamic Revival: The Politics of Ideas in the Middle East. New Brunswick: Transaction Publishers.

Landry, Donna & Gerald Maclean. 1996. The Spivak Reader. NY & London: Routledge.

Latief, Muhammad Adnan. 1990. Assessment of English Writing Skills for Students of English as a Foreign Language at the Institute of Teacher Training and Education (IKIP-Malang) Indonesia. The University of Iowa (unpublished Dissertation).

Legge, G.D. 1964. Indonesia. New Jersey: Englewood Cliffs.

Lewis, Bernard. 2002. What Went Wrong? Western Impact and Middle Eastern Response. Oxford: Oxford University Press. p: 100.

Linz, Juan J. and Alfred Stephan. 1996. Problems of Democratic Transitions and Consolidation: Southern Europe, South America, and Post-Communist Europe. Baltimore: John Hopkins University Press.

Lopez, Alfred J. 2001. Posts and Pasts: Theory of Postcolonialism. NY: State University of New York Press.

Lyotard, J.-F. 1986. (trans. By G Bennington and B. Massumi). The Postmodern Condition: A Report on Knowledge. Manchester: Manchester UP.

Maarif, Ahmad Syafii. 1985. Islam and Masalah Kenegaraan [Islam and the Problem of the State]. Jakarta: PT Pustaka LP3ES. Pp. 52-79.

Macaulay, Thomas Babington. 1972. 'Minute on Indian Education'. In Thomas Babington Macaulay: Selected Writings, edited by J. Clive and T. Pinney. Chicago and London: The University of Chicago Press.

MacLachlan, Gale, and Ian Reid. 1994. Framing and Interpretation. Carlton, Victoria: Melbourne University Press.

Marching, Soe Tjen. 2003. Indonesia Women's Autobiographies & Diaries in the New Order (published Dissertation from Monash University, forthcoming).

Martani, Jeanne Yanita. 1996. Directions for Reform: Perception of Indonesian Students towards English Language Curricula. University of Massachusetts Amherst (unpublished Dissertation).

Marty, Martin E. Marty and R. Scott Appleby. "The Fundamentalism Project: A User's Guide," in M. E. Marty & R. S. Appleby. 1991.

Fundamentalisms Observed, Chicago: The Chicago University Press, pp. vii-xiii.

Meiklejohn, JMD. 1897. The English Language: Its Grammar, History, and Literature with chapters on Composition, Versification, Paraphrasing, and Punctuation. Toronto: The W.J. Gage Co. Ltd.

Mernissi, Fatema. 1991. The Veil and the Male Elite, Feminist Interpretation of Women's Right in Islam. NY, Paris, Tokyo, Bonn, Amsterdam, Ontario, Sydney, Singapore: Addison-Wesley.

______________. 1995. Dreams of Trespass, Tales of a Harem Girlhood (autobiography)

Mestoko, Soemarsono. 1979. Pendidikan di Indonesia dari Jaman ke Jaman. Jakarta: BP3K Depdikbud.

McLaren, Peter. 1995. 'Post-colonial Pedagogy: Post-colonial Desire and Decolonized Community'. In Postmodernism, Post-colonialism and Pedagogy, edited by P. McLaren. Albert Park, Australia: James Nicholas Publishers.

McLaren, P.L. 1995. White terror and oppositional agency: toward a critical multiculturalism. In C.E. Sleeter & P.L. McLaren (Eds.). Multicultural education: Critical pedagogy, and the politics of difference (pp. 33-70). Albany: State Univ of New York Press.

Mehrotra, Arvind Krishna (ed.). 2003. A History of Indian Literature in English. London: Hurst & Co.

Milani, Farzaneh. 1992. Veils and Words: The Emerging Voices of Iranian Women Writers. New York: Syracuse UP.

Mills, Sara. 1997. Discourse. London and New York: Routledge.

_________. 2003. "Two Lectures" in Power/Knowledge, edited by C. Gordon.. London and New York: Routledge.

Minh-ha, Trinh T. 1991. When the Moon Waxes Red: Representation, Gender and Cultural Politics. NY & London: Routledge.

_____________. 1992. Framer Framed. New York & London; Routledge.

_____________. "Not You/Like You: Post-colonial Women and the Interlocking Questions of Identity and Difference" in http://humwww.ucsc.edu/CulturalStudies/PUBS/Inscriptions/vol_34/minh-ha.html

Ministry of Education and Culture. 1975 a. Kurikulum Sekolah Menengah Atas: Garis-Garis Besar Program Pengajaran, Mata Pelajaran Bahasa Inggris [Curriculum for Senior Secondary School: Syllabus for English Subject]. Jakarta: Balai Pustaka.

Ministry of Education and Culture. 1975a. Kurikulum Sekolah Menengah Atas: Garis-Garis Besar Program Pengajaran, Mata Pelajaran Bahasa Inggris [Curriculum for Senior Secondary School: Syllabus for English Subject]. Jakarta: Balai Pustaka.

Ministry of Education and Culture. 1975b. Kurikulum Sekolah Menengah Pertama: Garis-Garis Besar Program Pengajaran, Mata Pelajaran Bahasa Inggris [Curriculum for Junior Secondary School: Syllabus for English Subject]. Jakarta: Balai Pustaka.

Ministry of Education and Culture. 1986. Kurikulum Sekolah Menengah Atas: Garis-Garis Besar Program Pengajaran, Mata Pelajaran Bahasa Inggris [Curriculum for Senior Secondary School: Syllabus for English Subject]. Jakarta: Balai Pustaka.

Ministry of Education and Culture. 1987. Kurikulum Sekolah Menengah Pertama: Garis-Garis Besar Program Pengajaran, Mata Pelajaran Bahasa Inggris [Curriculum for Junior Secondary School: Syllabus for English Subject]. Jakarta: Balai Pustaka.

Ministry of Education and Culture. 1993a. Kurikulum Pendidikan Dasar: Garis-Garis Besar Program Pengajaran Sekolah Lanjutan Tingkat Pertama, Mata Pelajaran Bahasa Inggris [Curriculum for Basic Education: Syllabus for Junior Secondary School, English Subject]. Jakarta: Balai Pustaka.

Ministry of Education and Culture. 1993b. Kurikulum Sekolah Menengah Umum: Garis-Garis Besar Program Pengajaran, Mata Pelajaran Bahasa Inggris [Curriculum for Senior Secondary School: Syllabus for English Subject]. Jakarta: Balai Pustaka.

Mistar, Junaidi. 2005. "Teaching English as Foreign Language (TEFL) in Indonesia" in Braine, George (ed.). Teaching English to the World: History, Curriculum and Practice. Mahwah, New Jersey, & London: Lawrence Erlbaum.

Mohanty, Chandra Talpade. 2003. Feminism Without Borders: Decolonizing Theory, Practicing Solidarity. Durham & London: Duke UP.

Mohanty, Chandra Talpade; Ann Russo & Lourdes Torres (eds.). 1991. Third World Women and the Politics of Feminism. Bloomington & Indianapolis: Indiana UP.

Mohanty, Satya P. 1997. Literary Theory and the Claims of History: Postmodernism, Objectivity, Multicultural Politics. NY: Cornell UP.

Moore-Gilbert, Bart; Gareth Stanton & Willy Maley (eds.). 1997. Postcolonial Criticism. Essex: & NY: Addison Wesley Longman.

Morris, Richard. 1883. Historical Outlines of English Accidence, comprising Chapters on the history and Development of the Language, and on Word-Formation. London: Macmillan & Co.

Moussalli, Ahmad S. 2001. The Islamic Quest for Democracy, Pluralism, and Human Rights. Gainesville, FL: University Press of Florida.

Mujani, Saiful. 2003. "Religious Democrats: Democratic Culture and Muslim Political Participation in Post-Suharto Indonesia," unpublished PhD dissertation, The Ohio State University.

Mulia, Siti Musdah. "Syariat Islam Tidak Mungkin Merendahkan Perempuan" in Swara Rahima, Edisi 2: Kontroversi Posisi Perempuan dalam Syariat Islam.
http://www.rahima.or.id/SR/02-01/Opini.htm
[retrieved at 28 October 2006].

_______________. "Perda Syariat dan Peminggiran Perempuan (Ada Apa dengan Demokrasi di Indonesia ?)" in Kolom ICRP (Indonesian Conference on Religion and Peace). 11 Agustus 2006.
http://www.icrp-online.org/wmview.php?ArtID=178 \
[retrieved at 28 October 2006].

Mulya, R. Husna, Divisi Reformasi Hukum, Komnas Perempuan. Diskriminasi Terhadap Perempuan Dalam Kebijakan Daerah (Suatu Langkah Mundur dalam Upaya Perlindungan Hak-Hak Asasi Manusia di Indonesia). Jakarta, 15 September 2006.

Mumtaz, Khawar & Fareda Shaheed (eds.). 1987. Women of Pakistan, To Steps Forward, One Step Back?. London & NJ: Zed Books Ltd.

Ngi´g)´, wa Thiong'o. 1986. Decolonising the Mind: The Politics of Language in African Literature. London: James Currey.

Nieto, S. 1995. From brown heroes and holidays to assimilationist agendas: Reconsidering the critiques of multicultural education. In C.E. Sleeter & P.L. McLaren (Eds.). Multicultural education: Critical pedagogy, and the politics of difference (pp. 191-220). Albany: State Univ of New York Press.

Nieto, S. 2000. Affirming diversity: the sociopolitical context of multicultural education. NY: Longman.

Noer, Deliar, The Rise and Development of the Modernist Muslim Movement in Indonesia During Dutch Colonial Period (1900-1942), Cornell Uni, PhD Dissertation, 1963, pp. 51 and 59.

Nordholt, Henk Schulte (ed.). 1997. Outward Appearance: Dressing State & Society in Indonesia. Leiden: KITLV Press (Koninklijk Instituut voor Taal-, Land- en Volkenkunde).

Pedersen, J. and G. Makdisi. 1960—94. "Madrasa", in Encyclopedia of Islam, new ed. Leiden: Brill. 5:1123-27.

Pemandangan Alam Islam dan Muhammadijah 1932-1933, Jogjakarta, Hoofdbestuur Muhammadijah, n.d., pp. 118-128.

Penhallurick, Rob. 2003. Studying the English Language. NY: Palgrave Macmillan.

Pennycook, A. 2001. Critical Applied Linguistics: A Critical Introduction. Mahwah, NJ: Lawrence Erlbaum.

_________________. 1994. The Cultural Politics of English as an International Language. London: Longman.

________________. 1998. English as the Discourse of Colonialism. London and New York: Routledge.

________________. 1992. The Cultural Politics of Teaching English in the World. OISE, University of Toronto (PhD Dissertation).

Perren, GE (ed.). 1968. Teachers of English as a Second Language: Their Training and Preparation. London & NY: Cambridge UP.

Phillipson, Robert. 1992, rpt.2003. Linguistic Imperialism. Oxford: Oxford University Press.

Pieterse, Jan Nederveen & Bhikhu Parekh. 1995. The Decolonization of Imagination: Culture, Knowledge & Power. London & New Jersey: Zed Books.

Pieterse, Jan Nederveen. "The development of development theory: towards critical globalism". Review of International Political Economy 3:4 Winter 1996: 541-564.

Plasa, Carl. 2000. Textual Politics from Slavery to Postcolonialism: Race and Identification. London: Macmillan Press.

Pratt, Mary Louise. 1992. Imperial Eyes: Travel Writing and Transculturation. London and New York: Routledge.

Quran The Noble: Interpretation of the Meanings. 1996. Summarized in one volume by Prof Dr Muhammad Muhsin Khan & Prof Dr Muhammad Taqi-ud-Din Al-Hilali. Alharamain Foundation. Riyadh: Darussalam Publication.

Quirk, Randolph, Sidney Greenbaum, Geoffrey Leech and Jan Svartvik. 1972. A Grammar of Contemporary English. London: Longman.

RAHIMA Profile. http://www.rahima.or.id/English/index.htm [retrieved at 28 October 2006]

Rahman, Jamal D. Editor of HORISON literary magazine, "Menyemai Bintang di Padang Ilalang: Tentang Regenerasi Sastra Indonesia" which was presented at the Writers Meeting in Singapore 13 September 2003.

Ramage, Douglas E. 1996. Politics in Indonesia. London: Routledge.

Republika. Ahmad Syafii Maarif, "Demi Keutuhan Bangsa". Jakarta, 11 Juli 2006. http://www.republika.co.id/kolom_detail.asp?id=255993&kat_id=19 [retrieved at 28 October 2006].

Republika Online. Marwah Daud: "Isu Poligami Jangan jadi Kontroversi". Senin 11 Desember 2006 in http://www.icmi.or.id/ind/content/view/581/60/

Richards, Jack C., 2001. Curriculum Development in Language Teaching. Cambridge: Cambridge University Press.

Ricklefs, M.C. 1981. 1993. 2001. A History of Modern Indonesia Since c. 1200 (3rd ed). Hampshire: Palgrave.

Rosa, Helvy Tiana. 2001. Jaring-jaring Merah. Syaamil Publishing House.

________________. 2005. Short Stories: Maut di Kamp Loka and Hingga Batu Bicara. http://www.helytianarosa.com/dyna/galeri/ accessed at 10 June 2005.

________________. 2002. "FLP, Penulis dari 100 Kota" in Milad Forum Lingkar Pena 2002 in Jakarta, p. 2.

Sadtono, Eugenius (ed.). 1997. The Development of TEFL in Indonesia. Malang: IKIP Malang.

________________ . 1998. "Problems and Progress in Teaching English as a Foreign Language in Indonesia" in Linguistik Terapan, E. Sadtono (ed.). Malang: Penyelenggaraan Pendidikan Pasca Sarjana, IKIP Malang. 1-28.

Said, Edward. 1883. The World, the Text, and the Critic. Cambridge, Massachusetts: Havard University Press.

———. 1978, rpt.1995. Orientalism: Western Conceptions of the Orient. London: Penguin Books.

Saqeb, G.N. 1981. "Modernization of Muslim Society and Education: Need for a Practical Approach", in Education and Society in the Muslim World, ed. M.W. Khan. London and Jeddah: Hodder and Stoughton and King Abdul Aziz University. pp. 48-49.

Scherer, Savitti Prastiti. (1975) rep. 1985. Keselarasan dan Kejanggalan: Pemikiran-pemikiran Priyayi Nasionalis Jawa Abad XX [Harmony and Dissonance: Early Nationalist Thought in Java in the 20th century]. Jakarta: Penerbit Sinar Harapan.

Seel, Norbert M. & Sanne Dijkstra. 2004. Curriculum, Plans, and Processes in Instructional Design: International Perspectives. London: Lawrence Erlbaum.

Simon, R. 1992. Teaching against the Grain: Essays towards a Pedagogy of Possibility. Boston: Bergin & Garvey.

Sleeter, C.E. & Grant, C.A. 2003. Making choices for multicultural education: Five approaches to race, class, and gender (4th ed.). New York: Wiley.

Candraningrum, Dewi. 2006. "Indonesia as the Site of the Reproduction of Power: Inquiring the Neo-Imperial Ideology in the English Department" in Proceedings of the 10th ISSM International Conference 30 Sept-1 Oct 2005, Paris, France. Pp.: 192-201.

Candraningrum, Dewi. "Phases of Awareness: How did I become an English Teacher" in Journal of English Teaching Practice and Critique (ETPC). New Zealand, May, 2004, Volume 3, Number 1, Pp.: 59-70. http://education.waikato.ac.nz/research/journal/view.php?author=true&id=62&p=1

Sorabji, Cornelia. 1901. Love and Life Behind the Purdah. Oxford: Oxford UP.

Spivak, Gayatri Chakravorty Spivak. 1995. "Teaching for the Times" in Pieterse, Jan Nederveen & Bhikhu Parekh. 1995. The Decolonization of Imagination: Culture, Knowledge & Power. London & New Jersey: Zed Books.

______________________________. 2000. "Can the Subaltern Speak?" in Diana Brydon (ed.) Postcolonialism: Critical Concept. NY and London: Routledge.

______________________________. 2000. "Discussion: An Afterword on the New Subaltern" in Chatterjee, Partha & Pradeep Jeganathan (eds.). Subaltern Studies XI: Community, Gender and Violence. London: Hurst & Co.

______________________________. 2000. "Three Women's Texts and a Critique of Imperialism" in Diana Brydon (ed.) Postcolonialism: Critical Concept. NY and London: Routledge.

Stein, Mark. 2004. Black British Literature: Novels of Transformation. Columbus: The Ohio UP.

Stern, Gertrude. 1939. Marriage in Early Islam. London: Royal Asiatic Society.

Stierstorfer, Klaus. 2000. "Crossing Cultural Boundaries: Literature and Liminality in the EFL Classroom" in Antor, Heinz & Klaus Stierstorfer (eds.). English Literatures in International Contexts. Heidelberg: Universitaetsverlag C. Winter.

Stierstorfer, Klaus. 1999. "Intercultural Development in German EFL Teaching" in Heinz Antor and Kevin L. Cope (eds.). Intercultural Encounters-Studies in English Literature. Heidelberg: Universitaet Verlag C. Winter.

Stoler, Ann. 1995. "'Mixed-blood' and the Cultural Politics of European Identity in Colonial Southeast Asia" in Jan Nederveen Pieterse & Bhikhu Parekh, The Decolonization of Imagination: Culture, Knowledge & Power. London & New Jersey: Zed Books. Pp. 129-148.

Stowasser, Barbara F. 1994. Women in the Quran, Traditions, and Interpretation. New York: Oxford UP.

Strevens, Peter. 1980. Teaching English as an International Language: From Practice to Principle. Oxford, NY, Toronto, Sydney, Paris, Frankfurt: Pergamon Press.

Suminto, H. Aqib. 1985. Politik Islam Hindia Belanda [The Politics of Islam the Netherlands East Indies]. Jakarta: PT Pustaka LP3ES. Pp. 36-37, 193-98.

Sutton, P.W. & S. Vertigans. 2005. Resurgent Islam: A Sociological Approach. Cambridge: Polity Press. pp. 97-99.

Syahidah, Novia. Sebelum Jadi Penulis, Berkacalah! (Reflect, before you become a writer!),
accessed at 10 June 2005 in East Java PKS website

http://www.pks-jaktim.or.id
Syamsiyatun, Siti. 2007. "A Daughter in the Indonesian Muhammadiyah: Nasyiatul Aisyiyah Negotiates a New Status and Image" in Journal of Islamic Studies Vol. 18 No. 1: Pp. 69-94. Oxford Center for Islamic Studies.

Thomas, Murray R. 1968. "Indonesia: The English-Language Curriculum" in RM Thomas, LB Sands & DL Brubaker (eds.). Strategies for Curriculum Change: Cases from 13 Nations (pp. 279-322). Pennsylvania: International Textbook Co.

Thomas, Murray R, LB Sands & DL Brubaker (eds.). 1968. Strategies for Curriculum Change: Cases from 13 Nations. Pennsylvania: International Textbook Co.

Tibawi, A.L. "Philosophy of Muslim Education", in Islamic Quarterly 4, no. 2 (July 1957): 78-89.

Tiffin, Helen. 1994. "Teaching Post-Colonial Literary Theory" in Bridging the Gap: Literary Theory in the Classroom, J.M.Q. Davies (ed.). West Cornwall, CT: Locust Hill Literary Studies No. 17.

Vickers, Adrian. 2005. A History of Modern Indonesia. NY: Cambridge UP.

Vlekke, Bernard H.M. 1943. 1959. Nusantara: A History of Indonesia. The Hague & Bandung: W.van Hoeve Ltd.

Volkmann, Laurenz. "Intercultural Competence through Reading Yasmine Gooneratne's Novels" in Antor & Stierstorfer (eds.), 2000, English Literatures in International Contexts, Heidelberg: Universitaetsverlag C. Winter.

_______________. "Universal Truths or Ethnic Peculiarities? On Tensions Inherent in the Reception of Post-Colonial and Minority Literature" in Heinz Antor and Kevin L. Cope (eds.). Intercultural Encounters-Studies in English Literature. Heidelberg: Universitaet Verlag C. Winter. 1999.

_______________. 1991. Wildnis und Zivilisation: Britische Romanschriftsteller des spaeten 19. und des 20. Jahrhunderts und das Internationale Thema. Heidelberg: Carl Winter Universitaetsverlag.

Von Gronebaum, G.E. 1955. Islam: Essays on the Nature and Growth of a Cultural Tradition. Menasha: American Anthropological Association. P. 114.

Walder, Dennis. 1998. Post-colonial Literatures in English: History Language Theory. Oxford: Blackwell.

Walkerdine, V. 1989. Counting Girls Out. London: Virago.

Walther, Wiebke. 1993. Women from Medieval to Modern Times. Princeton & NY: Markus Wiener Publishing.

Ward, Stuart (ed.). 2001. British Culture and the End of Empire. Manchester and NY: Manchester UP.

Watt, W.M. "Cultural Clashes in a 'Perfect' World: The Challenge of Progressive Ideas to the Islamic World," Times Higher Education Supplement (June 13, 1986), p. 174.

Wertheim, W.F., 1969. "Indonesian society: the changing status system" in Andre Beteille (ed.). Social Inequality. Middlesex: Penguin Books.

Williams, Patrick, and Laura Chrisman, eds. 1993. Colonial Discourse and Post-colonial Theory: A Reader. New York, London, Toronto, Sydney, Tokyo and Singapore: Harvester Wheatsheaf.

Willinsky, John. 1998. Learning to Divide the World. Minneapolis and London: University of Minnesota Press.

Wilson, Kathleen (ed.). 2004. A New Imperial History: Culture, Identity and Modernity in Britain and the Empire 1660-1840. Cambridge: Cambridge UP.

Wirjosukarto, Amir Hamzah, Pembaharuan Pendidikan dan Pengadjaran Muhammadijah dalam Masa Pembangunan Semesta, 1962, p. 58.

Wood, Frederick T. 1950. An Outline History of the English Language. London: Macmillan & Co. Ltd.

Yadav, Alok. 2004. Before the Empire of English: Literature, Provinciality, and Nationalism in Eighteenth-Century Britain. NY & Hampshire: Palgrave Macmillan.

Young, Robert J.C. 2003. Postcolonialism: A Very Short Introduction. New York: Oxford UP.

Zahab, M.A. & Oliver Roy. 2004. Islamist Network: Afghan-Pakistan Connection. London: Hurst & Co. pp. 12-18.

Zainil. 1987. A Study of the Spoken English Proficiency of Students in the S1 Program of the English Department at the Padang Institute of Teacher Training and Education, Sumatera Barat, Indonesia. State University of New York at Buffalo.

Zonneveld, Peter Van. 1998. "H.J. Friedericy and the Indonesian Voice" in Cross/Culture 30: (Un)Writing Empire. Theo D.Haen (ed). Amsterdam: Rodopi.

Index

V

W

Y

Z